THE RACIALIZATION
OF AMERICA

THE RACIALIZATION
OF AMERICA

Yehudi O. Webster

St. Martin's Press
New York

First published in the United States of America in 1992

Printed in the United States of America

ISBN 0-312-07557-X

Library of Congress Cataloging-in-Publication Data

Webster, Yehudi O.
The racialization of America / Yehudi O. Webster.
    p. cm.
    Includes index.
    ISBN 0-312-07557-X
    1. United States—Race relations. 2. Afro-Americans—Census.
    3. Demographic surveys—United States. I. Title.
E185.615.W344   1992
327.73—dc20   92-1192
                                                     CIP

To my first teacher, my mother,
Elaine Webster

CONTENTS

ACKNOWLEDGMENTS

I am grateful to a wide variety of persons: Crécy, Jean-Claude, Nick, Richard, and Rosemary, who supported my bohemian existence and grew intellectually with me; John Rex, who made my studies at Warwick University possible and taught his graduate students to look for the larger theoretical picture; Harold Wolpe, who encouraged a quite distraught M.Phil student; Melvin Oliver, who was generous to a fault with his computer skills and advice; the library staff at Occidental College; and not least to my editors at St. Martin's: Laura Heymann, who offered indispensable suggestions for improvements of style and intellectual rigor, and Simon Winder, a model of patience and good humor.

—

Introduction

This book attempts a particularly ambitious task of identifying and refuting a general racial theory that has virtually dominated social studies and public policies for over two centuries. In order to analyze structural elements of this theory, terms such as white, black, Hispanic, Asian Pacific American, Native American, the black experience, Mexican Americans, and other racial-ethnic names must be presented. However, these terms are not used as descriptions of persons but as referents of classifications presented in texts on racial and ethnic relations.

In reviewing authors' works, the ground rules of intellectual exchanges that are observed in this text are as follows:

1. Comments do not focus on persons or their political motives, racial origin, or cultural attributes, but rather on the definitions of terms, premises, and the logical implications of the arguments advanced in their texts.
2. Distinctions among affirmation, denunciation, rejection, repudiation, and refutation are maintained.

Affirmation is an expression of endorsement of a proposition or argument. Denunciation refers to a moral relegation, or politically pejorative characterizations of arguments, or of the person advancing the arguments (the *ad hominem* fallacy). Rejection is an expression of disagreement with, opposition to, or dislike of ideas. Repudiation is constituted by a rejection of arguments on the basis of contrary personal observations and experiences. Denunciation, rejection, and repudiation are regressive and self-contradictory responses; they should form no part of intellectual exchanges and are distinguishable from refutation, which is a demonstration of logical flaws in an argument. The analysis in this book aspires either to affirm arguments or refute them. It should stand, or fall, on the basis of the ground rules outlined.

Almost every text in history and social sciences, not to mention media discussions of social relations in American society, refers to "race" or to "whites" and "nonwhites." Some scholars claim that race has always been a formative force in American society. However, this is an incomplete and most ambiguous assertion, insofar as it is not accompanied by a clarification of whether "race" refers to racism, racial policies, racial beliefs, or racial classification. The incompleteness of the assertion, as well as its popularity despite this incompleteness, is itself significant. It illustrates a certain tolerance of imprecise formulations and the adoption of a general racial theory of society whose logical flaws would ordinarily have had it consigned to a Museum of Contradictions.

Chapter 1 makes the case that it is neither race nor racism that bedevils American society, but rather that racial classification enjoys a privileged status in social studies. What is rarely mentioned is that races, generally defined as classes of people identifiable through common anatomical characteristics, are the product of racial classification and that the flaws in this classification produce substantial controversies and public policy failures. In other words, American society is being tied into painful knots by virtue of legislative, social scientific, and media practices of racially classifying persons. These practices are evinced in racial descriptions of past and contemporary social relations and socioeconomic conditions and experiences as well as in explanations of behavior in terms of either nonwhite biological deficiencies or a white moral deficiency, racism.

In terms of its longevity, the simultaneous admission of its illogicality, and consideration as a reality, race has all the hallmarks of myth. References to its realness are meant to consolidate and perpetuate its presence as something that cannot, or should not, be questioned. The very use of the term race and not "racial classification" is a means of preserving an ethos of mystery, intractability, and opacity. Why is race so appealing? it is asked. Why has this idea been so influential in human history? Actually, it is not race that has been influential. Rather, racial classification has been applied systematically and uncritically to human beings. It is social scientists who classify persons racially, announce that race is a social reality, admit that race cannot be defined satisfactorily, and claim to be dealing with the enigma of race.

Racial classification is itself part of a general racial theory of social relations in which persons are racially classified and their biological and moral attributes are presented as explanations of their behavior and historical developments. The development of this theory owes as much to eighteenth-century naturalist thinking as to the search for a justification of slavery that absolves slaveholders from any wrongdoing in the eyes of Christianity. Slavery was to be conceived as a natural phenomenon by virtue of the natural inferiority of blacks. As the theory was developed over the last two centuries, not only slavery but also ancient history and, indeed, the whole human past is racially interpreted. Archaeological findings are examined for racial implications. Egyptian, Asian, Greek, and Western civilizations are scrutinized for racial configurations. However, these discovered configurations are not part of the ancient past but rather a modern practice of describing persons as "whites" and "blacks" and tracing their ancestors through racial bloodlines. Thus, the racialization of the past is a backward extension of a contemporary practice, for scholars allocate persons to racial groups, then claim that history is an unfolding of relations between races.

Racial classification is further propagated in government estimates of social and demographic conditions. It figures eminently in federal, state, and local reports, as citizens are requested to confess to their racial membership on a variety of official documents. This official bombardment with racial names forms the first foundation of America's racialization, defined as a systematic accentuation of certain physical attributes to allocate persons to races that are projected as real and thereby become the basis for analyzing all social relations. The popularity and longevity of race derive from official practices of racially classifying citizens, their experiences, motives, and behavior.

This official racial classification was never benign. The collection of occupational data by race in 1890 coincided with the imposition of jim crowism. Contemporarily, racial classification serves various Republican and Democratic electoral interests. The creation and manipulation of "blacks" and "whites" are long-standing practices.

The second foundation of racialization is provided by social scientific research on race relations, in which the disciplines of history and sociology play an eminent role. For example, modern slavery is deemed a case of past race relations, and modern race relations are called "the aftermath" of slavery. Social scientists, then, have been actively engaged in the construction of the general racial theory. This involvement includes references to race as a riddle, a social reality, and a social construct. These claims supposedly obviate the need to consider the effects of racial research itself on how "actors" construct their identities and relations. Thus, social scientists are perhaps unwittingly part of the racialization of social consciousness. Throughout this book, their claim to be describing reality is critically examined for, given the multifarious definitions of "reality," it amounts to a further relapse into ambiguity.

The third foundation of racialization is the development of naturalist and liberationist variants of the racial theory. Starting in the seventeenth century, certain eminent naturalists, ethnologists, and anthropologists initiated a systematic construction of different races within the human species. Nature was conceived as an intrinsically hierarchical order whose gradations culminated in a First Cause, or the Creator. Nonwhites were the last link in "a great chain of being." In *some* of these "scientific" writings, the black race was deemed inferior and derived from a separate biological tree. Its enslavement was a natural outcome caused by the unequal biological endowments of the races. In the middle of the nineteenth century, amid an increasing clamor for abolition, discussions raged over the separate origins and comparative biological statuses of races. Some social philosophers developed the argument that inferior and superior races, representing types or species of human beings, produced different levels of civilization. In other words, historical and social processes are rooted in a natural order of things.

A naturalist variant of the racial theory was developed first; it presented a biological or genetic explanation of continental inequalities as well as processes of conquest, enslavement, and colonialism. This variant of the racial theory had its heyday in the late nineteenth century, when it was adopted by legislatures and defenders of "the peculiar institution." Naturalist writings contain different wings — social Darwinist, eugenicist, white supremacist, and sociobiological. They vary in their emphases on genetic factors in explaining nonwhite poverty but are united in their opposition to government intervention to alleviate nonwhite deprivation — the effect of alleged natural predispositions and attributes cannot be altered.

The liberationist variant also took root in the nineteenth century, in the form of abolitionist and Pan-Africanist writings. It rejects and repudiates naturalist justifications of slavery and colonialism. Indeed, these justifications are denounced as racism. This variant represents a racial-egalitarian school of thought. It is conceded that races are a product of nature, but any hierarchical ordering is rejected. The black race is said to be equal to the white, but has been victimized by slavery, colonialism, and white racism. This racism, or the racist nature of white people, is presented as the axis of oppressive historical processes. Hence liberationist writings outline a variety of measures for the eradication of racism and racial inequality.

The liberationist variant of the racial theory has been in ascendancy, especially since the 1960s, and is formative of antiracist struggles. Its exponents pursue the liberation of African Americans from what is regarded as historical patterns of white victimization. However, the liberationist school of thought is divided into various wings, which offer divergent interpretations of the so-called black experience. For example: a fundamentalist approach regards whites as inveterate racists; and conservative, radical/Marxist, and liberal perspectives raise doubts about the significance of racism in the formation of racial inequalities, seek to combine race and class, and question the advocacy of race-specific solutions to "inner city" problems.

Exposure to naturalist and liberationist writings contributes much to the proliferation of racial sentiments and the development of racial identities in the general population. Indeed, naturalist and liberationist

arguments are aimed precisely at generating racial divisions and organizations. The claims and counterclaims of racial victimization and
racial innocence and remedial suggestions foster and consolidate a
racial consciousness that is then decried and expected to be alleviated
through further racial analyses and remedies. Despair over the "worsening" state of race relations is expressed, even as government and
scholars combine to increase racial awareness. None of these writings
suggests the abandoning of racial classification.

The condoning of the inconsistencies in naturalist and liberationist
writings indicates the fourth and most critical foundation of racialization — a general tolerance of fallacies. Formal education systematically underdevelops the reasoning skills of the population. A citizenry
reared in a spirit of disregard for reasoning cannot but be taken in by
the claim that race is a reality. Few social scientists are taught the
philosophical ramifications of the theoretical-empirical distinction that
is used in social studies. Since philosophical issues are neglected in the
training of graduate students in social sciences, little attention is paid
to conceptual analysis and the logical structure of descriptions and
explanations embodied in social studies. As a result, a flawed racial
theory of social relations dominates educational, legislative, research,
and media institutions. It is this theory that underlies the claims that
American society comprises different racial groups, in conflict and in
relationships of victimization and oppression.

Social scientists do not generally consider the logical implications
of the claim that there is a real world that is separate and distinct from
theories. This is especially pertinent to race relations studies whose
most striking philosophical feature is their claim that race is a reality
that is dealt with by various theories and models. However, over the
last two decades, some philosophers have raised doubts about certain
traditional philosophical propositions, such as: language as a representation, or mirror, of things beyond language; knowledge as a relationship between a theorizing subject and a real object; truth as a reflection
of reality; and classifications as real, existing things. Their criticisms
have deconstructive implications for the notion that race is a social
reality that is investigated by social scientists. Some of the questions
that would be posed by a deconstructionist are: Are so-called race

relations still a socially constructed reality, if their study flouts elementary logical rules? Do aspects of social reality include the racial research activities of scholars themselves? If so, are so-called racial and ethnic relations not unrelated to these activities? Should studies of racial experiences not be terminated, if their "realness" escapes theoretical identification? If studies of racial experiences are a flawed project, their continuation is perplexing, unless their commercial and political nature is taken into consideration. The claim on reality is central to a political purpose of changing or conserving the status quo. However, what does this realpolitik imply for the scientific status and integrity of social sciences? And if no distinction can be drawn between scholarly work and "politics," what is nonpolitical?

Social scientists' lack of attention to philosophical issues produces a self-serving subdiscipline of racial and ethnic studies. Race is deemed "a social reality," which is then cited to continue studies of race relations. The results of research on race relations are fed into government, educational institutions, media, and political organizations. Their further utilization forms an intractable process of racialization. In other words, government institutions and scholars develop a racial theory of social relations in which experiences are racially described and explained. Racial solutions are developed for racial problems; these solutions, however, generate more racial problems. Jim crowism produced the civil rights movement, which called forth affirmative action, black power, and multiculturalism, which foster tensions between nonwhites and whites. Identical discussions of racial problems repeat themselves decade after decade, indeed century after century. Such are the fruits of racialization. Neither whites, nor blacks, benefit from it. The fact that it is not being abandoned suggests that behind the development and utilization of the racial theory is a fundamental philosophical-educational condition. Overall educational inputs do not cultivate respect for logical reasoning.

In keeping with the philosophical innocence of social scientists, the proof structure of the racial theory is based on realist categories. Logical rules are glossed over. The general result is not only controversies but also irrepressible contradictions. In most texts on racial and ethnic relations:

1. It is admitted that racial classification is vague and illogical, but government institutions and scholars continue to classify citizens as blacks and whites. The scholars' practice is hidden under a notion of socially constructed races. The government's usage is covert and authoritarian.
2. Terms such as culture and class are used, without any systematic analyses of cultural anthropological writings on culture, or of the logical deficiencies in Weberian and Marxian conceptions of class.
3. A moralistic and fatalistic focus is developed in which whites are racist and nonwhites are irrevocable victims of white racism, side by side with the suggestion that nonwhites take control of their own destiny.
4. A realist philosophy of science is utilized so that references to "reality" and "empirical instances" constitute proof of a valid argument and, conversely, arguments that make no reference to reality, or the "empirical," are rejected. The question that emerges then is whose reality? This, in turn, leads to endless relativist disputes and dogmatic claims that are expressed in demands for political correctness and the intellectual separatism of black and white perspectives.

In effect, no ground rules of intellectual exchanges are established. Hence, studies of race relations represent regressive and self-perpetuating speculations.

Coupled with the use of racial classification in social studies and the government's bombardment of citizens with racial identities, the U.S. system of public education effectively destroys critical thinking skills. Schools pay little or no attention to instruction in logical reasoning, but instead conduct various programs that accentuate racial and ethnic differences. Indeed, logic is approached with a certain suspicion and disfavor. Hence within the general population, faulty reasoning goes unrecognized. The entire citizenry embraces the classifications "black people" and "white people," without questioning their logical status. Specific educational inputs, then, underlie America's racialization.

Chapter 1 charts the development of a racial theory of social relations into a distinct field of study. It examines the early development of this theory in order to demonstrate that races are perceived through the use of certain criteria of classification. "Blacks" and "whites" are classifications of persons by persons, not creations of nature. Races are not things in themselves but the result of a specific type of classification. To think otherwise is to reify the concept of race. This reification, however, has roots in certain "scientific" practices and political economic considerations. The idea of a homogeneous white race was adopted as a means of generating cohesion among explorers, migrants, and settlers in eighteenth-century America. Its opposite was the black race, whose nature was said to be radically different from that of the white race and functioned as a biological justification of enslavement. Racial classification thereby became the politics of the day and the future; it was adopted by some legislators and social scientists to justify all subsequent relations between the descendants of slaves and masters. This adoption has had a long and virtually unchallenged career. Even recent emphases on culture and class are part of an effort to retain racial classification.

It is not race that has been the problem in American history. Rather, the founding fathers, legislators, social scientists, journalists, entrepreneurs, anti-abolitionists, and abolitionists appropriated a specific type of racial classification and suggested that it is the basis of their judgments and policies. Modern studies of history and society continue practices of adoption and dissemination of race. The processes of racialization grow uncontrollably and culminate in the periodic electoral successes of politicians offering remedies for racial problems that cannot be unambiguously identified. Self-characterized conservative, liberal, radical political economic, and Marxist scholars also outline a variety of mutually exclusive solutions to racial problems, for example, laissez-faire, affirmative action and antidiscrimination programs. In the disputes among these wings and between naturalist and liberationist variants, and in the government's periodic implementation of their recommendations, the racializing of social relations has proceeded unimpeded. No social issue can be raised without its racial qualification and compartmentalization. Courses on racial and ethnic relations are standard fare in educational institutions. In texts on racial and ethnic relations, students are presented with exhaustive historical-descriptive analyses of racial and ethnic experiences written from fundamentalist, Marxist, and liberal "perspectives." Media reports and commentaries on social problems invariably draw attention to racial configurations in social phenomena. It is these myriad investments in the racialization of society that utopianize suggestions of its termination.

The adoption of the racial theory for public policy purposes has led to its unrivaled development within social sciences. However, the development of racial classification and the reasons for its official usage are not generally analyzed. On the contrary, the practice of racial classification is glossed over by references to sociologist W. I. Thomas' dictum that if people define a situation as real, then it is real in its consequences. This allows scholars to present narratives of historical experience and statistical descriptions as *unchallengeable* truths, or as reflections of "reality." The reference to reality betrays racialization as a political project. A relativist controversy erupts when this question is posed: Which reflection or description of reality is correct? That which is most politically acceptable. Politically acceptable to whom? it may be further inquired. One's politics is as correct as any other's. Claims on reality, then, lead to endless political interrogation, and since nothing is resolved, they stifle one of the central purposes of education — the development of proficiency at refuting invalid arguments.

In naturalist writings, it is suggested that different and unequally endowed races are observed in the real world and cannot but have different and unequal social destinies, while in most liberationist writings, white racism is the scourge of the modern world. The career of racism mirrors theoretical-sociological as well as moral and political climates. In texts written during the immediate postwar period, racism was sociopsychologically conceptualized. By the mid-1960s, this approach was discarded in favor of an institutional emphasis. It was said that only whites can be racist, since they control the power structure. This emphasis on structures was, in turn, supplemented by Marxist and materialist analyses that identify racism in political economic and ideological contexts. Thus, definitions and qualifications of racism grow uncontrollably, changing according to the overall social scientific perspective being utilized to explain "race relations" and "migrant experiences."

Discussions of racism are plagued with equivocation, as the term is used to cover social conditions, beliefs, theories, actions, and their effects. Rules of consistency are sacrificed in order to interpret every aspect of black-white relations as an illustration of the evil nature of white people. So many racisms emerge that the term loses all analytical value. What this condition suggests is that social scientists need to pay more attention to definitions of terms, their consistent usage as well as to the premises and implications of arguments. Otherwise, sterile political disputes are bound to ensue, for example, over the origin and effects of racism in American society. But much of the controversy over the significance of racism can be avoided by conceiving racial classification *itself* as racism. Such classification necessitates references to biological attributes and racial motives in explaining behavior. Once persons are racially classified, there is no escaping the implication of operant racial motives. Whites can always be accused of racism, and there is no logical reason why blacks cannot be accused of it. The argument that blacks do not have the power to be racists is but a repetition of the liberationist claim that blacks are victims.

Chapter 2 follows up on the thesis that racism is a potent force in the history and organization of U.S. society. This thesis surfaces especially in the construction of racial minority experiences. Racist victimization is said to define these experiences. A variety of naturalist treatises and legal edicts did deem enslavement to be the destiny of "Negroes," and exclusion, segregation, decimation, relocation, and dispossession the natural fate of nonwhite races. Within the liberationist variant, these policies are manifestations of racial discrimination. Chapter 2 outlines an alternative interpretation, for, as specific policies toward "races" are necessarily based on a prior racial classification, racial discrimination is a product of racial classification. By implication, scholars should terminate the traditional moralistic focus on racism and address their own usage of racial classification and other elements of the racial theory.

Chapter 2 also deals with the principal theme in racial and ethnic relations texts — the experiences of racial minorities, who are identified as African Americans, Hispanics, Asian Americans, and Native Americans. It presents a critical summary of these experiences and exposes not only how social scientists adopt the racial theory to describe and explain events, which then become racial experiences, but also some of the inconsistencies and arbitrariness that result from social scientific claims on the real world. Texts on racial and ethnic relations do not provide readers with the theoretical basis or logical justification of the racial classification of persons and their experiences. In other words, such texts continue a dogmatic pedagogic tradition in which students are inducted uncritically into a racial vision of the world. This certainly does not stimulate the desire to challenge ideas and to pursue learning as an end in itself.

In racial and ethnic relations texts, readers are presented with masses of racial descriptions of social conditions, without a clarification of the theory that generates these descriptions or why they need to be known. Students are simply asked to read about various racial/ethnic experiences, about how Jewish, Italian, Polish, Irish, Asian-American, African-American, and other groups fared in American history and society. These "facts" generally are selected within a hidden thesis of racial minority and ethnic victimization. Although the facts provide the basis for a variety of multiple-choice questions, they are useless as a means of intellectual development. Students may memorize some of the historical facts and descriptions of "racial and ethnic oppression" without being nearer an understanding of how descriptions derive from theoretical perspectives and why U.S. society is described in racial terms that are not relevant to (for example) Brazilian society.

In omitting discussions of the racial theory, textbooks on racial and ethnic relations present arbitrary and logically indefensible claims that cash in on a self-generated racialization of society. Their descriptions can be condensed into a chapter or two, without losing the substantive but flawed argument that racial minorities are historical victims of whites. But which whites are the victimizers? One flaw in the image of (white) villains and (nonwhite) victims is evinced in the claim of so-called white ethnics that they too had been victims of racism. Because some white racists and oppressors can also claim to have been victims, racial and ethnic relations studies merely perpetuate moral accusations and counteraccusations; they cannot claim to be educating students, in the sense of cultivating critical thinking skills.

The summaries of so-called racial minority experiences in Chapter 2 form the basis of critical comments which demonstrate that racial and ethnic descriptions of events have no logical or educational justification. They are forms of propaganda, an indoctrination into a conviction that U.S. society has different racial and ethnic groups that are locked in a relationship of domination/oppression. They purport to tell it like it was, and is, in order to generate specific attitudinal and policy changes towards particular racial and ethnic groups. Racial ethnic descriptions must flout rules of consistency; they are part of a project of accentuating *selected* anatomical and cultural differences for moral-political purposes. In a society respectful of rationality and logical rules, this arbitrariness, counterproductiveness, and self-contradiction would have been sufficient to terminate racial classification and racial studies.

The organizing principles and focus of racial studies is the allocation of persons to white and nonwhite groups. Events in the lives of the nonwhites are interpreted through a prism of racially motivated victimization, but the operation of this type of motivation is not sustained. Throughout Chapter 2 it is emphasized that genocide against Native Americans, the enslavement of African captives, the subjugation of Asian Pacific Americans, and the colonization of Mexicans are racial experiences *only within the racial theory*. Racial descriptions of discrimination, oppression, poverty, exploitation and segregation are theoretically generated. Change the theory and the descriptions are transformed. This condition is evident in the growing number of studies that deny racism any decisive significance in modern U.S. society; that describe Asian Americans as a model minority; that combine class, race, and ethnicity and assert that some whites have, at some time, been victims of discrimination, oppression, poverty, exploitation, and segregation. Describing events as a racial experience is a particular way of interpreting phenomena. Abandon the racial theory and events can be conceptualized as class, or ethnic, or human experiences.

Theories produce their specific images, elements of empirical relevance, and policy solutions. A racial description of experiences, then, is a matter of theory choice. Hence, such experiences should not be presented as a social fact. If education is to move beyond indoctrination, the objective of social studies cannot be directed at raising group consciousness, through "telling it like it was," but at developing critical thinking skills on social relations. Texts on racial and ethnic relations do not contribute to this objective of a liberal arts education. The narratives of victimization and the data on racial minorities are not accompanied by any rigorous clarification of the underlying racial theory. Yet the language of protest against historical and contemporary violations of human and civil rights suggests a human-centered focus. Indeed, certain elements of the African-American, Hispanic, Asian Pacific-American, and Native American experiences do reflect "man's inhumanity to man." If the goal is the development of remedial strategies, one question that needs to be posed is: Does the racial description of inhuman treatment contribute to its longevity? Any such description is necessarily accompanied by a denunciation of whites, the very persons to whom appeals must be made for an end to oppression.

Chapter 3 addresses the incorporation of the concept of culture in race relations studies and its effect of a deemphasis on racism as an explanation of racial inequalities. A careful reader of race relations texts in the decades between 1960 and 1980 would notice a focus on ethnicity in the 1970s that indicated a shift from race to culture. More precisely, culture was appended to race, counterposed to race, and combined with race. Race relations studies and courses were renamed racial and ethnic relations. An ethnic group was defined in terms of cultural practices, a common identity, and "consciousness of kind." It is said to differ from a racial group, which is defined with reference to anatomical similarities. This focus on culture and ethnicity marks a development away from a bipolar racial classification. It was inspired by certain developments in cultural anthropology in the early twentieth century.

Some cultural anthropologists, principally of the Boas school, argued that it is not so much race as culture that should be the defining feature of social relations. Each race has its culture, and insofar as the racial group survives in its habitat, its culture is relatively equal to others. Boasian studies may have refuted the thesis of black cultural inferiority, which naturalists had championed. However, in attributing a culture to each race, they relativized and continued the racialization of culture. References to black and white cultures began to permeate both social scientific and humanities texts. Subcultures within each culture also became legitimate objects of study. Hence, whites were divided into white Anglo-Saxon Protestants (WASPs) and white ethnics (WETs). Empirical racial-ethnic comparisons were developed, with the black experience being at the bottom end of a pyramid of victimization. Some ethnic theorists subsequently proposed that ethnic immigrants had experienced similar patterns of victimization from other whites and that racial differences and racist considerations are not a sufficient condition for victimization. All whites cannot be said to be racist, and some whites (WASPs) are both racist and ethnocentric. In effect, intraracial cultural prejudices also generate discrimination and oppression. The American problem is not racism, or only racism, but racism *and* ethnocentrism.

In the ethnic perspective, patterns of victimization cut across race. Jews, Roman Catholics, and indeed all nonWASPs had suffered discrimination from the dominant WASPs. References to the experiences of ethnic groups and ethnocentrism emerged particularly in the 1970s, partly as a result of civil rights militancy and in opposition to legal reforms meant to benefit, principally, African Americans. Some scholars argued for a sharp distinction between white ethnics, the descendants of South and East European immigrants, and white Anglo-Saxon Protestants. In the literature on the revival of ethnicity, certain claims stand out:

1. White ethnics themselves have been victims of Protestant prejudices, nativism, and racism; they too deserve an affirmative response from the government.
2. Whites are not an homogeneous group. WASPs and white ethnics are as culturally diverse as blacks are from whites.

3. The historical experiences, socioeconomic circumstances, and political attitudes of whites are not uniform.
4. Jews, Roman Catholics, and the descendants of South and East European immigrants were, and still are, victims of nativism, anti-Semitism, and Protestant biases. These ethnics also had been ghettoized, stereotyped, and systematically deprived of their civil rights. However, they struggled against discrimination without any help from government.
5. U.S. society was, and remains, a sea of ethnically differentiated opportunities.
6. Black culture may itself be deficient and responsible for the growing black underclass.

These claims form the basis of the intense opposition to affirmative action for *racial* minorities, which is deemed "reverse discrimination." Clearly this solution to racial inequality could increase racial and ethnic tensions. The cure perpetuates the disease. Has the problem been misdiagnosed?

Ethnic and racial theorists share methods, but not criteria of classification. Like racial groups, ethnic groups are constructed on the basis of observed differences and similarities as well as self-identification. Cultural attributes are predefined as different from each other, and individuals are said to have "a consciousness of kind" on the basis of a common nationality, language, and religious affiliations. Roman Catholics, for example, become an ethnic group. However, there are significant differences among Italian, Polish, and Hispanic Catholicism. Hispanics are also presented as an ethnic group, even as it is claimed that they inhabit various tiers of cultural, economic, and political situations. Similar difficulties accompany the designations Asian Pacific Americans, African Americans, and Native Americans. Not surprisingly, some scholars protest vigorously against the use of "culture" alone to define ethnicity. However, the inclusion of other elements introduces significant internal variations, deviations, and inconsistencies. For example, many black cultures have been discovered in the United States — Southern, rural, youth, middle class — so that the so-called black community may be said to comprise different ethnic groups. Hence, black culture cannot be held responsible for deprivation.

The ethnic theory focuses on cultural rather than anatomical differences and draws attention to ethnic rather than racial experiences. American society is presented as a cultural mosaic, a society in which different cultures intermingle. In investigating America's ethnic diversity, a commonly posed question is: What is the genesis of ethnic affiliations? Various theorists identify ethnogenesis in human nature, social organization, and economic competition. Thus, an ethnic group can become indistinguishable from a race or a class. Differentiation according to ethnicity, therefore, lacks a principled focus. Indeed, both the genesis and the behavioral effects of ethnicity remain obscure. Ethnic groups are said to exist by virtue of cultural differences, just as racial groups reflect anatomical differences. Shelby Steele, author of *The Content of Our Character*, criticizes this incessant pursuit of differences and recommends a return to Martin Luther King's humanist vision. Because the number of cultural differences is indeed infinite, ethnic studies become a self-serving activity. But more ominously, an emphasis on cultural differences underlies revived tensions among groups of persons classified as African Americans, Jews, and Asian Pacific Americans.

Chapter 3 examines a culture-or-structure dispute that permeates various wings of the liberationist variant of the racial theory. Conservative and liberal wings are manifest in the writings of economists Thomas Sowell, Glenn Loury, and Walter Williams; Shelby Steele; and of William J. Wilson, a "liberal" sociologist at the University of Chicago whose much-heralded *The Declining Significance of Race* (1978) renewed controversies over the relationships among race, culture, and class. These authors draw on many arguments from E. Franklin Frazier's *The Black Bourgeoisie* (1957), Senator Daniel P. Moynihan's study of "the Negro Family" (1965), and ethnic revivalist writings of the 1970s that claimed that white ethnics had survived and transcended discrimination by virtue of their cultural fortitude.

So-called conservative scholars take issue with the civil rights pursuit of racial group equality, radical and fundamentalist accentuation of racism and capitalism, their support for remedial government intervention, and their overall ignoring of class differentiation and cultural tendencies in the black community. It is claimed that for specific cultural reasons, some Asian Americans and non-American blacks excel over African Americans and Hispanics as well as other Asian Americans and even some whites. Indeed, a "model minority" thesis is used to suggest that not government welfare programs but cultural cohesion and individual discipline are the keys to social mobility. Affirmative action and welfare programs are, therefore, unnecessary and even counterproductive for African Americans. Such arguments reflect a growing lack of confidence in racial classification and "race-specific" solutions, but they intensify disputes among all wings of the liberationist variant of the racial theory.

Chapter 3 critically analyzes points of divergence and compatibility among these scholars, but concludes that some familiar contradictions plague their analyses. For example, while demonstrating that there is no homogeneous, socioeconomic black community, they utilize the classifications blacks, the black family, and African Americans. Conservative, liberal and radical scholars also fail to analyze the multitude of weaknesses in the claim that races have their own cultures. In their writings, empirical data "proving" a worsening black situation are perpetually counterposed to empirical data justifying assertions of black economic progress. Charges of political incorrectness then take the place of refutation.

In Chapter 3, the roots of this stalemate are explored and explained in terms of disciplinary specializations and a more significant insensitivity to the philosophical ramifications of social sciences. The racial theory is one of many social theories; it comprises criteria of classification, conceptual arrangements, and explanations couched in arguments. Their coherence and validity depend on the logical rules used in their construction. In the development of the racial theory, however, attention to these rules has been neglected in preference for a claim on the real world. Since this claim has an aura of certainty and unchallengeability, criticisms were deflected onto the theorists, whose race, social origin, or politics can themselves become significant for the validity of an argument. Racial descriptions of "real" events are presented as both issues to be explained and proof of the racial descriptions' accuracy. Since there is no logical control over racial descriptions, the result is masses of conflicting empirical data on racial progress/regress. This development is not a sign of analytic depth but of an impasse. It also suggests the need for a movement beyond racial minority experiences, for the inability to resolve the competition over empirical data derives from their racial classification. Unending statistical wars are bound to result from race relations research.

Writings on "the revival of ethnicity," "the declining significance of race," and race-class analyses constitute major and related additions to the study of racial experiences. They derive from attempts to merge racial, ethnic, and class theories of society. The real world is said to contain intersecting elements of race, culture, and class. Hence, different classes and subcultures are discovered within the African-American population. The data on internal socioeconomic and cultural differences are used to repudiate the thesis of racially generated deprivation as well as the need for government affirmative action and welfare programs. Some blacks have "made it." Others have not. Racism, then, is not universally operative and has limited explanatory significance. For some theorists, however, this conclusion implies that race should be combined with class. On the other hand, does not such a combination constitute a dissolution of racial classification?

Can the concept of class rescue racial studies, which are increasingly becoming racial-ethnic and race-class studies? Chapter 4 explores the ramifications of race-class analyses. From the late 1970s, class approaches to race relations signaled an emergent trend in studies of the so-called black experience. However, this trend may be regarded as part of a larger movement of diffusion, if not dissolution of the racial paradigm. In Wilson's *The Declining Significance of Race*, class, in a Weberian sense, was deemed a more significant factor than race in modern urban America. This type of class analysis must be distinguished from political economic, Marxist, and materialist explanations. Indeed, four separate types of race-class combinations may be identified — Weberian, Marxian, Marxist, and materialist. Race-class combinations utilize both Marx's and Weber's writings on class to retain racial experiences as a viable object of study and at the same time discredit the idea of racial causation. In the Weberian perspective, race

and class intersect, while in Marxist analyses, racism and racial inequalities are effects of the exigencies of capitalism and its built-in class
relations. In either case, racial classification retains some analytical
value.

The reluctance to abandon the idea of racial experiences, even
while advancing evidence of a class structure, reflects attempts to save
the descriptions produced by the racial theory. Events and conditions
are racially described but economically explained, or economically
described and racially explained. The explanations are then criticized
as "idealistic," "economistic," "mechanical materialist," and "reductionist." This stalemate derives from an extraordinary conceptual
looseness. The extensive literature on, including criticisms of, Marxian, Weberian, and Marxist writings on class is ignored. The concept
of class itself is rarely defined, and there is no consistency in its usage.
Some of its "meanings" include the distribution of wealth, income,
property, relationship to the means of production, patterns of consumption, industrialism, and political domination. Given the legendary
amorphousness of "race," race-class combinations cannot but raise the
level of opacity of racial studies.

A more fundamental philosophical issue is at stake — the necessity of congruency between description and explanation. Racial descriptions require a racial explanation. Any class explanation of
racially described events can be accused of ignoring race. If the white
and black communities are stratified by class, this is not evidence of
the need for a race-class approach. Rather, it constitutes a demonstration of the limitation of racial classification. *Certain* legacies of early
physical anthropology and Victorian biology, as well as the ghosts of
Karl Marx and Max Weber, must be resisted. Their retention stultifies
the development of a viable theory of social change. Race-class analyses especially do not present adequate means of overcoming race-
class exploitation. The study of social relations is ripe for a movement
away from racial and class theories of society.

But what of the differences among human beings and the patterns
of racial and class inequalities in society? It is important to recognize
that these differences are produced by racial and class theories. Racial
classification draws attention to specific anatomical differences among

persons; this classification needs to be justified, because social studies cannot just point to differences, they must explain their significance. The social significance of different skin colors, hair types, and facial form may be a result of these attributes being used to allocate persons to races. Social scientists have hitherto not discussed the general racial theory that embodies racial classification. It is this oversight that allows references to race-class factors and experiences as things independent of theories.

This book critically engages the official, academic, and activist usages of racial classification and the incorporation of the concepts of class and culture in race relations studies. It exposes how social scientists, legislators, entrepreneurs, and publicists use racial classification to generate a racial ethos that is then claimed to be the basis of their practices. It deals subversively with this racialization of American society and, by implication, outlines conditions of deracialization. It demonstrates that official racial classification and studies of racial experiences do nothing but render social problems insoluble. Racial solutions, such as busing, affirmative action, black power, and multiculturalism, are bound to fail, because they heighten the very racial awareness that is said to have led to "racial problems" in the first place. Their failure is then conceived as proof that race is a hardened reality that has "a life of its own." Violent confrontations often emerge from the stalemate, and escalate into large-scale conflagrations. The periodic death and destruction, however, pale into insignificance compared to the chronic maiming of human beings, which is misnamed racial violence, racial oppression, and racial poverty. Racial classification of social problems is the principal source of the tolerance of waste and human destruction in American society. This conclusion does not imply that were it to be abandoned, social problems would disappear. Rather, the implication is that once racial classification is discarded, conclusive analyses can be developed on whose basis solutions could be constructed. Racially defined problems, by definition, cannot be resolved.

This book reintroduces philosophical issues into social studies. This reintroduction is made necessary by the innocent use of philosophical categories in studies of racial and ethnic relations. In explaining the behavior of observable whites and nonwhites, racial studies draw on a particular philosophical tendency that suggests that concepts represent a given of the real world. Racial classification is treated as a natural or a social given rather than as a human practice influenced by informal and formal educational inputs. The racializing practices of government, educational institutions, and media are thereby ignored. Social scientific research on race relations itself becomes part of an official cultivation of racial groups. *Not a single study of racial experiences questions the idea of the social reality of race.* This is not to suggest a conspiracy between government and social scientists but rather their voluntary ignorance of the realist tradition in philosophy and its relationship to social sciences. Racial, ethnic, and class studies represent, above all, the price paid for the neglect of philosophy in the training of social scientists.

Throughout this work, attention is repeatedly drawn to the regress involved in the social-constructionist conception of race, which is often presented as a justification of further racial classification and research. In the social-constructionist approach, it is argued that since laypersons are attached to race, public policies and social studies must deal with race as a social reality. Even if race is a reality (and it is not clear which of the many definitions of "reality" is being utilized), the question remains: How is this reality to be dealt with, subversively or subserviently? Public policies and academic research deal subserviently with race, then claim that laypersons are attached to race. The realness of race, therefore, may be said to be a result of this subservience. So intensely have people been bombarded with this thesis of race's realness that they are bound to be convinced of the unchallengeability of racial classification.

Studies of race relations survive because people are convinced that they reflect the real world. However, this conviction perpetuates so-called racial problems, because once the realness of race is endorsed, studies of racial problems become plagued with inconclusive disputes and interpretations of data and experiences. Therefore, discussions of solutions to racial problems are necessarily replete with cyclical references to political economic, cultural, and biological factors. For example, economic and educational deprivation in American society is analyzed racially and, as a result, benignly neglected. Any proposed cause of this "racial" condition is susceptible to an eternal doubting. Are whites racist, or is it that blacks themselves are at fault? Blaming the victim! Blame the victimizer. Social scientists have only blamed races. The goal should be to abandon them.

Race is not a riddle. References to reality, as defense and criticism of arguments, are precisely the source of the stalemate in explanations of racial experiences. One author's "reality" is another's "ideology." What is also abundantly clear is that government and social scientists are by no means innocent observers and recorders of racial and ethnic relations. They play critical roles in the racializing of experiences and social problems. The question of the 1990s, if not of the twenty first century, is: Can they be persuaded to terminate the racial classification of the population? This book is written in a spirit of both protest and hope. The hope may be unjustified, however. Insofar as scholars reach for "reality" and do not observe distinctions among denunciation, rejection, repudiation, and refutation, the fallacies in racial studies will be condoned. It is a measure of the neglect of philosophy in the cultivation of social scientists that some reviewers of this book will be tempted to refer to racial "realities," or to the author's political credentials, or to observed "experiences" of victimization to *reject* its refutation of the racial theory of society.

1

The Racial Theory: Development, Structure, Variants

Four theses, beliefs, or convictions dominate social studies as well as media discussions of social relations.

1. There are different races, for example, black people and white people.
2. There are different cultures that may be racially demarcated, because each race has its own culture.
3. White people are racists, or American society is racist.
4. Nonwhites are oppressed, excluded, and disadvantaged because of their race.

These propositions are often couched in the form of a claim that race is a major influence on, if not the dominant feature of, American history, culture, economy, and social policies and behavior. This chapter seeks to demonstrate that these propositions derive from a racial theory of history and society that furnishes the conceptual tools of racialization.

The concept of racialization is developed in the writings of Frank Reeves and Robert Miles.[1] This concept does qualify as a replacement for the idea of race relations, for race relations are racialized social relations. In *Racism*, Miles presents a cogent analysis of the origination of racialization, tracing it to the writings of Frantz Fanon and critically examining its usage by modern British sociologists. Miles' own analysis conceives of racialization as racial categorization and racial discrimination. He places it in contexts of racism, class struggle, and an imputation of otherness. However, none of the current sociological conceptions of racialization identifies or challenges its most significant constituent, which is the claim that race is a social or a political reality. They do not highlight this philosophical aspect of racialization and ignore the roles of empirical social sciences and official practices that request racial self-classification from the general population. They thereby omit mention of the specific academic and government practices that render racialization processes a success and, at the same time, present possibilities of their reversal.

The social scientific aspect of racialization embodies an organization of studies of past and present social relations around racial classifications, which are presented as "real" and then justified as an object of study in terms of their reality. Racialization is, therefore, racial classification with built-in features of self-perpetuation. Anthropologist Colette Guillaumin makes a striking observation:

> The fact that at one point in the history of the last few centuries certain social relationships came to be called "racial" does not necessarily mean that they are so. For that to be the case, "race" would have to be a concept with a practical basis, found in "reality." But is not. What are called "race relations" refer to two different kinds of facts; either to relationships regarded as racial by those directly involved (Nazi Germany and the Republic of South Africa are two examples of this belief being given legal form), in which case such relationships are indeed, ideologically speaking, racial, or to intergroup relations described as "racial" by anthropologists or other outside observers.[2]

Guillaumin's references to the legal practices of government and the classifying practices of outside observers — that is, social scientists — touch the core of the self-perpetuating nature of racialization, which is rooted, then, in social scientific references to the reality of race, official requirements of racial self-description, electoral utilization of "blacks" and "whites," and public policies addressed to racial problems.

Institutional mechanisms of racialization are powerfully in operation in U.S. society. Community activists as well as Republican and Democratic party strategists capitalize on a racialized social climate generated by academic and official usages of racial classification. Legislators, social scientists, and political activists have chosen to utilize a racial theory to analyze past and present social relations. This theory was developed primarily as a natural defense of slavery and continues to flourish in educational institutions, as social scientists describe contemporary social relations as an aftermath of slavery and teach generations of students that race is the axis on which U.S. society turns.

The choice of the racial theory for contemporary social studies is supported by foundations and corporations, which invest comparatively vast sums of money in research on the experiences of racial and ethnic groups. Given this financial backing, social scientists are able to ply government, media, and citizens with an abundance of racial data. What is enigmatic is that in conducting their "research," social scientists group "actors" racially but then announce that race is a potent factor in society. These research practices, then, are self-serving. As long as they continue, racial problems will be discovered and be further investigated to generate a racially charged climate in which any encounter between persons who are classified as white, black, brown, or Asian can lead to so-called racial tensions and confrontations.

THE PRIVILEGED STATUS OF RACE IN SOCIAL STUDIES

Race is generally said to be a dominant influence in American society, a reflection of the slave past in which whites had ruthlessly oppressed blacks. This assertion permeates studies of history and social relations; it is often voiced enigmatically, disparagingly, and regretfully. These very forms of expression impute an aura of mystery to race. For example, Congresswoman Eleanor Holmes Norton writes: "With persistence even tenacity, 'race' lingers in American life, seeming to mock us like a disquieting riddle. It is our longest running unresolved problem. . . . The racial riddle has defied American logic."[3] Why is race such a powerful political and behavioral force in society? This question is badly posed, however. It is not "race," but a *practice* of racial classification that bedevils the society. Race is a riddle only as the result of a choice not to specify precisely what the term means. It is not race that, as philosopher David Goldberg suggests, "has served as a central category of natural and social recognition and self-representation."[4] Rather, government and social scientists choose to promote the racial classification of citizens, and this practice is hidden behind equivocal references to race.

Claims about the dominance of race reflect an extraordinary laxity in conceptual analysis within studies of race relations. Strictly speaking, race refers to what is produced through racial classification, for example, Caucasians, or the white race, Negroes, and Mongoloids. A virtual tradition of equivocation allows "race" to be used to mean racism, racial differences, racial classification, racial policies, racial behavior, racial motives, racial stratification, racial explanation, racial attitudes, and racial anything. The underlying thrust of these various usages of race is the preservation of the racial classification of persons, experiences, and social phenomena. The riddle of race cannot be solved if its meanings shift randomly and indiscriminately.

But, it may be asserted, there *are* anatomical differences among human beings. This is an indisputable assertion. However, because there are so many differences, the question is: Which differences are to be selected and used as a means of demarcating groups? Classification by anatomy is simply one of the chosen means of classification in social studies. The development of classifications is a critical first move in scientific analyses, for classifications depict the specific differences of the phenomenon or phenomena being analyzed. Nevertheless, as similarities among phenomena may be considered equally significant as differences, references to any particular differences must be justified. Analysts cannot merely point to differences on the grounds that they are natural phenomena. They may be natural, but the reasons why they are selected must be made explicit. In other words, all classifications are made for a purpose or purposes that must be made clear.

Human beings are both different and similar, and they possess innumerable attributes. Hence, some of the critical questions facing social theorists are: Is it legitimate to place human beings in mutually exclusive categories that are based on only a few of their attributes? Why is skin color presented as a decisive criterion of racial demarcation? Usage of other criteria of classification has led to the discovery of many numbers of races. This suggests that races are not objects in a so-called natural world but constructs developed within a given theoretical structure. Classifications, such as black people and white people, are traceable to a body of centuries-old writings that place a "white race" at the center of history.[5]

A modern invocation of race as the great mover and shaker of American history is illustrated in a typical sociology textbook. The authors, D. Stanley Eitzen and Maxine Baca Zinn, write:

> Throughout human history race has been used as a criterion for differentiation. If any factor makes a difference in American society, it is race. Blacks, Native Americans, Mexican Americans, Asian Americans, and other minority racial groups have often been systematically excluded from residential areas, occupations, and organizations, and even sometimes denied equal rights under the law. . . . Racial strife has occurred throughout American history. Slave revolts, Indian battles, race riots, and lynchings have occurred with regularity.[6]

Such descriptions permeate sociological studies of American society in which racial conflicts are presented as the centerpiece of history. However, it is important to note that it is the authors of the text who are describing certain events in racial terms. Admittedly, "everyday actors" use racial expressions and explanations. This usage, however, could be a function of the dissemination of racial categories by educational and official institutions. Thus, the prevalence of racial sentiments in public life does not obligate social scientists to follow suit. Social studies cannot be said to be a reflection of the so-called everyday world, if they themselves contribute to its construction.

A second significant feature of the claim that race is a powerful influence in American history and society is its implicit reification of the concept. Race is mentioned as a sort of deus ex machina, a live thing that acts on human beings and determines the course of events. This reification of race effectively obscures the human choice involved in the use of a specific social theory to justify, for example, an exclusion from resources and rights. Elements of this racial theory are also used to protest against this exclusion. If this reification of race were to be abandoned, it could be proposed that race is and has not been a significant force in American society. Rather, what would be claimed is that a racial theory of society has been developed by natural and social scientists. This theory was, and continues to be, chosen by political representatives, community activists, social scientists, and laypersons for various purposes. Indeed, the very claim that race is a potent force in society reflects this choice. It is itself part of the dissemination of racial classification.

Neither the past nor contemporary social relations needs to be racially described. Class, or culture, could be the chosen prism through which events are analyzed. But more significantly, how accurate is the racial description of past events? As sociologist Michael Banton writes:

> It is of greatest importance to appreciate that relations between reds, whites, and blacks in the New World were not described in racial terms until the latter half of the nineteenth century. To begin with, the various groups were identified by labels which related to their cultural or physical characteristics; they were called Spaniards or Indians, blacks or mestizos. Then groups of common ancestry were referred to as races, but the word 'race' was used simply to designate the group and played no part in any attempt to explain the nature of the individuals who were members of it.[7]

However, it should be made clear that reds, blacks, and whites are classifications, not a reference to actual persons. Banton's remarks imply that Eitzen and Baca's claim that "throughout human history race has been used as a criterion of differentiation" is not only inaccurate but also a case of "presentism," the reading of the past as a reflection of the present. Nor is the present characterized by relations among red people, black people and white people. These descriptions derive from the racial theory of society and could be discarded in favor of class or ethnic descriptions.

In their rejection of any emphasis on the concepts of ethnicity and class, Michael Omi and Howard Winant advance the proposition that contemporary social relations *must* be read through a prism of race:

Most theories are marked by a tendency to reduce race to a mere manifestation of other supposedly more fundamental social and political relationships such as ethnicity and class. Our doubts about this literature derived from this reductionism — an inability to grasp the uniqueness of race, its historical flexibility, and immediacy in everyday experience and social conflict.[8]

To construct an ethnic or class picture of society is to be "reductionist." Here race is given an ontological essence and primacy over ethnicity and class; it is portrayed as an elemental force that cannot but color the future. Thus, the authors continue: "Race will always be at the center of the American experience."[9] Does this prophecy mean that all future generations of Americans will be concerned about race? Could such a prediction not be self-fulfilling? What is the relationship between the predicted centrality of race and the continued use of racial classification by social scientists?

Racial classification has been raised to an extraordinarily privileged status in social studies; it has been interpolated and extrapolated to color all social phenomena. Both demographic studies and the popular weeklies predict whites becoming a minority by the middle of the twenty-first century and proclaim the "browning" and an "Asianization" of America.[10] The two related questions that are not raised are: How will nonwhites react to the implication that America is "white"? Will not the prediction of an impending minority status generate white fears and support for pro-white politicians who promise to look after future white interests? The privileged status of race in social studies surely fertilizes support for such politicians.

Because race is presented as a major force in history and contemporary society, analysis of its origins represents much-trodden ground. Various scholars claim that the term "race" first appears in ancient Egyptian, Greek, Roman, Biblical, and European writings.[11] Nevertheless, given the variety of usages and translations of race, the issue of its first mention cannot be resolved. What emerges from studies of the history of the race concept is that, over the last three centuries, a general racial theory of history and society has been developed. It comprises racial classification of persons as well as race-specific descriptions of events, their causes, and racial solutions to social problems. Hence, it is not race that should occupy the analytic efforts of social scientists. Race refers to what is produced through racial classification. What requires analysis is the structural components of a social theory organized around a racial classification of persons.

Racial classification is a core feature of social studies; it is, however, the least analyzed and thus it is uncritically propagated through racial research. Most studies of race relations simply ignore the critical literature on the formation and ramifications of "the idea of race." Michael Banton and Jonathan Harwood's works, however, are a significant exception.[12] In *Racial and Ethnic Competition*, Banton suggests that seventeenth-century political treatises conceived race primarily as a categorization of vaguely formulated "lineage differences." However, two centuries later "races" were conceived as permanent types. Banton notes that, apart from a denotation of lineage, race was used as an index of social class as well as national, civilizational, and cultural achievements. Over the last three centuries, then, the meaning of race has shifted from vague, literary, linguistic, national, and folk references to a systematic biological taxonomy and an explanation of behavior, inequality, and social change. Biological attributes came to be used to define a race and explain civilizational developments. As Banton concludes:

> The word "race" is currently used in several quite different ways. . . .
> There are three contexts in which people try to use it in a precise way:
> the biological use of race as sub-species, the sociological attempt to
> define the characteristics of racial minorities, and the legal or adminis-
> trative use of categories like racial group. Then there are folk concepts
> of race which probably vary from one group to another; they draw upon
> the old literary sense of race as lineage or descent and take a powerful
> impress from the nineteenth-century sense of race as type, though they
> are now also influenced to some extent by developments in scientific and
> administrative practice.[13]

According to Banton, folk references to race were part of the English intellectual tradition before the contact with Africans. Definitions of race as "permanent types" radically altered the merely descriptive usage of race. As a taxonomic category, race denotes a distribution of certain biological attributes. As a type, it is a "subspecies" to which individuals naturally belong. It is, therefore, utilized to explain their temperament, behavior, socioeconomic achievements, and all social phenomena.

Early biologists were the social scientists of their times, because their racial descriptions of the human species contain explicit behavioral correlations. Racial attributes were cited to explain social conditions, which then become a natural state of affairs. In the process of their construction, races are deemed part of nature; they are alleged to have been "discovered," not constructed by an emphasis on particular anatomical attributes. This assumption of the naturalness of race is connected with the pursuit of an explanation of a particular social condition — inequality. Races, as unequal biological entities, must be said to have their peculiar cultures, psychologies, and unequal economic circumstances. It is this implicit and explicit correlation of nature and behavior that makes racial classification part of a sociobiological enterprise, or a biological theory of history and society. Thus, race, cannot be dismissed as simply analytically useless; it is the product of a form of classification that is embedded in a wider theoretical context.

THE RACIAL THEORY: EARLY DEVELOPMENTS

In the development of a social theory based on the observation and measurement of biological endowments and their correlation with behavior and social conditions, the conquest and enslavement of the "darker races" are conceived as laws of natural history, and, given the powerful reputation of the natural sciences, the idea of race rises to incomparable explanatory eminence. However, the connection between biology and race was not always maintained. Races have been demarcated according to not only physical attributes such as skin color, hair type, facial form, stature, skull shape, and eye structure, but also language, religion, and customs. However, other biological and cultural characteristics may be regarded as more significant so that any number of different races can be discovered. Moreover, the differences between the discovered races may be less than differences within a given race.

Some scholars have suggested that race is an erroneous and unscientific category that should have no place in social studies. As sociologist S. Carl Hirsch writes:

> Some scientists see only three races while others list three hundred. Most estimates are somewhere between, the common numbers being five, six, nine, thirty. There is an important group of anthropologists who have abandoned the term "race" altogether. They see it as "a dangerous four letter word," more troublesome than useful. One leading biologist states that most of the world's people are so racially distinct that they are members of no race.[14]

As part of political struggles, however, the term race is retained and its vagueness is conceived as a reflection of the slippery nature of social reality. Its anatomical mainstay, skin color, was reinforced but subsequently overshadowed by cultural as well as political and economic referents. One could be black without looking black. The percentage of "black blood" necessary for being black varied in the Southern states. One's race could be changed by crossing state lines. In eugenicist writings some whites are deemed a race distinct from other whites. These peculiarities have led some social scientists to regard race as a socially constructed reality and an ideology. It should, however, be called the most equivocally used construct in social studies.

The allocation of persons to races has been placed in the context of an Other representation through the signification of biological attributes. This signification, however, is a two-way street. As Robert Miles writes: "Ascribing a real or alleged biological characteristic with meaning to define the Other necessarily entails defining Self by the same criterion."[15] But why are Others constructed? The major exponent of the concept of the Other, existentialist philosopher Jean-Paul Sartre, grounded otherness in "the practical intersubjectivity of group formation." Otherness is said to be a manifestation of the human condition. We are condemned to define self and, by this token, to define Others. The human world is a process of perpetual construction of Others, a signification of difference and recognition of self through this signification. Otherness, then, derives from an immanent philosophical anthropological state of reciprocal alienation. Sartre writes: "In short, I produce myself through the Other and for myself as an inessential passing mode of the intersubjectivity of my group in so far as I operate with and on the Other on behalf of this group."[16] This explanation of the origin of Otherness implies unavoidability and could be used to suggest that perception of races is rooted in an essential psychological propensity. Racialization, then, would be an ineradicable feature of human societies.

Observation of difference may be essential to self-recognition, but it does not imply that white and black self-consciousness is either inevitable or universal. In *Before the Mayflower*, historian Lerone Bennett writes of self-conceptions in Virginia's early settlements:

> Of all the improbable aspects of this situation, the oddest — to modern blacks and whites — is that white people did not seem to know that they were white. It appears from surviving evidence that the first white colonists had no concept of themselves as white people. The legal documents identified whites as Englishmen and/or Christians. The word white, with its burden of arrogance and biological pride, developed late in the century, as a direct result of slavery and the organized debasement of blacks.[17]

However, racial classification is not an inevitable accompaniment of debasement. *Some* political economic conditions may be correlated with its emergence. What is universal in racial classification is a certain disregard for logical reasoning.

In allocating themselves to a race by virtue of their skin color, some human beings initiated the racialization of themselves and others. But their racial self-definition reflects flawed reasoning — an equation of a part with the whole. As the philosopher S. Morris Engel defines this error: "What is true of the part is not necessarily true of the whole. To think so is to commit the fallacy of composition. It is to compose the whole out of its parts. The whole, as the old saying has it, is more than the sum of its parts."[18] The color of one's skin — a part of one's body — cannot entail color of personhood. Illogical reasoning underlies the claim: I am a white, or a nonwhite, because my skin is white or nonwhite. However, insofar as logical reasoning is scorned, or illogical reasoning tolerated, such self-definitions will be difficult to abandon. The longevity of racial classification lies, ultimately, in specific formal and informal educational processes.

The Other does not precede the Self. Who *I* am categorically defines who or what *you* are. Human beings are perhaps the only species that asks itself: Who, or what, am I? Answers to this question vary enormously; they are influenced by ecological phenomena, economic conditions, and random events in specific societies. Human beings have named themselves after their gods, territory, the shapes of surrounding mountains, other animals, ways of obtaining the means of life, and anatomical attributes. For example, "I am a European. I was born on a particular land mass named Europe." "I am white because my skin is white." These identities are recorded and passed on from generation to generation; they become a self-perpetuating basis of community and group formation — we.

Classification of the human species is an extension of the answer to the who-am-I, or the who-are-we, question. Mythical stories, imaginary tales, worldviews, and complex social theories are constructed around self and group classifications that identify others and justify particular behaviors. One such construction is the racial theory, whose analytic nucleus is classification of persons according to their anatomical characteristics. This theory runs parallel with other social theories — ethnic, class, and human-centered — that to varying degrees inform perceptions, social studies, and public policies. Figure 1.1 presents elements of racial, ethnic, class, and human-centered theories of society.

The first column comprises general analytical components of theories — criteria of classification, causation, objects of victimization, criteria of stratification, proof structure, and means of conflict resolution, or solutions. Subsequent columns indicate the specific components of a given theory.

This figure indicates that racial, ethnic, class, and human-centered theories contain distinct and mutually irreducible conceptual arrangements. Indeed, race, ethnicity, and class are competitive, rather than supplementary, theories of social relations. More recent writings on

Figure 1.1
A TYPOLOGY OF SOCIAL THEORIES

	Racial	Ethnic	Class	Human-Centered
Criteria of Classification	anatomical	cultural	economic	species
Causation	race and racism	ethno centrism	capitalism	reasoning
Objects of Victimization	races	non-WASPs	working class	all human beings
Stratification	racial power	WASP hegemony	class structure	universal insecurity
Proof Structure	reality	reality	reality	logical rules
Conflict Resolution	racial reforms	acculturation	socialist revolution	educational reforms

race relations, however, suggest a complementarity and an interpenetration of race, culture, and class. Chapters 3 and 4 address issues of race-ethnic and race-class combinations.

In terms of popularity, official usage, and diversity, the racial theory stands head and shoulders above other social theories. Unlike the others, racial classification has had the blessing of "science" and the backing of government. Natural scientists are believed to have observed, not constructed, races. This implicitly justifies the government's racial classification of citizens and the social scientists' research on the relations between races. In conducting this research, social scientists endorse and popularize the "scientific" discoveries and official racial decrees. Their activities, then, are a major contribution to the racializing of social relations. The obviousness of racial differences is a function of their study and propagation; it is the principal effect of studies of race relations. In order to make this less obvious effect obvious, radical and reflexive studies of studies of so-called race relations need to be initiated.

The idea of a "racial theory" indicates a set of integrated propositions on racially classified persons, events, situations, causes of behavior, problems, and solutions. "Racial classification" refers to the use of anatomical, biological, or genetic criteria to form distinct populations. "Racial causation" refers to the imputation of a determining status to racial attributes in the explanation of behavior. The combination of racial classification and causation marks the racial theory as a merging of biological and social sciences. Its criteria of classification produces major racial stocks, primarily Negroid, Caucasoid, and Mongoloid races. As an explanation of history and society, the theory presents causal accounts of relations among races in global historical and domestic contexts.

In the early development of the theory, each race is said to have a culture, or civilization — African, European, and Asian — separate and unequal. Human society is described as a cluster of unequal civilizations produced by unequally endowed races. These propositions surfaced in the pro-slavery treatises of the 1830s, but mushroomed especially in mid-to-late nineteenth-century defenses of inequality, slavery, and colonialism.[19]

The "scientific" embryo of the racial theory is discernible in eighteenth-century biological classifications of the human species. Among the classifications of humankind developed by zoologists and physical anthropologists, Carl von Linnaeus' is significant in its pioneering status. In his *Systema Naturae*, first published in 1735, six subspecies are identified according to skin color, civilization, and continental location. Linnaeus is not averse to offering psychological commentaries on the natural differences discovered among these "races." European man is as intelligent and moral as African man is black and "phlegmatic." Each race is said to have its peculiar temperament, with homo-Europeus being the most astute and energetic. In *On the Natural Variety of Mankind*, published in 1776, anthropologist Johann Blumenbach utilized color, culture, and geographic location to construct five races. Caucasians were regarded as the human prototype.

Blumenbach's classificatory criteria bear a striking similarity to those used in the U.S. Census.

In 1800 the botanist Georges Cuvier constructed a hierarchical racial classification — whites, yellows, and blacks — that emphasized the role of nature in racial formation and cultural development. In his *Inequality of Human Races*, Arthur de Gobineau presented a racial ladder occupied by Caucasian, Mongoloid, and Negro races. Negroes are on the last rung, as the least developed race within the species. Michael Banton refers to de Gobineau and a series of other late-nineteenth-century "typologists" as those who developed "a theory of history purporting to explain the differential patterns of human progress."[20] In their writings, racial typology became part of a general racial explanation of variations in behavior as well as in social inequalities and social change. Races were biological types that corresponded to psychological and social differences. De Gobineau's ladder is not set up on strictly biological grounds.

His ladder signals a transformation of racial classification into a three-tiered hierarchy of racial-civilizational achievements. His equation of "race" and honor crosses the boundary between biology and psychology:

> The negroid variety is the lowest, and stands at the foot of the ladder. The animal character, that appears in the shape of the pelvis, is stamped on the negro from birth, and foreshadows his destiny. . . . The yellow race is the exact opposite of this type. The skull points forward, not backward. The forehead is wide and bony, often high and projecting. The shape of the face is triangular, the nose and chin showing none of the coarse protuberances that mark the negro. . . . We come now to the white peoples. These are gifted with reflective energy, or rather with an energetic intelligence. When they are cruel, they are conscious of their cruelty; it is very doubtful whether such a consciousness exists in the negro. The principle motive is honor. I need hardly add that the word honor, together with all the civilizing influences connoted by it, is unknown to both the yellow and the black man.[21]

De Gobineau identifies three "races" but posits a "subrace" of Aryan Nordics, a superior group within the "white race." What is being suggested is that "whites" themselves are not equally biologically endowed. Because European nations are not equal in their accomplishments, the white race has its weak spots, as it were, and ultimately, miscegenation will cause its degeneration. Thus, de Gobineau's analysis spawns eugenicist and white supremacist wings of the racial theory.

Although de Gobineau's writings are in no sense original, their influence on social and political thought down into the twentieth century is striking. Fear of a yellow peril, horror at miscegenation, and Nazi contempt for Semites can all be found in de Gobineau's propositions on race and historical change. In early twentieth-century eugenicist versions of this idea, social mobility is said to reflect the qualitative genetic structure of the races. It is not the case that certain genes produce anatomical characteristics which identify a race, rather, genes themselves are racially stratified, even among whites, as eugenicists would propose.[22] Hence, all white people are not biologically and culturally equal. In 1916 Madison Grant would publish *The Passing of the Great Race* in which whites are themselves racially stratified. The lower stock of Alpine and Mediterranean types were deemed inferior to those of Teutonic and Anglo-Saxon ancestry and unacceptable as American citizens. His influence may have led to restrictions being placed on East and Southern European immigration through the 1921 and 1924 Immigration Acts and a National Origins Quota Act in 1929. These whites were to be excluded from the white American race.

In late nineteenth-century anthropological and international political economic writings, the construction of the racial theory was intensified. Racial elements were regarded as the alpha and the omega of global developments. Some racial classifications were developed to demonstrate that nonwhite races spring from a different species and were incapable of independently taking the first steps toward civilization. Given this biological superiority of the white race, its culture must also be most advanced. Indeed, the discovery of hierarchical racial differences was intended to demonstrate Europe's cultural superiority. Defenders of slavery and colonialism will claim that slavery and colonialism were a blessing to Africans. The ranking of races justified slavery in terms that brook no refutation — natural biological endowments. Racial classification, then, is part of a larger blueprint of civilizational development, cultural differences, economic organization, and continental inequalities.

It has been suggested that the science of zoology, as developed by the zoologist Linnaeus and applied to the human species to generate various subspecies, took early American statesmen by storm.[23] The notion of a subspecies provided a natural justification for slavery. The Negro was a justifiable "species" of property. His "savagery" cleared the conscience of the framers of the Declaration of Independence and the signatories of the American Constitution. They could keep slaves in the "prison camps" called plantations and simultaneously demand their own freedom from British "tyranny." Slavery was the Negro's fault, an effect of a "Negro nature." In historian Reginald Horsman's words:

> While the Revolution helped to stir some to an attack on slavery, the necessity of justifying the institution in what was now regarded as the freest country in the world under a government theoretically based on the natural equality of mankind, eventually helped produce a specific, intellectual condemnation of the Negro race as separate and inferior. If slavery was to continue then it became essential to demonstrate that the fault lay with the blacks, not the whites.[24]

The lofty ideal that "all men are created equal" was never meant to include all human beings. If there were any remaining doubts about who was "human," racial classification facilitated a dehumanization so that certain persons became Negroes. Negroes, as historian Earl Conrad has suggested, were invented.

Nineteenth-century social studies teemed with racial explanations of events and social conditions. In *Democracy in America*, a work published in 1832 and often cited as a classic in historical observation, Alexis de Tocqueville set the tone of natural, racial predestination:

> It is obvious that there are three naturally distinct, one might say almost hostile, races. . . . Among these widely differing people, the first that attracts attention, and the first in Enlightenment, power, and happiness, is the white man, the European, man par excellence; below him come the

Negro and the Indian. These two unlucky races have neither birth, physique, language, nor mores in common; only their misfortunes are alike.[25]

De Tocqueville's claim on the obviousness and naturalness of races was made over a century and a half ago, before studies in philosophy challenged the epistemological assumption of a distinction between observation and conceptualization. That different numbers of races are discovered by different observers suggests, in fact, that races are not things in nature that are observed by the naked eye. They are a product of the racial classification constructed by observers. As Michael Banton writes: "People do not perceive racial differences. They perceive phenotypical differences of colour, hair form, underlying bone structure, and so on. Phenotypical differences are a first order abstraction. . . . Race is a second order abstraction."[26] The clue to the understanding of assertions of the obviousness, naturalness, and hierarchical characteristics of "races" lies in a philosophical climate that had not yet assimilated the philosopher Immanuel Kant's thesis that the order in nature is produced through reflection by the human mind.[27] The same may be said of racial differences.

RACIAL CLASSIFICATION AND RACIAL SATURATION

There are four principal usages of racial classification.

1. To identify a biologically separate group of human beings. Governments express an endorsement of this "scientific" finding by administratively classifying the population into different races.
2. To explain historical achievements and social conditions. The comparative life situations of persons are demarcated according to their racial features and traced to their genetic or racial psychological attributes.
3. To conduct research. Race is characterized as a socially defined population — blacks and whites, for example — with a specific type of social relations deserving of a subfield in social studies.

4. To locate an individual or self in a larger collectivity. This is evinced in the use of race as a subjective expression of membership in a group.

In analyzing mass racial awareness, attention must be paid to the relationship among these various usages. For example, the combination of social scientific and official practices may be a key factor in citizens' expressions of race membership.

Despite frequently expressed doubts about its scientific status, racial classification enjoys considerable eminence as a research category. Its usage in historical studies has been especially far-reaching. The past is racially conceived and divided. There is white history and nonwhite history as well as European, African, and Asian civilizations. In textbooks on prehistory, something called Western civilization invariably appears at the apex of human achievements. The historical contributions of so-called nonwhites to the development of contemporary civilization are denigrated or made invisible. The umbilical philosophical and scientific connections among Africa, Greece, Rome, and Europe are effaced or marginalized. Artistic, aesthetic, and literary creations are deemed primitive and uncivilized merely by virtue of being produced by persons classified as nonwhite and non-European. The history of the modern world is also racialized. The enslavement of certain Africans becomes a racial act, a case of "white over black," and contemporary social relations an extension of "our racial past." Thus, the racialization of the present is hidden by references to "history."

From cradle to grave, a governmental, media, and academic race-relations complex maintains varying levels of saturation with racial identities. Citizens are placed in racial groups on the basis of particular anatomical attributes as well as racial self-evaluation. Then, in further social studies and research, race is deemed a social reality. Its basis is located in a variety of conditions, such as: capitalism, the class structure, poverty, unavoidable group conflict, sociobiological impulses, the slave past, and human nature. By implication, the activities of government and social scientists bear no responsibility for the generation of race consciousness. But official practices of giving a citizen a racial identity, academic research on race relations, public policies on race relations, school courses on race relations — can these be unrelated to mass racial awareness? The reluctance of social scientists to consider the possibility that the social reality of race is constructed by official, academic, and other institutional practices is surely the nadir of irresponsibility.

Once set in motion by official edicts, racial classification is not only self-perpetuating but also self-justifying. The practice is justified by the racial consciousness it creates. On a variety of official documents, citizens are requested to state their race or ethnicity. In census tabulations, they are asked to respond, indeed, to confess to their race, to examine their skin color, the color of their blood, their type of hair, and the breadth of their nostrils to allocate themselves to racial groups. Race, then, is presented as a natural fact, as a matter of observation and quantification. Most social scientists participate in this racialization of society by avoiding discussions of racial classification, despairing at the power of race, and conducting research on race relations on grounds that race is a social reality. In these conditions, laypersons are not empowered intellectually to question or challenge racial classification.

Can flawed and inconsistently used classifications be a reflection, or grasp the nature, of social reality? Michael Omi and Howard Winant write:

> For example, consider the U.S. census. The racial categories used in census enumeration have varied widely from decade to decade. Groups such as Japanese Americans have moved from categories such as "nonwhite," "Oriental," or simply "Other" to recent inclusion as a specific "ethnic" group under the broader category "Asian and Pacific Islanders."[28]

It is, indeed, paradoxical that while saturating citizens with confused racial categories, government representatives, so-called conservative and liberal scholars, and racial liberationists are critical of the longevity of race. Paradoxical because citizens are expected not to discriminate, to treat one another as human beings while at the same time they are forced to see themselves as belonging to different groups.

A final saturation by default is evinced in educational inputs that exclude instruction in logical thinking. A citizenry incapable of recognizing fallacies cannot discern the absurdities in racial classification.

Indeed, a demonstration of the absurdity of race names and the destructive consequences of their propagation fails to reach either laypeople or legislators. Racial classification and research are defended on the grounds that there are real biological differences and that race consciousness is a social reality which must be dealt with. This type of defense effectively obscures the official and academic racialization of social relations. Thus, it is extraordinarily difficult to find social scientists who would admit to their role in constructing racial perceptions of social relations.

Observation and classification are both part of a theoretically grounded process. For example, the observation of races derives from the use of the anatomical criteria of classification that are specific to a racial theory of society. Similarly, to perceive classes is to utilize economic criteria of classification. The influence of theories on perception cannot be overemphasized. We do not see with our eyes but with our minds. That is to say, a particular thinking process guides an observer's eyes to specific features, which are then "seen." It is in this sense that the philosopher Karl Popper makes the claim that all observation is "theoretically impregnated."[29] The sighting of races is a function of usage of specific criteria of classification.

The 1890 U.S. Census established the official tradition of collecting racial data. The purpose was far from benign. It is no accident that this decade witnessed the most intense attempts to build a segregated racial order. Indeed, the latter part of the nineteenth century signalled a profound policy entrenchment of the naturalist variant of the racial theory. As historian Mark Aldrich writes:

> The period from 1860 to WW1 was the years of the white man's burden and the yellow peril, of Anglo-Saxon concern with race suicide; of the emerging Southern caste system characterized by lynching, disfranchisement of Negroes, jim crow laws; and of the increasingly open exclusion of blacks from the American Federation of Labor.[30]

It was in this same period that the idea of race relations became firmly entrenched in social studies. Races were identified as biological types of persons whose different natures determined their behavior — which, however, was also influenced by social structure. Sociological studies of race relations were initiated by universities, where social scientists examined the natural and social structural conditioning of race relations.

Modern social studies also endorse a focus on measurable physical differences by singling out race relations for study. Various kinds of explanations proliferate. Some analysts point to deficient black genes, white racial consciousness, racism, and biologically based kinship preferences. Others emphasize legacies of slavery, the class structure, culture, and xenophobia. Don Nakanishi writes:

> Research on American race relations is at a critical divide. After a decade or more of collectively debunking demeaning myths and stereotypes about minority life, as well as challenging an array of earlier, order-based theories such as assimilation, the field has come to reflect a rich mosaic of new paradigmatic tendencies and goals. Race, which has always been a fuzzy concept, can no longer be analyzed on its own slippery terms. Instead, it now must be conjugated with often equally muddy notions of class and gender.[31]

However, the mosaic of paradigms does not reflect the richness of social sciences, but the "slippery" and "fuzzy" status of the category race. Why has this confession of its amorphousness not prevented social scientists from studying race relations? One answer suggests that amorphousness is functionally significant for the growth of explanatory models — genetic, sociobiological, internal colonial, power-conflict, economic-class, family-disorganization, cultural-deficiency, white racism, and urbanism. Various solutions also proliferate — reparations for nonwhites, black capitalism, affirmative action and welfare programs, separatism, racial extermination, black power, miscegenation, genocide, repatriation, and multiculturalism. The intrinsic vagueness of race provides the basis of studies of race relations and the growth of a research industry that produces "solutions," which, in turn, become problems requiring solutions.

Given the imprecise status of racial classification, racial relations are an analytical playground. Indeed, the adjective racial is rarely appended to relations. The object of study is race relations, relations between races, not relations that are somehow, or have become, racialized. The mystery of race can be analyzed perpetually. Researchers can have a field day, which stretches into long nights of contemplation of race relations. There is no wake-up call, as the realness ascribed to race results in racial classification becoming a sacred cow of social studies. Its sacredness is evinced in the oft-made claim that race is impossible to abandon. Thus, racial classification surreptitiously acquires a canonical status, which is reinforced by race-specific public policies.

The incorporation of race by educational and research institutions and investments in racial research is not logically justifiable, given the arbitrary status of racial classification. Indeed, from its inception, racial classification was plagued with analytic difficulties. It has been pointed out repeatedly that anatomical criteria such as skin color, facial form, and hair type cannot be decisive as means of demarcating racial types, for there are different gradations of each of these characteristics. Over a billion people — the populations of India, Pakistan, and Indonesia — do not fit the threefold categorization into Caucasoid, Mongoloid, and Negroid. Even more disturbing is the fact that in some classifications, language, skull shape, and culture are also racial identifiers. Not surprisingly, then, intense debates over the number and status of races took place among early travellers, zoologists, ethnologists, and physical anthropologists.

How many races can be counted? Answers range from 3 to 113. Are races so different as to be different species? Are some naturally superior to others? At what point in human evolution did the subspecies become separated, and separate and biologically distinct types (the monogenetic-polygenetic debate)? Are races pure and fixed for all time, or fluid and interrelated? Each answer poses a fresh set of equally puzzling set of questions. Some scholars resigned from the task of discovering what is a race, deeming it a scientific error, a fallacy, a myth, and an ideology. Yet, these doubts have not prevented the U.S. government from institutionalizing racial classification. What is even more perplexing is that scholars bemoan the rise of racism and ignore government's incessant cultivation of racial and national otherness. For example, an endorsement of some notion of racial purity is implicit in the official demarcation of racial and ethnic groups. U.S. citizens are repeatedly requested to state their racial origin, *not origins*, despite over three hundred years of so-called miscegenation.

Why have educators and political representatives not sought to terminate racial classification? Some answers that suggest themselves are: the sharp distinction between natural and social sciences, the conception of natural science as "hard" and the subsequent relegation of social sciences to a "soft" intellectual sector, the noncultivation of respect for logical rules, the political usefulness of a natural explanation of inequalities, and the electoral virtues in having polarized groups that can be played off against each other. Insofar as the whole society loses, in the forms of an "internal war" and diagnostic confusion over social problems, the disrespect for logical rules must be regarded as most significant. Even if public tolerance of racial classification is innocent, given the manifold absurdities of racial classification, this tolerance cannot be separated from certain philosophical-educational conditions.

Allocation to a race is a comparative exercise, and racial cut-off points are clearly not bounded by any canons of consistency or attention to logic. Consider the circular reasoning. Why is a person called black? Because he, or she, is not like whites. And whites? They are defined in terms of their difference from blacks. The arbitrariness is also worthy of note. If the original human being was white, all contemporary blacks have white ancestors. If she was black, present-day whites have black predecessors. If so, however, why are they called whites in the first place? The origin of this arbitrary label is in a racial classification of prehistoric human figures that is as absurd as a dog-breeder's dispute over the breed — the result of a contemporary practice — of the first dog. One implication of these conclusions is that races are not produced by nature, but by a signification of certain anatomical attributes. Nature produces physical variations. Race names such as whites and blacks are derived from hypotheses about biology and social development.

Racial classification is grounded in an overall theory of society that claims that (a) races exist in nature, (b) social, including transnational, inequalities are reflections of racial attributes, and (c) white convictions of nonwhite inferiority underlie policies that generate racial inequalities, oppression, and deprivation. These propositions have been subjected to moral and political evaluations. That is to say, they are not tested primarily for their logical consistency but in terms of their significance for black people and white people. Their advocates and critics are designated racists, conservatives, and antiracists. Such polarized designations stymie the resolution of disputes over so-called race relations. However, they are an inevitable development, which exposes the counterproductiveness of racial classification. Given this practice, scholars themselves can be racially classified and their writings evaluated in terms of whether they are for or against a given racial group. Indeed, because race is said to be of immense behavioral significance, the race of scholars must be taken into account in evaluating their propositions. However, the race of the evaluator is also open to examination. Charges and countercharges of racial partisanship are bound to plague discussions of so-called race relations. Thus, the endorsement of racial classification underlies the longevity of the disputes over racial problems in American society. The problems thereby remain unresolved.

SOME PROCESSES AND PERILS OF RACIALIZATION

The proposition that race is a pervasive feature of American society has been shown to be unacceptably vague and a cover for further racial classification. An alternative analysis could point to practices that racialize discussions of social relations — the official imposition of racial classification, social scientific racial research, the deficient reasoning skills of the population, and conservative-liberationist struggles for political power through promises of justice and progress for whites and blacks. Politicians periodically capitalize on the racial ethos generated by government as well as formal and informal educational institutions. Republican and Democratic election organizers manipulate well-established racial correlations to maintain and augment the support of voters.[32] In the electoral strategies of both parties, race is tied in with crime, affirmative action, welfare, and taxes, as is done in government publications and social scientific discussions. Democrats aspire to retain the so-called black vote by championing racial fairness, racial equality, and civil rights, while Republicans seek to milk white voters' fears of loss of jobs through affirmative action, unsafe streets and homes, and progressive taxation. These votes are critical at the margin, and hence there will be no let up on race-baiting in U.S. politics.

Once in office, politicians must reward their constituents, so that all three branches of government become involved in furthering racial measures. These interventions are often referred to as "the politics of race," but this is a misnomer. It is not race that is being politicized; rather whites and blacks are being manipulated and victimized. This racializing of electoral processes may be said to be a clear manifestation of divide and win, not rule. It is not at all certain that Democrats, or Republicans, rule. It seems more likely that they are themselves ruled by certain social scientific traditions — laissez-faire and Keynesian economic theories, deterrence theory in foreign policy, and the dictum that the ends justify the means.

The development of racial classification was initiated as a justification of certain political economic decisions and arrangements. Its continuation reflects the quality of an intellectual environment that is permeated with anti-intellectualism and money-grubbing. Despite easily accessible literature demonstrating the absurdity and self-destructive consequences of racial classification, community activists vie over corporate funding for racial reform activities, demand racial slices of educational resources and employment opportunities, and jump-start their legislative careers through involvement with racial issues. Media reportage on social problems invariably cites the race of protagonists and the racial proportions in all social phenomena from AIDS to space travel. Film and other artistic creations address even interpersonal relations as racial issues. In effect, citizens are inundated with information about their racial and cultural differences and encouraged to struggle and compete as racial groups — today blacks versus whites, tomorrow blacks versus browns and yellows. The chickens come home to roost in the form of violent confrontations, but those responsible for their breeding are rarely affected.

At the center of racialization is usage of a racial theory whose eminence in intellectual life and public policies is egregiously undeserved. In discussions of social relations, the most frequently posed questions are: What is the state of race relations? How will they unfold during the 1990s and beyond? Various reports suggest that "hate crimes" are on the increase.[33] Predictions of large-scale violence are made, on the grounds that an intensified racism is rearing its ugly head once more. This explanation is unsatisfactory, for racism has so many different meanings that the presentation of any alternative explanation of race relations can incur the response: "That's what I mean by racism." This unfalsifiable status of "racism" will be addressed subsequently. What is more to the point here is that the source of the potential for mass racial confrontations is much more complex. Some of the reasons why a public encounter between two or more persons could escalate into group confrontation are: (1) racial self-classification and classification of the encounter itself; (2) a depressed economic climate; and (3) an increasingly popular electoral utilization of race. In other words, the initial encounters between citizens are not of race; they are made racial.

Conditions such as a recession-driven economic deprivation, a conviction of being wronged and fiscally cheated, and the belief that race is somehow related to these wrongs secrete a collective anger and hostility toward a given race. Thus, an even more significant question must also be raised: To what extent are predictions of mass racial turbulence self-fulfilling? Any mention of race or racial to describe persons and social encounters generates insoluble disagreements. Such descriptions are irremediably vague. Hence, the racially defined and self-defined participants in the encounters cannot resolve verbally their disputes. Virtually all media debates over race relations become exchanges of acrimonious accusations. Racial descriptions, then, simply charge the climate with racial perceptions and frustrate the protagonists. A nonverbal resolution of their disputes emerges as a form of release from unbearable tensions.

In the development and propagation of the racial theory, racial interpretations of social phenomena are pervasive in the media. A quarrel between a police officer and a youth will be racially reported if certain anatomical differences are evident. Indeed, these persons are already so racially hypersensitive that this conflict spells potential "racial" riots. A conflict of interests between a "black" customer and a "Korean" shopkeeper or a "Cuban" police officer portends mass racial demonstrations and violence. Such conflicts of interests take place every moment of the day and are racially described in the media. Hence, the potential for escalation into racial riots is omnipresent. However, in discussions of so-called racial conflicts, the questions not asked are: How do racial descriptions of these individuals and their encounters affect outcomes? Does not the general practice of racially classifying citizens contribute to a self-perpetuating racial polarization? Social conflicts are being racially described because persons are racially classified.

Contrary to what some social scientists claim, this practice is initiated by official institutions. As sociologist Alain Touraine writes:

> On the one hand, the state unifies society from the top downward, by inserting social organization within the framework of the political system and within the field of historicity. It stamps the practices of social life, which on the surface seem relative and changing, with the seal of the absolute, for it is the supreme power and, in Weber's famous phrase, holds the monopoly of legitimate political violence.[34]

More precisely, then, it is Congress, educational institutions, the Census Bureau, and media that "stamp" citizens with the labels whites, nonwhites, and racial minorities. Citizens are not in a position to resist, unless some social scientists and educators initiate a subversion of racialization. What is practiced is subservience and collaboration with government's racialization of social relations. Social scientists, then, are dutifully involved in racialization, but they frequently proclaim their innocence by referring to the force of "the real world." What price their innocence? If anything is to be learned from the "ethnic explosions" in East and Central Europe, it is surely this: The cultivation of group differences, coupled with an educational neglect of logical reasoning competencies, is a recipe for violent social dissolution.

Government and academic institutions, social political activists, and lay citizens make extensive use of racial classifications and explanations. However, an apparent break with racial classification in social studies was initiated in 1978 with the publication of William J.

Wilson's *The Declining Significance of Race*. Wilson argued that race had lost some of its force as a shaper of decisions in modern industrial America.[35] Class differentiations among blacks are so acute that there is no homogeneous black community. Segmental black social mobility, side by side with a worsening of the black underclass situation, suggests that class is a more significant variable in modern urban America. A shifting combination of cultural and structural conditions now generate novel patterns of racial inequality.

Wilson's retention of the traditional focus on "black poverty" indicates that his break with racial classification was only apparent. In fact he maintains racial classification while claiming that race is of diminishing importance. However, no specific definition of race is offered. Wilson's analysis simply plays on various meanings of the word race — racism, racial classification, racial prejudice, racial con-sciousness. . . . If race is taken to mean racial classification, Wilson's thesis is wholly inaccurate. How can race be said to be of declining significance in light of extensive studies of racial experiences as well as the emphasis on racial cultures that passes as multiculturalism?[36] The underlying issue is that some scholars continue to use race equiv-ocally, criticizing its presence, while conducting research on race. Some authors question the causal significance imputed to race, but claim that racism is a powerful ideological force in the real world. This last claim may be denied, but not as a means of seeking "to opt out of history," as Henry Louis Gates, director of the W.E.B. Du Bois Center at Harvard, suspects. The concepts of both race relations and history need to be rescued from the reification implicit in the notion that they are entities that control or have an impact on human beings.

To opt for the racial theory is to choose to preserve the status quo. First, with the classification of so-called inner city residents as blacks comes an implication that their race, or the white race, is responsible for their poverty. The construction and implementation of solutions thereby face a significant hurdle because the identification of the race of the poor, and the designation of race as an influential factor in behavior, give succor to generalizations such as: Whites are racist. Or, something must be biologically or culturally wrong with blacks, if they continue to be overrepresented among the poor. The suspicion that the black poor may be responsible for its poverty necessarily accompanies the qualification black. Second, racial opposition to antipoverty, antidiscrimination, and welfare programs is implicit in their racial description. But it is an impotent opposition because the racist-social causation of poverty can be perpetually challenged with a racial-genetic causation. It follows that studies of racial groups are counterproductive for those being studied. Even if these studies do not present race-specific explanations and solutions, the very selection of racial minorities for study consolidates the racial consciousness that underlies discrimination in the distribution of resources. The identified minorities are constantly reminded that they are victims because of their race and given that race is an unchangeable condition, these minorities are encouraged to regard their socioeconomic conditions as also unchangeable. Thus, the racial identification of poverty contributes to its longevity.

It is generally asserted that "actors" do define themselves and situations racially. Race is a social construct, a phenomenon that must be accounted for by social scientists. These assertions, however, are incomplete. What should be added is that racial classification is an officially engineered and electorally exploited construct whose popularity reflects poorly developed reasoning skills. Mass racial self-definitions are based on capricious references to anatomical attributes; they therefore indicate a tolerance of arbitrariness. These definitions must, therefore, be linked to educational conditions in U.S. society. Nor should their political utilization be ignored. To claim that race is a social construct and omit mention of the political manipulation of the persons classified as black people and white people is to be part of that manipulation.

Social scientists have generally toed the political line and participated in the adoption of a general racial theory of society. Black and white people are presented as victims and villains on the strength of the observation that racial classification has accompanied countless acts of violence. The most frequently described acts of victimization are the conquest and decimation of the Native American population; enslavement of Africans; U.S. amalgamation of Mexican territory; colonization of African, Asian, and American countries; and persecution of Asian-Pacific immigrants. In most race relations writings, whites are identified as the villains in these processes of destruction and deprivation. In keeping to the tradition of ignoring reasoning processes in the analysis of human conduct, these questions are not asked: Who are whites? Is there any logical justification for this designation?

Insofar as it indicates blood lineage, whiteness implies an hereditarian thinking that links the past and the present. "I am white, therefore, whites were my ancestors. I am descended from them." Radical social studies would pursue the issue: How do persons come to define themselves by their skin color, as whites? This self-definition is not ordained by laws of nature. Social scientists have rarely posed the even more significant question, which is: How is the white self-identification related to atrocities in American history — causally, ideologically, or only incidentally? Instead, most texts on race relations announce that white people are racists. But the designation of whites as racists could be as fatalistic as the belief that nonwhites are inferior.

Only within premises that white people are a given of nature and are naturally, morally flawed can there be a refusal to examine their actions as human choices. White skin — and it is surely debatable that this is the skin color of "white people" — is a product of certain biological-ecological processes. However, "white people" is a human-made classification of persons. It refers to human beings who have adopted a white identity or have had it imposed on them; this white identity, however, is a product of an erroneous reasoning process — the equation of skin color and personhood. A rectification of this error leads to the conclusion that human beings, not white people, committed the atrocities against other human beings, not black, brown, red, and yellow people. The actions of all the parties involved were human choices based on their reasoning processes. The refusal to examine human behavior as a manifestation of human reasoning makes a critical contribution to the racialization of American history.

In early racial theorizing, a white race almost replaced God as the creator of the world. As "Lords of Humankind," this race was empowered to extract wealth from other people and continents, govern them, and decide on the moment of their readiness for freedom. Countless acts of human destruction were committed in the name of the natural superiority of the white race. Race, or, more precisely, hierarchical racial classification, was bought lock, stock, and barrel. In writings on society in the last quarter of the nineteenth century, race not only explained continental inequalities, it also justified disfranchisement, segregation, denial of civil rights, and various forms of deprivation. Even opposition to these conditions cites race and racism as the defining features and scourge of American society. But more precisely, it is racial classification, its political utilization, and the quality of education that requires analysis, for the fact that a system of classification, a theory of society, so riddled with fallacies can preoccupy the nation for so long suggests the presence of severe reasoning problems. In other words, the widespread use of racial classification indicts education's neglect of instruction in logical reasoning and conceptual analysis. This conclusion has an optimistic implication. One of the means of resolving America's so-called racial problems is a relatively costless rethinking of social sciences and a philosophical reshaping of curricula.

TWO VARIANTS OF THE RACIAL THEORY

A general racial theory can be constructed from the writings of a variety of eighteenth- and nineteenth-century publicists and social thinkers such as Carl von Linnaeus, Arthur de Gobineau, Houston Chamberlain, Lothrop Stoddard, and Madison Grant. Some of these writings claim a natural scientific status. Others are treatises on history, anthropology, and even sociology. Together they move racial classification beyond biology. It becomes part of a general theory of racial behavior, civilization, and comparative socioeconomic achievements. So influential has been this racial tradition that modern scholars do not critically analyze racial classification, even as some despair at the effects of race. The social theory that has been constructed around racial classification also passes unrecognized. The idea of an overall racial theory, a theory competing with other social theories such as ethnic, class and human-centered, should displace references to race and draw attention to classificatory criteria in social studies.

Classification on the basis of anatomical differences and racial causation are core components of the racial theory. The population is divided into racial groups whose behaviors and cultures are explained with reference to their biological and genetic attributes. The overall premises are that races are a product of nature and that human behavior and history are a reflection of these natural conditions. In effect, scientists and social philosophers constructed various types of races and sought to explain their history, relations, and destinies as biologically determined outcomes. Some scientists investigated the Negro's origin as part of demonstrating that this race was a distinct species, that it was naturally inferior, and that, therefore, slavery was justified. As Benton notes in the mid-nineteenth century, Darwin's *Origin of the Species* refuted the proposition that the so-called Negro race is a distinct species, but not the idea that it was naturally inferior to the white race.

The early attempts at racial classification rely on an anthropocentric conception of nature, that is, nature is presented as a humanlike entity. It (she) is not regarded as a construct devised by human beings to make sense of their observations. Rather, it is a creative force in itself and even a determinant of human behavior. The idea of natural selection signals a high point in the development of naturalist philosophy and natural sciences.[37] The search for natural laws in social processes, including human nature, became a preoccupation of a variety of scholars, and the concept of nature played a critical part in the development of a hierarchical racial classification. Biology, the queen of nineteenth-century sciences, was both a natural and a social science, but its explanatory pivot was nature.

Given the thesis that nature is responsible for variations among and within organisms and for their behavior, survival, or extinction, it follows that science should pursue studies of the nature of races, or the natural cause of a given race's fate. Thus, a striking feature of pro-slavery writings is frequent references to nature and the Negro's natural inferiority and instability. These references, often deemed racial determinism, formed the causal or explanatory element of the racial theory. Its descriptive centerpiece is racial classification; its image of history is of racial confrontation, competition, victimization, deprivation, inequality, *and race-specific behavior.*

The major questions pursued by eighteenth- and nineteenth-century classifiers such as Carl von Linnaeus, Georges Cuvier, François Bernier, Johann Blumenbach, Robert Knox, and Arthur de Gobineau are: What is the role of nature in the making of black people? Why are they so different from whites? Whence their color? Are they of the same species as whites, kin to them, equal to them? The most popular answers to the last three questions were negative. A white race was conceived as the norm as well as the basis for comparative racial judgments. Racial difference means different from whites because whites are assumed to be the race. Persons are called "people of color" because whites are said to be without color. It is whiteness, then, that sets the standard. People of color are investigated in order to ascertain how they stack up in relation to white people. Even most enlightened eighteenth-century minds, such as Voltaire, Rousseau, Jefferson, and Montesquieu, questioned the comparative human status of Negroes. However, historian George Fredrickson writes: "Despite the fact that Jefferson speculated in the 1780's about the possibility that blacks were inherently inferior in some respects to whites, no one in the United States actually defended institutionalized inequality on the basis of racial theory until well into the nineteenth century."[38] Late nineteenth century writings on society fleshed out the earlier, hierarchical racial classifications and used them to assess civilizations and inequalities. Judging by the subsequent frequency of references to Negro inferiority, these writings were immensely influential on social studies, legislative practices, and public policies.

During the last half of the nineteenth century, the racial theory was further amplified by proponents and opponents of slavery and colonialism. As both these phenomena were racially justified, opposition to them became a defense of the Negro or African race. It grew into a liberationist variant of the racial theory that endorses racial classification but rejects the allegation of Negro inferiority. The analytical components of this liberationist variant can be traced to early abolitionist and Pan-Africanist writings.[39] The liberationist school of thought, then, comprises a variety of perspectives on "the black experience" and prescriptions for racial justice. Most of its advocates conceive white racism as the cause of centuries of racial exploitation and oppression. White scholarship is also identified as a practice of political, historical, and cultural distortions. Black scholarship, however, would attend to the liberation of black people, which includes the removal of white falsifications, correction of omissions, and political organization for the eradication of racial victimization, racial discrimination, and oppression.[40]

In liberationist writings, the so-called nonwhite races are urged to struggle continually against white racist policies and attitudes, which are presented as the primary cause of black suffering. The beginning of the twentieth century witnessed the mushrooming of this variant of the racial theory. Its advocates launched attacks against the naturalist tenet that identifies genetic deficiencies in nonwhite populations as the determining elements in their behavior and comparative underachievements and naturalist strategies of racial disfranchisement and segregation. The writings of the Boas school of cultural anthropology initiated a persuasive repudiation of racial determinism, and the works of W.E.B. Du Bois, Marcus Garvey, and scores of other thinkers provided intellectual ammunition, and organizational leadership, and gave birth to complex perspectives on "black liberation."

The cardinal thesis of most contemporary liberationist writings is that white society is shot through with racism, racial discrimination, and racial inequalities. It is observed that nonwhites congregate in the lower echelons of occupational, residential, educational, and corporate hierarchies. This does not imply that some whites are not also socially, economically, and politically victimized. Rather, the argument is that racial minorities are victimized *because they are nonwhite*. Thus, Native Americans, Hispanics, African Americans, Mexican Americans, and Asian Pacific Americans are disproportionately represented among the poor and the powerless. They are racial minorities, victims of historical patterns of racial discrimination and oppression because of their racial and/or cultural characteristics.

The data generated by the liberationist variant of the racial theory indicate that nonwhites experience high unemployment, low income, substandard housing, inadequate education and training, miscarriages of justice, media stereotypes, social rejection, civil rights abuses, immigration maltreatment, and health care neglect. Some descriptions of these conditions contain mild and even neutral language. Others present poignant and painful images of suffering. However, there is a general agreement that racial inequalities and disadvantages permeate American society and that racism is of some behavioral and policy significance. According to the more militant liberationist analyses, the correlation between nonwhite skin and conditions of deprivation is not a coincidence. American society is consciously and unconsciously racially oppressive. Nonwhites should resist by organizing and struggling for political power, legal reforms, and ameliorative economic policies, or even initiate a race war. Separation of the races is also an option and may even be inevitable.

Writings within the liberationist variant comprise various perspectives — conservative/meritocratic (Thomas Sowell, Walter Williams, Glenn Loury, Clint Bolick, Shelby Steele), liberal (William J. Wilson, Bernard Boxill, Thomas D. Boston), radical/Marxist (Oliver C. Cox, Robert Allen, Manning Marable, Victor Perlo, Carl Boggs), cultural nationalist/Afrocentric (Harold Cruse, Maulana Karenga, Cheik Anta Diop, Molefi Asante, Asa Hilliard III), fundamentalist (Malcolm X, Frances Cress Welsing, Leonard Jeffries, Hakim Madhabuti), and separatist (Marcus Garvey, Elijah Muhammad, Louis Farrakhan). Liberal and conservative perspectives are analyzed in greater detail in Chapter 3, while the radical/Marxist or race-class wing of the liberationist variant is further discussed in Chapter 4.

The following caveats must be introduced in order to avoid any misunderstanding of these categories. First, the term liberationist is not pejoratively used; it depicts a theme of concern with progress and justice for black people, or African Americans. This concern is common to all the perspectives. Second, this listing of authors is not exhaustive. Third, the writings of any particular author often not only span different perspectives, but also present overlapping arguments, especially because there is a consensus that racism is an active force in American society. Fourth, the disagreements within these writings reflect, inter alia, different social scientific disciplines, although many writers cross disciplines at will. For example, elements of Marxism and conflict sociology underlie the radical/Marxist perspective, while Weberian sociology and Keynesian economics are seminal to the liberal analysis. Laissez-faire economics informs the conservative-meritocratic perspective, while the disciplines of psychology and history are represented in the fundamentalist approach, which focuses on the workings of a racist white mind in the history of the post-Columbus world. Disciplinary boundaries and specializations underlie some of the internal liberationist disputes over "the black experience." Finally, the terms used to identify these different perspectives by no means validate, or invalidate, any of their arguments. "Fundamentalist," for example, refers to the axiomatic status of the premise about the racist nature of white people and American society.

The divergent perspectives within the liberationist variant are also extensions of disputes among "classical" works in social sciences. This is all the more reason why social scientists should establish ground rules of intellectual exchanges. For example, as indicated in the introduction, distinctions should be maintained among affirmation, denunciation, rejection, repudiation, and refutation. In the interest of conclusiveness in intellectual exchanges, scholars should refrain from denunciation, rejection, and repudiation. It follows that the disputes among those scholars concerned with the liberation of black people cannot be resolved without a recognition of their doctrinal, philosophical, and disciplinary roots. Indeed, these disputes replay dissensions among free market, Keynesian, and Marxist economics, order and conflict perspectives in sociology, psychohistorical and materialist-structuralist analyses, cultural and political economic explanations of human behavior, and the problem of the status of "empirical proof" in social studies. Insofar as these issues are not explicitly addressed, the disputes are bound to remain unresolved.

Advocates of the naturalist variant suggest that racial inequalities should be explained as a manifestation of the inferior or deficient genetic makeup of nonwhites. In the liberationist variant, this explanation is itself deemed racist, for the explanation of white behavior in terms of racism is central to the liberationist school of thought. However, the preeminence of racism diminishes along the separatist-conservative spectrum of liberationist perspectives. For example, in separatist and fundamentalist perspectives, white racism is presented as a historical destroyer of black people, and whites are depicted as irredeemable racists. Evidence of their racism is provided by statistical indices of rampant racial discrimination and chronic disparities between the consumption levels of nonwhites and whites. The state of black America is said to be suggestive of "genocidal" white racist intentions. White racism goes beyond class prejudice. Only a deeply embedded belief that blacks are inferior beings could tolerate the astronomical level of destruction unleashed by slavery and contemporary racial oppression. It is white racism that rationalizes white privileges and motivates whites toward the destruction of black people. The claim that white people, are inveterate racists is the stronger of the second fundamentalist assertion that American society is plagued with racism and racial discrimination.

By contrast, in liberal and meritocratic writings, racism is simply one of many factors shaping the black experience. The fundamentalist emphasis on racism is criticized as simplistic. In the liberal perspective represented in the writings of William J. Wilson, racism, a force behind slavery, still persists as an "ideology." But it is a problem, not *the* problem facing blacks. Rather, changing urban institutions and economic processes now constitute the principal obstacles to the socioeconomic advancement of certain segments of the black population. Wilson argues that race and racism are conditions that operate only periodically. In the contemporary industrial period, the socioeconomic conditions confronting the black underclass derive from the changing technostructure of an economy being dislocated by global competition.

In the liberal perspective, racial inequalities are regarded as the consequence of a combination of irrational public policies and a racist ideology that, however, is of decreasing significance. This perspective shares with the conservative perspective the contradiction of deemphasizing race and simultaneously studying blacks. Indeed, the standard, conservative and liberal repudiation of the radical/Marxist, fundamentalist, and Afrocentric stress on racism is expressed in the question: If racism is so pervasive, why are some blacks "making it"? In Shelby Steele's *Content of Our Character*, it is argued that even if whites are racist, moral condemnation of them does not absolve blacks of their own responsibilities. Blacks must cease to wallow in self-defeating psychoses of paranoia and victimization and dependency on government welfare interventions. Blaming the victimizer leads to self-immobilization, not liberation.[41] The disputes among so-called liberals, radicals, and conservatives are analyzed in Chapter 3.

Criticisms of so-called black conservatives abound in the militant and civil rights advocacies of liberation through moral condemnation of whites and appeals to the government for redress through affirmative action and antidiscrimination laws. The arguments and counterarguments are reminiscent of the early twentieth century disputes among W.E.B Du Bois, Booker T. Washington, and Marcus Garvey; they are significant in their longevity and philosophical implications. But they represent controversy rather than conclusive intellectual exchanges, because they are characterized by infinitely regressive statistical wars over the reasons for and extent of black progress and personal-political denunciations. These disputes, however, negate (1) the implication of homogeneity in the term black scholarship, (2) the analysis of whites and blacks as undifferentiated socioeconomic entities, and (3) the claim that any particular description of socioeconomic conditions reflects the real world. This realist claim is the bane of empirical studies. Divergent and competing "realities" cannot be equally credible. How many realities can there be, and if an infinite number, which one is to be taken as definitive? Then the question arises: Real according to whom? This philosophical quandary continues to haunt studies of race relations that claim a purchase on the real world.

In radical/Marxist writings, racism, in conjunction with capitalism, is held responsible for racial discrimination, oppression, and exploitation — endemic features of the black experience under capitalism. These race-class analyses propose that blacks are exploited as members of a class and because of their race. In this sense, white racism dovetails with capitalism to superexploit the black working class. Another version of radical/Marxist perspective claims that black and white workers have different relationships to the means of production and thus constitute different working classes. This perspective is examined in Chapter 4.

The Afrocentric analysis of race relations is exemplified in the writings of Cheikh Anta Diop, although it is preceded by a wealth of pan-Africanist and cultural nationalist theses in the writings of Marcus Garvey, W.E.B. Du Bois, George James, J. A. Rogers, Harold Cruse, and Maulana Karenga. Diop's writings, however, constitute the most extensive exposition of the liberationist variant of the racial theory, in the context of the role of blacks in ancient history.[42] As in the works of Du Bois and Garvey, the goal of liberating blacks from both historical falsifications about Africa and from racial oppression is explicitly stated. Diop develops an Afrocentric prehistory of race relations. Following is a summary of its main theses on the relationship between race and ancient history.

1. The human species was originally African (that is, black).
2. Ancient Egyptians were black.
3. Modern blacks and whites are offshoots of original black and white races, which can be linked to Egypt and Europe, respectively.
4. The white race is a relatively recent mutation of a black human prototype.

In the pursuit of black liberation, the ancient past is to be reconstructed within an Afrocentric focus. The black race must be at its center. However, politics apart, the "truth" must be told about ancient civilizations. Thus, advocates of "a black Egypt" further claim that ancient Egypt was the fountainhead of Western civilization, including its philosophical, scientific, and technological achievements, and that Egypt's achievements, in turn, are indebted to Nubian and Ethiopian civilizations up the Nile. Black people, then, cannot be biologically inferior to white people. Thus, the Afrocentric perspective *repudiates* the cardinal naturalist tenet that blacks are so genetically backward that they have never produced civilization.

Afrocentricity embodies a project of positive historical self-discovery, as a necessary prelude to political and socioeconomic liberation. Blacks throughout the world are to "rediscover their historical memory." As Diop writes:

There is for us the necessity to organize instruction of history in view of the cultural renaissance. We must construct a new Afro-American cultural personality within the framework of our respective nations. Our history from the beginning of mankind, rediscovered and relived as such, will be the foundation of this new personality.[43]

The political cast of the Afrocentric perspective entails an endorsement of racial classification and an imputation of cultures to races. As in the general racial theory, the terms, black people and white people have no fixed conceptual status. Black people are claimed to be the ancestors of white people and, for political purposes, a race distinct from white people. In other words, the Afrocentric analysis fails to address the issue of genetic similarities among anatomically defined races. It seeks merely to repudiate specific naturalist assertions about black inferiority and civilization. Thus, it does not challenge racial classification, but rejects any causal connection between civilization and racial "intelligence."

No specific racial characteristic is to be held responsible for advances in civilization. Diop writes:

I can say that all studies to make a hierarchy of intelligence among the races have been failures. The truth is, man has the same origin. His adaptation to different climates does not permit a hierarchy of intelligence. Only superficial changes of appearances have occurred. All races have the same intellectual capacities.[44]

Races are not specially endowed. Diop does not propose a hierarchical racial classification; he asserts that in the origination of humankind in Africa, black skin and, hence, a black race, was biologically first. A white race derives from Cro-Magnon Man, who was a descendant of black-skinned women who migrated to Europe. Diop writes:

The man born in Africa was necessarily dark-skinned due to the considerable force of ultraviolet radiation in the equatorial belt. As he moved toward the more temperate climates, this man gradually lost his pigmentation by process of selection and adaptation. It is from this perspective that the appearance of Cro-Magnon Man in Europe must be seen. In the Solutrean he is seen after 20,000 years of adaptation and transformation

from the Grimaldian negroid in the condition of the final Würm glacia-
tion. Therefore, Cro-Magnon Man did not come from anywhere. He is
rather the product of mutation of the Grimaldian negroid where he was
found and no pre-historical archeology has provided any other explanation for his appearance.[45]

Diop's retention of racial classification is part of an Afrocentric
political project, and it results in a logically flawed analysis. Why are
black and white civilizations being studied, if racial attributes have no
significance for the development of civilizations? Indeed, how did
these civilizations become racial phenomena? The error in de
Gobineau's claim that Negroes had no civilization was not historic-
factual but conceptual. Black and white races were conceptualized
prior to their "observation" in prehistory.

Diop's effort to identify white and black races, 5 million years ago
when facial forms were surely Simian must rest solely on skin color,
a "modern" concern. It amounts, then, to sheer speculation, because
there are no records of the skin color of these "men." Nevertheless, the
speculation involves a confusion of genotype and phenotype. Climatic
conditions are said to have forced a lightening of skin color in the
Grimaldian negroid, which mutated into Cro-Magnon Man, which led
to a white race that is distinct from the black race and at the same time
a descendant of this race. The two races may be said to be genotypically
kindred extensions of one species. However, one significant implication of the linear color descendancy is that all kinds of phenotypical
races can be demarcated anywhere on a spectrum of skin colors. A
yellow or a brown race in Egypt may be said to have been the actual
builders of that civilization. Diop's Afrocentric history attempts to
marry positively blackness and "civilization." As Greek civilization
was white, so Egypt's, its alleged fountainhead, can be shown to have
been black. However, the so-called whites who built Greek civilization
had black ancestors and, therefore, could be called blacks. Similarly,
the so-called black Egyptians were descendants of "white" Cro-Magnon Man. In effect, Egyptian and Greek civilizations cannot be classified according to the race of their builders; they were neither black nor
white.

Naturalist and liberationist arguments revolve around relations between blacks and whites and their roles in history. They identify races acting in history, rather than decisions taken by persons who are classified as races. Certain arguments are divergent, however. Some distinctly naturalist tenets are as follows:

1. Races are naturally unequally endowed.
2. Socioeconomic inequalities are derived from nonwhite genetic deficiencies.
3. Race relations problems need no special solutions, except perhaps segregation, and especially not government interventions for racial equality.

By contrast, liberationist writings assert:

1. Races are biologically equal.
2. Racial discrimination, poverty, and oppression are caused by a moral deficiency within whites, their racism.
3. Race relations need government intervention; indeed, racial inequalities are a product of interventions from white governments.

Naturalist and liberationist writings share these theses:

1. Races are found in nature; they are not the product of human classification.
2. The history of the world is a history of racial contact, confrontation, and conflict.
3. Race relations and racial inequalities are an observable social reality.

In the naturalist variant the comparative history and achievements of groups are explained in terms of their biological or genetic attributes. In de Gobineau's writings, for example, non-Nordic Aryans — that is, less-achieving groups within white societies, are identified as racially inferior to Nordic Aryans. White and nonwhite races are presented as scientifically established facts; they are systematically studied and said to have their own civilizations, cultures, psychologies, and life situations that are determined by their natures. The influence of this variant is discernible in much of nineteenth-century legislation that legalized "separate but equal" institutions. Disfranchisement, jim crowism, repatriation, and separatism are standard, naturalist solutions to problems between the races. The Supreme Court decision of *Plessy v. Ferguson* (1896), which made segregation the law of the land, expresses the legal triumph of the idea that black and white races are born to be unevenly polarized.

In explaining social conditions, the naturalist variant emphasizes innate racial differences, while the liberationist school of thought cites the racist nature of whites as the cause of the destruction of nonwhite civilizations and of racial inequalities. It is against these atrocities that liberationist protests have been raised. However, liberationist writings do not refute naturalist tenets; they are involved in repudiation, the presentation of other facts, observations, and experiences, not refutation. A process of refutation requires examination of criteria of racial classification and the logical structure of the arguments involved in the explanation. Users of the liberationist variant of the racial theory cannot engage in this. Rather, they develop diverse versions of race relations that necessarily retain the classifications whites and blacks. Some advocates of racial liberation attribute a marginal causal efficacy to racism. Others accuse whites of being inveterate racists.

Like the liberationist, the naturalist variant comprises diverse versions — eugenicist, social Darwinist, white supremacist, and sociobiological. They are all deemed "conservative" by virtue of their emphasis on a natural state of affairs that manifests itself in socioeconomic inequalities. Each has been characterized as racist by adherents of the liberationist variant. However, if racism is taken to mean a belief in the genetic inferiority of blacks, this accusation does not apply to all versions of naturalist writings. One suggests that the inferior genetic makeup of nonwhites is the cause of their socioeconomic deprivation. Another cites cultural deficiencies, which may or may not be biologically determined. Thus, racial welfare policies, especially government interventions, are merely tilting at windmills. Inequality is part of the natural order of survival and success of the fittest; it is not so much racial as meritocratic and "altruistic." Finally, the sociobiological perspective proposes that genetically based affinities underlie racial kinship systems which are inherently discriminatory. Racial inequality

Figure 1.2
VARIANTS OF THE RACIAL THEORY

	Naturalist	Liberationist
Classificatory Criteria	anatomical	anatomical
Causation	black genetic deficiencies	white racism
Objects of Victimization	whites	blacks
Stratification	white power	black power
Proof Referent	empirical data reality	empirical data reality
Solution	laissez-faire segregation separatism	anti-racist legal, cultural, and political econo- mic reforms

is a product of the altruistic behavior of groups in pursuit of the survival of their kin.

Figure 1.2 illustrates structural components of naturalist and liberationist variants of the racial theory.

Liberationist and naturalist variants of the racial theory diverge, specifically, at levels of causation and solution. In the liberationist variant, racism is the causal force in white behavior and the ultimate source of black suffering. Adherents of the naturalist variant deny this assertion, arguing that, because blacks are naturally inferior, they cannot hope to have equality with whites and should be grateful for the contacts with the superior white race and civilization. Naturalist writings also deny that whites are oppressors. Whites are merely fulfilling their natural destiny. Ku Klux Klan and other naturalist representations claim that, in contemporary U.S. society, whites are in danger of becoming victims of a black-liberal government coalition.[46] Indeed, some assert that there is no race problem, as such. Black poverty is to be explained in terms of black genetic and cultural deficiencies. The two races are destined to live separately; their enforced integration will result in race war. In the interest of both maintaining supremacy and ensuring survival, whites should prepare for inevitable racial confrontations or organize themselves to seize political power. These arguments may be reminiscent of Nazi demagogy. However, what should be noted is that as long as official racial classification continues and as long as social scientists and liberationist advocates persist in describing social conditions through the prism of a black-white polarity, some political aspirants will also develop extensions of naturalist ideas. As Louisiana state representative David Duke realizes, if these ideas can be polished into a program for the defense of so-called white interests, certain electoral successes can be attained.

Disputes between *and among* naturalist and liberationist advocates should be called more accurately controversies because they cannot be resolved. What can be conclusive about discussions in which, at any time, a participant may claim "truth" because of being more in touch with a particular racial "reality" or by citing selected personal experiences and observations? For example, realistic proof of the proposition that "blacks are lazy" would be a television camera roaming through a housing project in a certain part of Brooklyn. Proof of widespread racial discrimination consists of surveys of employers' practices that produced different patterns of rejection for black and white applicants. However, given that the applicants were professional actors, objections can be made to their performances. Did they overplay or underplay racial issues during the interviews? Are their qualifications equal in terms of the stature of their alma mater, major, grades, references, mannerisms, and regional accents? Were gender differences controlled, as unemployment among black males is higher than among black females? The empirical tug of war continues, and no winner can emerge because the source of the disputes is not in people's experiences but in premises on how the society operates.

Each variant of the racial theory endorses the racial classification of persons so that the race of disputants itself easily becomes an element in disputes and in research. Can whites be nonpartisan about issues affecting the black race? A negative answer is suggested by the overrepresentation of nonwhite researchers in racial studies. But, by this token, the knowledge they produce is also partisan. It should come as no surprise that most recommendations for improving race relations, or eradicating racism are systematically ignored by policymakers. These recommendations do, however, provide the basis for more discussions, conferences, symposia, publications, and a periodic heightening of controversy over "worsening" race relations. The disputants do not examine the possibility that the controversies themselves perpetuate racial perceptions and policies, or perceive the contradiction in simultaneously disseminating explanations of race relations and decrying the presence of racial consciousness.

In the naturalist variant, genetic attributes are held responsible for racial achievements and underachievements. For example, it is argued that the Negro's genetic inferiority caused enslavement and its aftermath of socioecomic inequalities. This explanation has been endorsed in documents of slaveowners, state legislatures, colonial governments, and certain contemporary "scientific" studies. In 1969 psychologist Arthur Jensen proposed that the inferior genetic endowments of blacks are responsible for their educational underachievement. Jensen presented a series of cross-racial intelligence tests to demonstrate the related thesis that black Americans were genetically inferior to whites.[47] Some reviewers of Jensen's propositions have accused him of racism, refuted his conception of intelligence as a measurable element that can be equated with test scores, challenged the cultural representativeness of both his tests and his racial samples, and exposed a flawed methodology within the proposed correlation between race and IQ.[48]

A critical weakness in Jensen's research pertains to its circular conception of race. Races are defined with reference to anatomical characteristics, which are a product of genes, which are responsible for the anatomical elements that define a race. Jensen writes:

> Races are more technically viewed by geneticists as populations having different distributions of gene frequencies. These genetic differences are manifested in virtually every anatomical, physiological and biochemical comparison one can make between representative samples of identifiable racial groups.[49]

The implicit methodology needs to be analyzed. Races — persons with different anatomical features — are observed with the naked eye.

Representative racial samples are selected, by fiat. These different racial representatives are then tested for comparative gene frequencies that show them to be of different races. In other words, the races were defined prior to the genetic measurements. Whites are as different from blacks as apples are different from oranges. Proof? Go pick some apples and oranges and compare them. Yet, how is the picker to know what to pick? A person cannot observe races without being told of the qualities that make a race.

Jensen's comparisons were not based on the geneticists' (which?) conception of race. The number of genes in a human organism has been estimated at tens of thousands. The gene frequencies that produce different degrees of pigment, hair type, eye color, and facial form exist side by side with gene loci that are responsible for millions of similarities within the human species. Blacks and whites share a vast number of genes. Their anatomical differences can be repudiated by reference to their other genetic similarities. A skin-color, facial-form, and hairtype race may be a nonrace, if skull shape is taken as a racial criterion. Thus, in identifying races, Jensen necessarily abandons genes as the basis of racial demarcation and relies on popular observation. As he confesses:

> Socially we usually have little trouble recognizing a person's race, based on overall physical appearance. If a group of persons were asked to classify racially the various people they observe on the streets of any large city in the United States, there would undoubtedly be very much agreement among their classifications. And if the persons so classified were asked to state their racial background, there would be high agreement with the observers' classifications. This is the social meaning of race used by the proverbial "man in the street." It is also the form of racial classification used in the vast majority of studies of racial differences in IQ.[50]

Some pages later, the author also admits that: "The average American black has received about 20-25 percent of his or her genes from Caucasian ancestors."[51] Thus Jensen discards genes as the basis of race but retains them as a unit of heredity. This implies that each of the children tested represented not a race but individually unique gene frequencies. If racial genes are not abandoned, then, it may be argued that the mixture of white, red, and black genes among the U.S. population surely makes it a hybrid race. Jensen's selection of a representative of a race is an arbitrary act. His "American blacks," then, are genetically disguised whites, unless white genes do not make a person white.

What significantly enjoins both variants of the racial theory is the proposition that race is a biological or a social "reality." As de Gobineau wrote: "I was gradually penetrated by the conviction that the racial question overshadows all other problems of history."[52] In 1898 W.E.B. Du Bois restated this thesis in his oft-quoted: "The problem of the twentieth century is the problem of the color line." Du Bois also recognized that racial classification is nonsense. He wrote: "Three, five, twenty races were differentiated, until at last it was evident that mankind would not fit accurately into any scientific delimitation of racial categories; no matter what criteria were used, most men fell into intermediate classes or had individual peculiarities."[53] There is no color line, only lies about color. Indeed, Du Bois writings demonstrate that the problem is not color but an absurd racial classification.

Races are not produced by a simple observation of color differences. People may notice these differences, without allocating persons to races. In studies of race relations, it is claimed that actors attach significance to certain physical differences to make race a social reality. What is not exposed is the reasons for and sources of this attachment. Attempts at such an exposé would be suicidal. They would have to address the practices of social scientists, community activists, foundations, corporations, lobbyists, and journalists.

Once race is officially endorsed, special interest groups intervene to demand resources for certain races or protection of the position of others, because the identification of racial proportions in the population leads inevitably to demands for proportional racial representation in especially the upper echelons of institutions. In the resulting racial dogfights, citizens become hypersensitized about anatomical differences and cannot see the human forest for the racial trees. This condition of enforced racial awareness is then referred to as a social reality and a justification for further racial research and policies on race. The official racial classification, liberationist and naturalist research, and public policies on racial problems are not conceived as themselves generative of racial awareness. This lack of self-reflexiveness makes nonsense of the claim that race relations studies are aimed at (changing) social reality. If they were, surely such studies would be especially conscious of their social consequence of conservation. Race relations studies cannot lead to the amelioration or eradication of racial problems; indeed, they create and feast on them.

SOCIOLOGY'S INCORPORATION OF
RACIAL CLASSIFICATION

It is a tribute to the reign of biology as the queen of nineteenth-century sciences that the works of the so-called classical sociologists, Karl Marx, Max Weber, and Emile Durkheim, contain numerous references to races. Indeed, it is testimony to the influence of the naturalist variant in the nineteenth century that these three "founding fathers" of sociology mention "inferior" and "uncivilized" races.[54] In the development of an American sociological tradition heavily influenced by Herbert Spencer's social evolutionist and eugenicist treatises, competition between Negroes and whites becomes a social scientific object of study. Their relations were, naturally enough, race relations. Sociology did not present race as a human categorization of certain physical attributes but as a manifestation of nature's purpose and a measure and explanation of social inequality and behavior. Race was considered eminently applicable to social change and useful for social control. The history of human interaction was interpreted as a story of racial-cultural contact, competition, confrontation, and victimization. Explanations of racial outcomes reached into economics, culture, morality, and, above all, biological endowments. Late-nineteenth-century sociologists and social reformers and, indeed, the whole intelligentsia unhesitatingly appropriated racial classification.

It has been further claimed that the writings of Max Weber are especially significant for race relations studies.[55] Indeed, some of Weber's writings deal explicitly with relations among ethnic groups.[56] Sociologist John Rex's construction of "a Weberian approach" to race relations makes reference to Weber's historical comparative investigations of slavery; his writings on class stratification, status honor, the relationships among slave labor, estates, and wage labor; as well as his conception of sociology's purpose. Rex concluded that sociology is ideally poised to investigate race relations. Early American sociology, then, was not in breach of the Weberian sociological tradition in focusing on racial and ethnic groups. In the 1920s, the writings of Robert Park and his associates at the University of Chicago initiated the development of a specific subdiscipline — the sociology of race relations.[57] Its mission was to investigate the experiences of the various races interacting in America's growing urban conglomerates. Racial groups were defined both as a fact of nature and a social fact. Race relations and urban sociological studies would record the empirical features of racial and cultural contacts. Such studies, then, become an extension of the early biologists' project of finding a natural explanation of relations among races.

Sociological studies were formed within an ethos of concern with unequal racial destinies, racial competition, racial experiences, and racial mixing. One of their purposes was to chart the course of the contacts and relations among races and cultures, because each race was supposed to have its own culture. Writing in 1958, sociologist Brewton Berry captures the early sociologists' passion for racial and cultural differences:

> Race has always been one of the major concerns of sociologists. The first two sociological books published in the United States, a century ago, dealt with the problem. . . Sociologists were fascinated by the task of classifying mankind, of studying the physical and mental characteristics of races, and of measuring these differences. They spent their efforts in the futile attempt to explain social phenomena in biological terms. The second period witnessed a shift to a cultural frame of reference.[58]

The presence of races in the New World was considered a phenomenon worthy of intense study. How will Negroes fit into the proto-European societies emerging in the Americas? The research interests of early-twentieth-century American sociology not only reflect but also justify this concern with racial arrangements and contacts. It was argued that even if the concept of race is ambiguous, it has some meaning for social actors and, hence, race relations should be studied. Even if racial differences are insignificant, culture differences are obvious and undeniable.

Sociologists do not generally seek to refute racial classification, although doubt is often cast on the scientific status of race. In most texts on race relations, it is suggested that the discovery of races is not based on a pursuit of an objective system of classification. By implication, biology is no more "scientific" than sociology; it may even be a servant of political overlords. Colette Guillaumin argues that because natural sciences took their research cues from social needs and problems, as defined by the powers-that-be, racial demarcation may be said to reflect relationships of power. She writes: "There still remains the obsessional linking of physical characteristics with social relationships or, more accurately, the invention of physical characteristics to go with the social relationships of domination. Wherever there is a power relationship, a somatic trait is found or invented.[59] The purpose of racial classification is the explanation or justification of socioeconomic differentiation, forms of domination, and policies that lead to socioeconomic disparities. Its underlying suggestion is that racial characteristics account for different customs, aptitudes, and social organization. The subordinated group is in its natural place. This invocation of "nature" obscures the choices that led to the subordination.

Guillaumin argues that racial classification of the human species represents a naturalization of particular social relations for purposes of social control. In identifying social conditions in biological attributes, the former are given an aura of essentiality and unavoidability. The classification into races represents a triumph for "somatic determinism," the argument that social relations are based on mutual assessments of physical images for likeness. It also marks a victory for biology as queen of not just natural sciences. In the development of the racial theory, specific physical differences are singled out as defining a race, and are used to account for levels of social development. The development of civilizations is conceived as a product of biological evolution and race-specific endowments. Racial classification is part of an explanation of social developments; it is, therefore, not a product of sciences that deal with something outside of society called "nature."

With the allocation of human beings to races, biological sciences cannot be deemed nonsocial, or natural, as opposed to social, sciences. As Guillaumin writes:

> The modern idea of race derives not from observation in the field of natural sciences but from the instigation of society and politics. Political and social theories, not only those of professional thinkers, but also popular ones of which the latter have taken advantage raised questions to which the natural sciences sought to find answers in the form of roots or traces. . . . [60]

Two significant implications of these remarks are that, first, race membership is not a natural scientific term, because the distinction between biological and social sciences is questionable. Second, the notion of race membership represents an attempt by biological scientists to explain how human organisms function in society. To achieve this objective they had to claim that persons belong to their biological attributes. Studies of race relations continue an investigation of the social fate of biological entities while asserting that human beings are more than just biological entities. Recognizing this inconsistency, sociobiologists claim that their project of bringing nature back in is a necessary part of social studies.[61]

Arguing that a genetically based idiom of survival underlies racial discrimination and inequality, sociologist Pierre L. van den Berghe suggests that sociobiology should not be a pejorative term, for insofar as it is accepted that human beings are both biologically and socially constituted, all studies of human behavior are sociobiological. In van den Berghe's words: "Sociobiology is, in fact, little else than a more theoretically grounded, and less descriptive brand of ethology informed by behavior genetics."[62] Biology is not an asocial science. The biological makeup of human beings covers a wide variety of material substances, such as protons, neutrons, electrons, hormones, and genes. Each influences behavior, but the extent of its influence is indeterminable, because behavior is mediated by social structure and culture.

Sociobiology purports to reduce the area of indeterminacy surrounding the question of the interaction between nature and society. However, as in van den Berghe's analysis, nature invariably triumphs. The reference to the social is only rhetorical, as social structure and culture are stripped of all influence. Ethnic and racial stratification are conceived as an elongation of a kinship system, which is, in turn, an effect of genetic arrangements. The behavior of racial groups is conceived as an effect of their genetic attributes. The social is reduced to a cocoon in which genetic traits manifest themselves, even to the extent of forming the cocoon. Whites are, therefore, said to be biologically programmed to favor their kin. Races are competitive because behavior traits are linked to alleles within genes that predispose individuals to pursue a particularistic and selfish altruism. It is then concluded that racial affiliation and discrimination against outsiders are derived from the genetically based predispositions of social animals, as they compete over scarce resources and seek to "maximize inclusive fitness." As van den Berghe writes: "Animals, in short, are nepotistic, i.e. they prefer kin over non-kin, and close kin over distant kin."[63] By extension, it is suggested that members of a given race will be naturally favorably disposed toward one another as part of an attempt to duplicate their genes and "maximize inclusive fitness." Both racial altruism and racial discrimination are extensions of "the idiom of kinship" and, by implication, ineradicable.

This type of sociobiological analysis is not faithful to its combinational designation because it grounds behavior in "a genetic mechanism." It does not resolve the issue of social and biological interaction, except to note that behavior is influenced by considerations of kinship; it represents the natural explanation of racial behavior to which eighteenth- and nineteenth-century biologists aspired. Nature is a kind of God that explains even the unnatural. If it is pointed out that whites have ruthlessly exterminated other whites, tribes their fellow tribesmen, races their blood sisters, families, their kith and kin, sociobiology falls back on a "selfish gene " that is smart enough to behave altruistically; or is it an altruistic gene that is so deceptive as to act selfishly? If altruism is a cleverly disguised egoism, sociobiology's genes are very much like "rational man." So then the question must be raised:

Which comes first, genes or a rationalistic culture? In seeking to identify the genetic roots of biologically identified groups, sociobiology becomes an extension of the biologists' project of grounding behavior in nature.

SOCIALLY CONSTRUCTED RACES AND RACISM

Sociological studies of race relations present three interesting sets of developments regarding racial classification. They deal with the scientific, or objective, status of race; the relationship between sociological and biological studies of social relations; and the socially constructed nature of race. Not surprisingly, modern sociological studies shy away from an explicit endorsement of biologically defined races. Given that race relations unfold in a normative social order, they cannot be defined independently of culture and actors' perceptions. Or, should race be discarded altogether, once class, for example, is seen to be of behavioral significance? These issues were raised but not settled by Robert Park, who is often referred to as the founding father of the sociology of race relations. His book, *Race and Culture*, is acknowledged as a seminal study of race relations.

Texts on race relations invariably contain definitions of racial groups *and* a caution against acceptance of scientific definitions of race. In *Race and Ethnic Relations*, sociologist Martin Marger writes: "Whether the idea of race is meaningful in a biological sense remains a controversial and seemingly unresolvable issue. But whatever its biological validity, the importance of race for the study of intergroup relations clearly lies in its social meaning."[64] Studies of race relations are valid because races are socially constructed. That is to say, who is identified as white or black depends not on biology but on actors' definitions of the situation. By implication, the flawed nature of objective or scientific racial classifications need not prevent relations from being racially identified and studied. If people define their relations as racial, then, there is a racial reality to be studied. However, what must be considered is that such studies themselves popularize racial classification and racialize human experiences. Leaving aside the question of scientific or objective races, social scientists could be investigating a product of their own practices.

In most race relations texts it is admitted that objective or scientific definitions of races are arbitrary and inconclusive. Racial membership is susceptible to selective anatomical emphases, regional conventions, society-specific customs, and political imperatives. These configurations are captured in the thesis that race is a social construct. Lucius Outlaw, a professor of philosophy at Haverford College, draws attention to cultural, scientific, and political economic "complexes" underlying the classification of persons as members of a race. He writes: "Racial categories are fundamentally social in nature and rest on shifting sands of biological heterogeneity. The biological aspects of 'race' are conscripted into projects of cultural, political, and social construction. 'Race' is a social formation."[65] Similarly, in the power-conflict model of race relations, the assignment of persons to racial categories is said to reflect political economic arrangements; it is a form of group mobilization in struggles over scarce resources. Sociologist Joseph Feagin writes: "From the social definition perspective characteristics such as skin color have no unique or self evident meaning; rather they primarily have social meaning, so much so that one might even speak of social races."[66] The idea of social, or socially constructed, races is an important one in the field of racial and ethnic relations. The basic point is that race is, or may be, scientifically unacceptable, but it is subjectively meaningful. Sociology must deal with the meaning of race for social actors.

A particular definition of sociology's purpose underlies the notion of social races. In defining sociology, Max Weber emphasizes subjective meanings in accounting for social action: "Sociology . . . is a science which attempts the interpretive understanding of social action in order thereby to arrive at a causal explanation of its course and effects. In 'action' is included all human behavior when and in so far as the acting individual attaches a subjective meaning to it."[67] Utilizing this Weberian insight, sociologists generally claim that Americans attach some meaning to race. Indeed, racial consciousness is said to be extraordinarily acute in American society. Hence, it cannot be ignored by sociologists. This emphasis on an actor's consciousness, then, has affinities with a Weberian sociological perspective in which subjective states are investigated and causally related to social action. Race is socially constructed by the meanings attributed to it and the actions to which it gives rise.

The social constructionist approach enjoys considerable eminence in sociological studies of racial and ethnic relations. Its own methods of construction and implications are rarely questioned. As a result, one neglected area of study is the institutional mechanisms and practices that provide the information underlying "meanings." What are actors told about race? In other words, what roles do government edicts on race and academic studies of race relations play in the widespread attributing of meanings to race? Given the comparatively astronomical intellectual and financial investments in racial research and its dissemination, it is difficult not to conclude that racial studies and public policies on race relations are a major transmission belt of the racial meanings social scientists cite to justify race relations studies. Hence, the meanings attached to race cannot be claimed as the reason for continuing race relations studies; they are produced by the studies themselves. In effect, sociologists claim to be studying race relations but suggest that relations are being racialized by particular institutional, structural, and cultural conditions. The claim, then, is inaccurate. Racialized relations, not race relations, should be considered the object of study. And the relations are racialized by social scientists themselves. *De fabula narratur.*

The "social" in the term social races needs to be unpacked, if it is not to serve as a cover for institutional practices of racialization. The idea of race relations is itself a social construct, in the sense of being a specific classification of social relations. Social studies cannot be a procedure of identifying racial groups and serializing their experiences as historical victims and villains. Such a project would be an obstacle to the appreciation of different social scientific theories and their shaping of perceptions and policies. Whatever the meanings actors attach to race, what cannot be denied is that it is social scientists who attach racial names to actors. As would be demanded of the discovery of "classes," the criteria of classification that generate these racial names must be logically justified. Why identify persons according to the color of their skin, the length and type of their hair, and the shapes of their lips and noses? The realist or social constructionist characterization simply allows social scientists to continue to operate with a flawed racial classification.

In the study of race relations, a wide variety of explanations compete, without resolution of their differences. However, when doubts are raised about continuing racial studies, they are quelled with reference to the mass popularity of race. But how does race become popular? To claim that the expansion of public policies on race relations, and the development of race relations research are unrelated to popular racial thinking is to absolve these institutions of any social responsibility. A radical and philosophically sensitive sociology would investigate the collaboration between government and social scientists in the racialization of society. The reference to "social meaning" may turn out to be a self-serving legitimization of racial studies.

The subjective contestability of human classification poses difficulties for the allocation of a human being to a race. Human beings can protest against being allocated to a race, on grounds that they comprise an infinite number of attributes. Indeed, race can refer only to an aggregate of anatomical attributes, not to human beings. Races are neither natural-factual things nor persons, but a classification of selected anatomical attributes. A person does not belong to a race. His or her attributes do. The whole enterprise of studying race relations is based on a philosophical error, because race is presented as a depiction of persons. Even if, as Max Weber insists, the sociologist does have the right to choose any segment of social reality for study, that does not make races, whether social or otherwise, an object for social studies. The real or contrived nature of race is not unrelated to the practices of social scientists. In investigating race relations, the everyday usage of race, and official racial classifications become intellectually consolidated. Race-names such as whites, Orientals, Negroes, and Indians are given a scholarly stamp of approval and enshrined in legislative documents. It is this usage of a racial theory of social relations that requires study. Admittedly, a variety of what may be called atrocities have been committed in the name of race. But this does not obligate students of society or opponents of human suffering to themselves use racial classification.

The social constructionist perspective draws on a phenomenological sociology whose methodological point of departure is the actor's subjective orientation. The argument is that because actors attribute meaning to race, sociological studies of race relations are justified. Despite its unscientific status, race has meaning for everyday actors, and racism, an ideological legacy of slavery and colonialism, permeates American society. Race must, therefore, be taken into account in the analysis of social relations. By contrast, Marxist-oriented scholars shy away from what is regarded as an idealist emphasis on race. Its pervasiveness is said to be either an ideological smokescreen or a reflection of material conditions. Indeed, how are social scientists to ascertain that it is racial and not economic situations that really concern actors even as they voice racial sentiments, especially because these sentiments are intensified during periods of high unemployment, recessions, and hard times? Are there not objective, material dimensions of subjective meanings?

Weber's methodological directives on the means of resolving the difficulties in the relationship between subjective and objective domains of meaning include references to statistical probabilities, value neutrality, ideal-types, and sociological empathy.[68] The criticisms of Weber's recommendations are extensive;[69] they are also similar to criticism of the explanation of white behavior in terms of prejudice, or a racist value. One criticism points to a regress into psychological reductionism. The sociologist Richard A. Schermerhorn writes:

> If we begin with the matter of prejudice, any approach to the field from this viewpoint has a subtle tendency to psychologize group relations by seeing them as personality process writ large. . . . If research has confirmed anything in this area, it is that prejudice is a product of situations, historical situations, economic situations, political situations; it is not a little demon that emerges in people because they are depraved.[70]

Other criticisms of prejudice as an explanation cite an absence of logical entailment, arbitrariness, definitional regress, and historical redundancy.[71] If racism is defined as a prejudiced belief, its discovery faces insurmountable methodological difficulties. Because the belief resides in minds that are being examined by other minds, "subjective" biases necessarily creep into its identification. Thus, any statement by a white person about blacks, or action that affects blacks can be deemed racist by an observing black mind. However, the accused white person can claim to be motivated by other considerations. In effect, a conflict between subjective and objective evaluations plagues the processes of discovering prejudice and its relationship to behavior. If racism is defined as the behavior that results from the belief, its discovery becomes ensnared in a circularity — racism is a belief that produces behavior, which is itself racism.

The idea of institutional racism appears to avoid these criticisms; it abandons the methodological-individualist focus and locates racism in institutional contexts and decisions that are made without conscious racist considerations.[72] However, this institutional relocation does not escape the difficulty of identifying racist motivations. One critical analysis of the concept of institutional racism suggests that institutional arrangements are created by human choices.[73] Thus, they are shaped by the goals and decisions of the institution's personnel. Institutions are not extraterrestrial entities separate from the aspirations, interests, and values of their members. If racism is practiced by institutions, it is because it resides in the individual perceptions of those who formulate and implement policies. However, in moving away from an emphasis on individual motives into subconscious forces and institutional arrangements, nonracial elements are being invoked. Institutional racism may be economically inspired. Therefore, it may be argued that the corporate structure within institutions generates socioeconomic deprivation among those who are forced to labor for others.

If racial oppression is an unintended effect of corporate choices, then neither the actors nor the institutions are consciously racist. Corporate racism may be deemed classism. Yet the reference to class raises critical issues of primacy and definitional consistency. Is racism an effect of class stratification, or is it prior to class formation? It is classism, not racism, which is peculiar to class structures. As will be demonstrated subsequently, the shift from race to class relations cannot retain racism but it does lead to the development of a focus on the economic determinants of racism and its specific location in capitalism.[74] Racism is conceived as "negative beliefs" about a group, beliefs that are not necessarily restricted to relations between races. But this strips racism of its theoretical specificity; it is transfigured into ethnocentrism, classism, nationalism, or even an adjunct of sexism. Racism becomes a superordinate evil, reflective of the nature of white men, or of any "oppressor" who is of a different "race." This explains the emergence of antiracism, a movement of moral passion generally aimed exclusively against whites. If race is a discourse, it is a moralistic and activist discourse embodying not logical arguments but assertions jockeying for moral ammunition and positions of political correctness.

The materialist analysis of racism has some affinity with the institutionalist focus, for the consciousness of individual actors is rejected as the starting point for the study of racism. It examines racism's emergence as an ideology, its interaction with the class structure, economic decisions, and public policies. Capitalism and remnants of a racist ideology are said to generate the specific economic conditions facing blacks in the modern world. Racism is essentially an ideological accompaniment of global capitalist development. Thus, racism is traced to a material substructure. However, the materialist analysis is weakened when it confronts the question of the origin of the material substructure. Negative beliefs about a group could have predated exploitative and repressive policies toward that group. Some historians claim that "Negro slavery" was conditioned by prior racial beliefs.[75] But a more fundamental weakness is evident. The multiplicity of definitions of racism also needs to be explained materialistically. Which racism is related to political economic and ideological relations within capitalism? Moreover, if racism refers to negative beliefs about a group defined as a race, the nature of "negative" needs to be clarified. Some beliefs about blacks may be adjudged "positive" and, hence, do not qualify as racism. Racism is necessarily conceptually imprecise. How can the actual state of the white mind be captured, when it is admitted that this mind is "contextualized" by an infinite number of ideological interests, economic relations, political considerations, and "cultural" representations?

Racism has inseparable analytical connections with racial classification. Both have been defined in contrasting ways and rejected for
being vague and nonexplanatory. Racial classification demarcates
human beings and social relations. Racism refers to, and categorizes,
ideas, beliefs, motives, events, actions, policies, and social conditions.
Why does it have this broad range of referents? The reason is that it
was constructed to explain white behavior, to identify white beliefs,
and link them with white policies and actions. Racism and racial
classification are analytical components of a general racial theory of
society.

RACISM AND ANTIRACISM

Working within a naturalist ethos, eighteenth- and nineteenth-century
social philosophers constructed a racial hierarchy in which a so-called
white race stands at the apex of civilization and culture. This race was
said to represent nature's highest achievement. Other races are subspecies, and verge on being subhuman. Each race has its peculiar genes
that are responsible for its historical destiny. Thus, racial or genetic
attributes may be cited to explain continental and social inequalities.
Races are not just different genetic populations but unequally endowed
populations with different moral natures, naturally programmed to
compete for scarce resources. These assertions have exhibited a remarkable survivability through the centuries, and in Nazi, Ku Klux
Klan, and even certain modern "scientific" pronouncements. Their
longevity gives credibility to the claim that racism permeates the
history of the post-Columbus world, and the construction of antiracist
programs. However, because such programs involve the dissemination
of polarized conceptions of black and white experiences, they generate
the racial divisions that underlie racial tensions.

Once persons are racially classified, racial attributes and motives
must be invoked to explain their behavior. Racism is the concept
developed and popularized, especially from the mid-twentieth century,
to depict the morally deviant nature and motives of white people.[76] It
is part of the liberationist variant of the racial theory, functioning as
the cause, or explanation, of white behavior and policies. Just as the

advocates of the naturalist variant of the racial theory proclaimed the genetic inferiority of blacks, so liberationist protagonists insist that whites are morally depraved and make antiracism the center of the struggle for the liberation of black people. Every naturalist assertion of a genetic, nonwhite inferiority is met with a counterproposition that a white moral deficiency, racism, is responsible for racial problems. However, in making racism responsible for whole sets of relations between whites and nonwhites, it becomes necessary to define it at a variety of levels. Thus, racism acquires a multiplicity of meanings centered around cognitive processes (statements, beliefs, motives), practices (exclusion, discrimination, victimization, domination), and their alleged effects (poverty, inequality, subordination).

Whites have a variety of attributes and interests and, hence, a range of motivations. Their behavior is influenced by a plethora of laws, norms, expectations, and other elements of social organization. Thus, the racist causation has been shown to be a spurious correlation between an idea and action. The social consequences of any white actions that affect blacks in any way can also be designated racism. Indeed any white response to blacks can be deemed racism. Hence, there are paternalistic, tokenist, unconscious, and condescending racisms. Racisms are the shadows accompanying races.

In the race relations literature, the term racism refers to theory, beliefs, attitudes, actions, policies, and practices; it is intrinsically pejorative, as it seeks to capture and denounce the evil deeds of whites, or a white ruling class, or a racially exploitative capitalism.[77] These myriad referents are unavoidable, for all relations between racially classified persons necessarily contain racial interests, motives, perceptions, and effects. If the actions and their effects are adjudged "bad," then the actors and the ideas that motivate them are also "bad."

The moralistic status of the concept of racism is illustrated in Robert Miles' comments:

> If racism brutalises and dehumanises its objects, it also brutalises and dehumanises those who articulate it. Racism is therefore simultaneously a mediation between human beings similarly and differentially located in a class structure and a denial of their humanity, even if that denial is

unequal by virtue of the relations of domination and subordination implicit in the mediation.[78]

These formulations suggest a conception of racism as an antihuman element that affects human beings, who are at the same time class agents in particular political economic and ideological conjunctures that must be investigated empirically. Hence, the application of racism is not to be restricted to whites. Racism is analytically independent of race. Miles writes further that

> it is mistaken to limit the parameters of racism by reference to skin color, because various "white" groups have been objects of racism. Furthermore, the expression of racism is not confined to "white" people. There is no doubt, for example, that many of the statements made by the American "black" Muslim leader, Louis Farrakhan, warrant description as racism. . . . [79]

These formulations seek to separate the concepts of race and racism. By this token all human relations, including class relations, and all social formations may be conceived of as being affected by racism, which Miles conceives of as a dehumanizing expression of Otherness. Moreover, if as Miles argues, the concept of race has no analytic value, it is inconsistent to refer to racism's presence in relations among members of the same race. His description of Louis Farrakhan's statements as racism could itself be deemed part of a white racist plot to discredit a "black Muslim leader." If social sciences are to retain such a moralistic and politically pejorative category as racism, social studies cannot avoid being perpetually dogged by issues of racial partisanship and political correctness.

Most definitions of racism have endorsed racial classification. Indeed, racial classification is the only stable element in these definitions. Miles' analysis seeks to avoid an endorsement of racial classification but "to justify the retention of racism as a key concept within the social sciences."[80] But racial classification cannot be separated from racism. The concept racism pertains to the (bad) thoughts and actions of races and, like race, its definitions are so multifarious that so-called blacks can be called racists. On the other hand, black racism is rejected by psychologists Gerald Pine and Asa Hilliard: "Racism is a mental illness characterized by perceptual distortion, a denial of reality, delusions of grandeur (belief in white supremacy), the projection of blame (on the victim), and phobic reactions to differences. A colonizer may be racist, but a victim cannot be so."[81] Thus, it is frequently asserted that nonwhites are not racists; they are victims and merely respond, often in a prejudiced fashion, to the white racist power structure. Will the "real" racists please stand up and be counted?

Sociologist Howard Schuman's definition of racism is exceptional; it links racism inextricably with racial classification or the construction of races: "The term racism is generally taken to refer to the belief that there are distinguishable human race races not only in superficial physical characteristics but also innately in important psychological traits. . . ."[82] This definition avoids any moral and political evaluation of ideas, persons, and actions. Schuman's definition may be stripped of its reference to belief, and racism would then be defined as the construction of racial distinctions. The practice signifies differences by assigning a person to a race on the basis of selected anatomical attributes. In the construction of races, skin color, hair type, facial form, and other attributes are used to identify a racial essence, which explains the behavior of the persons classified as races. It follows from this definition that to refer to persons as nonwhites, blacks, and whites is a racist practice.

In race relations studies, the explanatory and operational references to racism seek to capture the moral attributes of whites or the negative beliefs and inhuman false ideas (ideology) that motivate them in the commission of bad things (discrimination, exclusion, victimization) to blacks. On this moral plain, only accusations survive, and they are repeated ad infinitum. In the liberationist and antiracist literature, racism is a white thing, an accompaniment of a villainous whiteness. Thus, an anatomy of racism becomes an investigation of white people, and the study of white people is a study of racism. However, because white people operate in socioeconomic and political contexts, such studies are bound to produce racialized colonial and imperial histories and analyses of capitalism. Nevertheless, given the now all-embracing psychological and structural reach of racism, nonwhites can hardly escape the accusation of also being under its influence. They too are racists. All of American society is considered racist. Racism is said to be present even in relations among whites. But then, what is *not* racist? To borrow from Karl Marx's comment on religion: Racism is the sigh of a logically malnutritious variant of the racial theory, the heart of philosophically starved social sciences; it is the opium of racially classified people.

Racism's context is a racial theory of history and society. An expression of opposition to racism is part of "the discourse of race," because it presupposes the existence of races, and legitimizes references to them. But if, as Miles argues, racism is unrelated to race in the biological sense, if it is an ideological miasma, a process of signification that "occurs in a material and historical context as a component element of allocative and exclusionary mechanisms," then it does have an everlasting future within social sciences. Allocative mechanisms are, by definition, exclusionary. Migration between localities, regions, and countries is unavoidable. So the creation of Others — the alleged core of racism — is assured, and opposition to racism is eternal. Miles must suggest that it should be the centerpiece of social sciences.

Antiracist programs are counterproductive and self-perpetuating. If racism is intrinsic to white people (nonwhites can be, whites *are*), these programs are necessarily directed at white people. Thus, antiracism builds white defensive and offensive mechanisms and perpetuates racial consciousness on both sides of the barricades. In this sense, it engenders a protracted process of overcoming self-created odds. It is one of the sources of the longevity of racial thinking and interest formation. How can white people shed their supremacist sentiments, while being told to retain their identity as whites, an identity inextricably linked with the notion of being the superior race? Antiracism maintains the core of the racial theory, the racial classification of persons. But if nonwhites are also racist, what U.S. society needs is deracialization, a termination of racial classification. It would be based on a recognition that a flawed racial theory has been powerfully influential on self-images, the perception of persons, decisions, and public policies.

All studies of blacks and whites must come to rest on alleged natural attributes, such as genes and xenophobia, or moral states such as racism. Claims of black genetic inferiority and of white racism are the respective causal thrusts of naturalist and liberationist variants of the racial theory. Studies of race relations and the struggle against racism are part of the same racial intellectual tradition. Naturalist and liberationist controversies over the history and state of race relations merely consolidate the racialization of social relations. The two schools of thought feed on each other and, given their domination of public debate and public policies, breed a racially conscious population. Official and party electoral practices also contribute. Every event and situation between the birth and the death of person is quantified and recorded in black and white. A mass, polarized racial consciousness results, which politicians magnify and utilize at random. Finally, an educational system devoted to producing workers and consumers rather than cultivating human minds in a spirit of critical thinking provides the basis for the acceptance of the fallacies in racial classification. In this sense, America has not racial problems but philosophical educational deficiencies that manifest themselves in the racialization of social relations.

NOTES

1. See Robert Miles, *Racism* (London: Routledge and Kegan Paul, 1989), pp. 73-77. Frank Reeves, *British Racial Discourse* (London: Cambridge University Press, 1984); Michael Banton and Jonathan Harwood, *The Race Concept* (New York: Praeger, 1975); and several books by Banton, *The Idea of Race* (London: Tavistock, 1977), *Race Relations* (London: Tavistock, 1967).
2. Colette Guillaumin, "The Idea of Race and Its Elevation to Autonomous Scientific and Legal Status," in UNESCO, *Sociological Theories: Race and Colonialism* (Paris: UNESCO, 1980), p. 37.
3. Eleanor Holmes Norton, "Foreword," in Gail E. Thomas (ed.), *U.S. Race Relations in the 1980's and 1990's: Challenges and Alternatives* (New York: Hemisphere Publishing Corp., 1990), pp. xvii-xviii.

4. David Goldberg, "Introduction," in David Goldberg (ed.), *Anatomy of Racism* (Minneapolis, MN: University of Minnesota Press, 1990), p. xiii.

5. See Thomas F. Gossett, *Race: The History of an Idea in America* (New York: Schocken Books, 1965); Earl Conrad, *The Invention of the Negro* (New York: Paul Eriksson, Inc., 1966); Leonard Lieberman, "The Debate over Race," in James Curtis and John W. Petras (eds.), *The Sociology of Knowledge* (New York: Praeger, 1970), pp. 569-585.

6. D. Stanley Eitzen and Maxine Baca Zinn, *In Conflict and Order: Understanding Society* (Boston: Allyn and Bacon, 1991), p. 47. See also Ian Robertson, *Sociology*, 3rd ed. (New York: Worth Pub., 1987), chapter 11; and Thomas Sowell, *The Economics and Politics of Race: An International Perspective* (New York: William Morrow, 1983), p. 15.

7. Michael Banton, *Racial and Ethnic Competition* (Cambridge: Cambridge University Press, 1983), p. 32.

8. Michael Omi and Howard Winant, *Racial Formation in the United States* (New York: Routledge and Kegan Paul, 1986). p. ix.

9. Ibid., p. 3.

10. See Thomas (ed.), *U.S. Race Relations*; "The Changing Face of America," *Time*, July 8, 1985, pp. 36-94; "Beyond the Melting Pot," *Time*, April 9, 1990, pp. 28-31; Dinker I. Patel, "Asian Americans: A Growing Force," in John A. Kromowski (ed.), *Racial and Ethnic Relations 91/92* (Guildford, CT: Duskhin Pub. Group, 1991), pp. 86-91.

11. See Jacques Barzun, *Race: A Study in Modern Superstition* (New York: Harcourt Brace and Co., 1937), Ashley Montagu, *Man's Most Dangerous Myth: The Fallacy of Race* (New York: Columbia University Press, 1945), Michael Banton, *Racial Theories* (Cambridge: Cambridge University Press, 1987).

12. See several works by Michael Banton: *The Idea of Race: Racial and Ethnic Competition; Racial Theories*. See also Michael Banton and Jonathan Harwood, *The Race Concept*; Miles, *Racism*.

13. Banton, *Racial and Ethnic Competition*, pp. 57-58.

14. S. Carl Hirsch, *The Riddle of Racism* (New York: Viking Press, 1972), p. 172.

15. Miles, *Racism*, p. 75.

16. Jean-Paul Sartre, *Critique of Dialectical Reasoning: Theory of Practical Ensembles*, trans. Alan Sheridan-Smith (London: New Left Books, 1976), p. 570.

17. Lerone Bennett, Jr., *Before the Mayflower: A History of Black America* (Chicago: Johnson Pub. Co., 1982), p. 40.

18. S. Morris Engel, *With Good Reason: An Introduction to Informal Fallacies* (New York: St. Martin's Press, 1986), p. 113.

19. See Lieberman, "Debate Over Race"; Philip D. Curtin, *The Image of Africa: British Ideas and Action, 1789-1850,* vol. 2 (Madison, WI: University of Wisconsin Press, 1964); Robert Pois (ed.), *Race and Race History and Other Essays by Alfred Rosenberg* (New York: Harper Torchbook, 1974).

20. Banton, *Racial and Ethnic Competition,* p. 44. According to Banton, the first use or discovery of races is attributable to seventeenth-century biologists and social theorists. However, a host of eighteenth- and nineteenth-century biologists and social philosophers made race fashionable as a classification of the human species. The extent to which these writings influenced social, immigration, and foreign policies can hardly be ignored —their principal arguments and conclusions are repeated by slave owners, entrepreneurs, legislators, and the lay public. See also Curtin, *Image of Africa,* chapter 15.

21. J. Arthur de Gobineau, *The Inequality of Human Races* (New York: Howard Fertig, 1967), pp. 205-207.

22. See Gossett, *Race*; Stephen Jay Gould, *The Mismeasure of Man* (New York: Norton, 1981).

23. See John C. Greene, "The American Debate on the Negro's Place in Nature, 1780-1815," *Journal of the History of Ideas* 15 (June 1954), pp. 384-396, Reginald Horsman, *Race and Manifest Destiny: The Origins of American Racial Anglo-Saxonism* (Cambridge, MA: Harvard University Press, 1981).

24. Horsman, *Race and Manifest Destiny,* p. 101.

25. Alexis de Tocqueville, *Democracy in America* (New York: Anchor Books, 1969), p. 317. The extent to which America's "founding fathers" were influenced by the idea of race may be further illustrated. In an 1862 address to a group of "black leaders," Abraham Lincoln opined: "You and we are different races. We have between us a broader difference than exists between any other two races . . . on this broad continent not a single man of your race is made the equal of a single man of ours." Cited in Banton, *Idea of Race,* p. 1.

26. Banton, *Racial and Ethnic Competition,* p. 8.

27. See Gordon Nagel, *The Structure of Experience: Kant's System of Proof* (Chicago: University of Chicago Press, 1983).

28. Omi and Winant, *Racial Formation,* p. 3.

29. See Karl Popper, *Objective Knowledge: An Evolutionary Approach* (Oxford: Clarendon Press, 1972).

30. Mark Aldrich, "Progressive Economists and Scientific Racism: Walter Wilcox and Black Americans, 1895-1910," *Phylon* 40, no. 1 (Spring 1979), p. 1.

31. Don Nakanishi, "Convergence in Race Relations Research," in Phyllis A. Katz and Dalmas A. Taylor (eds.), *Eliminating Racism: Profiles in Controversy* (New York: Plenum Press, 1988), p. 160.

32. See Thomas B. Edsall and Mary D. Edsall, *Chain Reaction: The Impact of Race, Rights, and Taxes on American Politics* (New York: W. W. Norton, 1991).

33. See Camille A. Clay, "Campus Racial Tensions: Trend or Aberration?" *Thought and Action* 5, no. 2 (Fall 1989), pp. 21-30; Manning Marable, "The Beast Is Back: An Analysis of Campus Racism," *The Black Collegian* 19, no. 1 (September/October 1988), pp. 52-54; Susan Lang, *Extremist Groups in America* (New York: Franklin Watts, 1990).

34. Alain Touraine, *The Self-Production of Society*, trans. Derek Coltman (Chicago: University of Chicago Press, 1977), p. 219.

35. See William J. Wilson, *The Declining Significance of Race: Blacks and Changing American Institutions* (Chicago: University of Chicago Press, 1978).

36. See Dinesh D'Souza, *Illiberal Education: The Politics of Race and Sex on Campus* (New York: Free Press, 1991). Arthur Schlesinger, Jr., *The Disuniting of America: Reflections on a Multicultural Society* (Knoxville, TN: Whittle, 1991).

37. See Cynthia E. Russett, *Darwin in America: The Intellectual Response 1865-1912* (San Francisco, CA: W. H. Freeman and Co., 1976).

38. George M. Fredrickson, "Toward a Social Interpretation of the Development of American Racism," in Nathan Huggins et al. (eds.), *Key Issues in the Afro-American Experience: Vol. 1, to 1877* (New York: Harcourt Brace Jovanovich, 1978), p. 251.

39. W.E.B. Du Bois' writings, which span over sixty years, stand out as the foundation of the liberationist tradition. See his: *The Conservation of Races* (Washington, DC: American Negro Academy, 1897); *The Souls of Black Folk* (Chicago: McClurg, 1904); *The World and Africa: An Inquiry into the Part Which Africa Has Played in World History* (New York: International Publishers, 1980). See also Benjamin Quarles, *Black Abolitionists* (New York: Oxford University Press, 1969); Sterling Stuckey, *Slave Culture: Nationalist Theory and the Foundations of Black America* (New York: Oxford University Press, 1987).

40. See Glenn Loury, "Internally Directed Action for Black Community Development: The Next Frontier for the Movement," *Review of Black Political Economy* 13, no. 1-2 (Summer-Fall 1984), pp. 31-46; Thomas Sowell, *Civil Rights: Rhetoric or Reality?* (New York: William Morrow and Co., 1984); Clint Bolick, *Changing Courses: Civil Rights at the Crossroads* (New Brunswick, NJ: Transaction Press, 1988); Theodore Cross, *The Black Power Imperative* (New York: Faulkner, 1984); Bernard Boxill, *Blacks and Social Justice* (Totowa, NJ: Rowman and Allanheld, 1984); Thomas D. Boston, *Race, Class and Conservatism* (Winchester, MA: Unwin Hyman, 1988); O. C. Cox, *Caste, Class and Race: A Study in Social Dynamics* (New York: Monthly Review Press, 1959); Manning Marable, *How Capitalism Underdeveloped Black America: Problems in Race, Political Economy and Society* (Boston, MA: South End Press, 1983); Cedric Robinson, *Black Marxism: The Making of the Radical Black Tradition* (London: Zed Press, 1983); Robert Allen, *Black Awakening in Capitalist America: An Analytic History* (New York: Anchor Books, 1969); Sidney Willhelm, *Who Needs the Negro* (Cambridge, MA: Schenkman, 1970); Amy Jacques-Garvey (ed.), *Philosophy and Opinions of Marcus Garvey* (New York: Atheneum, 1970); Robert Blauner, *Racial Oppression in America* (New York: Harper and Row, 1972); Malcolm X, *Malcolm X on Afro-American History* (New York: Pathfinder Press, 1967); Stokely Carmichael and Charles V. Hamilton, *Black Power* (New York: Vintage Books, 1967); Harold Cruse, *The Crisis of the Negro Intellectual* (New York: William Morrow, 1967); James A. Kushner, *Apartheid in America* (New York: Associated Faculty Press, 1980); James A. Geschwender, *Racial Stratification in America* (Dubuque, IA: William C. Brown, 1980); George G. M. James, *Stolen Legacy* (San Francisco: Julian Richardson Associates, 1976); Maulana Karenga, *Essays in Struggle* (San Diego: Kawaida Publications, 1978); *Introduction to Black Studies* (Inglewood, CA: Kawaida Publications, 1982); Chancellor Williams, *The Destruction of Black Civilization: Great Issues of a Race from 4500 B.C. to 2000 A.D.* (Chicago: Third World Press, 1976); Molefi Kete Asante, *Afrocentricity: The Theory of Social Change* (New York: Amulefi Pub. Co., 1980); Haki R. Madhubuti, *Enemies: The Clash of Races* (Chicago: Third World Press, 1978); Frances Cress Welsing, "The Cress Theory of Color-Confrontation," *The Black Scholar* 5, no. 8 (May 1974), pp. 32-40; Raymond L. Hall, *Black Separatism in the United States* (Hanover, NH: University Press of New England, 1978), chapter 6; Sidney Willhelm, "Black/White Equality: The Socioeconomic Conditions of Blacks in

America, Part II," *Journal of Black Sociology* 14, no. 2 (December 1983), pp. 98-112.

41. See Shelby Steele, *The Content of Our Character: A New Vision of Race in America* (New York: St. Martin's Press, 1990).

42. See Cheikh Anta Diop, *The African Origin of Civilization* (New York: Lawrence Hill and Co., 1974), and *The Cultural Unity of Black Africa* (Chicago: Third World Press, 1978). But see also Martin Bernal, *Black Athena: The Afroasiatic Roots of Classical Civilization: Vol I, The Fabrication of Ancient Greece* (New Brunswick, NJ: Rutgers University Press, 1987).

43. Chejkh Anta Diop, "Speech by Cheikh Anta Diop," in Ivan van Sertima (ed.), *Great African Thinkers: Vol. I. Cheik Anta Diop* (New Brunswick, NJ: Transaction Press, 1987), p. 320.

44. Ibid., p. 291.

45. Cheikh Anta Diop, "Africa: Cradle of Humanity," in Ivan van Sertima (ed.), *Nile Valley Civilizations* (Atlanta: Morehouse College, 1984), p. 27.

46. See Lang, *Extremist Groups in America.*

47. Arthur R. Jensen, *Genetics and Education* (New York: Harper and Row, 1972).

48. See Paul Gomberg, "IQ and Race: A Discussion of Some Confusions," *Ethics* 85, no. 3 (April 1975), pp. 258-266; J. R. Flynn, *Race, IQ, and Jensen* (London: Routledge and Kegan Paul, 1980); Peter Medawar, *Pluto's Republic* (New York: Oxford University Press, 1982), pp. 167-183.

49. Jensen, *Genetics and Education*, p. 159.

50. Arthur Jensen, *Straight Talk about Mental Tests* (New York: Free Press, 1981), p. 197.

51. Ibid., pp. 210-211.

52. De Gobineau, *Inequality of Human Races*, pp. 14-15.

53. Du Bois, *The Conservation of Races*, p. 9.

54. See Carlos Moore, "Were Marx and Engels White Racists? The Prolet-Aryan Outlook of Marxism," *Berkeley Journal of Sociology* 19 (1974), pp. 125-155; C. Stephen Fenton, "Race, Class and Politics in the Work of Durkheim," in UNESCO, *Sociological Theories*, pp. 143-181.

55. See John Rex, "The Theory of Race Relations — A Weberian Approach," in UNESCO, *Sociological Theories*, pp. 117-142.

56. See Max Weber, "Ethnic Groups," in Talcott Parsons, Edward Shils, Kaspar D. Naegele, and Jesse R. Pitts (eds.), *Theories of Society*, vol. 1. (New York: Free Press, 1961), pp. 305-309; Max Weber, *Economy and Society*, vols. 1

and 2, edited by Guenther Roth and Claus Wittich (London: University of California Press, 1978).

57. See Robert Park, *Race and Culture* (New York: Free Press, 1950); E. Franklin Frazier, "The Impact of Urban Civilization Upon Negro Family Life," in Paul K. Host and Robert J. Reiss, Jr. (eds.), *Cities and Society* (New York: The Free Press, 1951), pp. 490-499; Robert Faris, *Chicago Sociology 1920-1932* (Chicago: University of Chicago Press, 1970); Robert Nisbet, *The Sociological Tradition* (New York: Basic Books, 1966).

58. Brewton Berry, *Race and Ethnic Relations* (Boston: Houghton Mifflin, 1958), pp. 18-19. If the prevalence of racial research is an indication of being fascinated, some sociologists still are mesmerized by racial classification.

59. Colette Guillaumin, "The Idea of Race," p. 54.

60. Ibid.

61. See Pierre L. van den Berghe, *Man in Society* (New York: Elsevier, 1975), and "Race and Ethnicity: A Sociobiological Perspective," in Norman Yetman (ed.), *Majority and Minority: The Dynamics of Race and Ethnicity in American Life* (London: Allyn and Bacon, 1985). For persuasive criticisms of sociobiological studies, see John and Janice I. Baldwin, *Beyond Sociobiology* (New York: Elsevier, 1981), chapters 2 and 3; Martin Barker, "Biology and the New Racism," in Goldberg (ed.), *Anatomy*, pp. 18-37, Ashley Mongtagu (ed.), *Sociobiology Examined* (New York: Oxford University Press, 1980).

62. Van den Berghe, "Race and Ethnicity," in Yetman (ed.), *Majority and Minority*, p. 55.

63. Ibid.

64. Martin Marger, *Race and Ethnic Relations* (San Francisco: Wadsworth, 1991), p. 22. See also Graham Kinloch, *The Dynamics of Race Relations: A Sociological Analysis* (New York: McGraw-Hill, 1974); John Rex, *Race Relations in Sociological Theory* (London: Weidenfeld and Nicholson, 1983).

65. Lucius Outlaw, "Toward a Critical Theory of 'Race'," in Goldberg, (ed.), *Anatomy*, p. 68.

66. Joseph Feagin, *Racial and Ethnic Relations*, 2d ed. (Englewood Cliffs, NJ: Prentice-Hall, 1984), pp. 6-7.

67. Max Weber, *The Theory of Social and Economic Organization*, trans. A. M. Henderson and Talcott Parsons (New York: Oxford University Press, 1947), p. 88.

68. See Max Weber, *The Methodology of Social Sciences*, trans. Edward A. Shils and H. A. Finch (New York: Free Press, 1949).

69. See Theodore Abel, "The Operation Called Verstehen," *American Journal of Sociology* 54, no. 3 (November 1948), pp. 211-18; Anthony Giddens, *New Rules of Sociological Method: A Positive Critique of Interpretative Sociology* (New York: Basic Books, 1976); Barry Hindess, *Philosophy and Methodology in the Social Sciences* (London: Humanities Press, 1977).

70. R. A. Schermerhorn, *Comparative Ethnic Relations: A Framework for Theory and Research* (New York: Random House, 1970), p. 6.

71. See Hubert M. Blalock, Jr., *Toward a Theory of Minority-Group Relations* (New York: Wiley, 1967); Banton, *Race Relations*; Pierre L. van den Berghe, *Race and Racism: A Comparative Perspective* (New York: Wiley, 1967); William Wilbanks, *The Myth of a Racist Criminal Justice System* (Monterey, CA: Brooks/Cole, 1987).

72. For a distinction between individual and institutional racism, see Carmichael and Hamilton, *Black Power*; Blauner, *Racial Oppression*; Alphonso Pinkney, *The Myth of Black Progress* (Cambridge: Cambridge University Press, 1986), chapter 4.

73. See J. S. Butler, "Institutional Racism: Viable Perspective or Intellectual Bogey," *The Black Sociologist* 7, nos. 3/4 (1978), pp. 5-25. For other criticisms, see Miles, *Racism*, chapter 2.

74. See Victor Perlo, *The Economics of Racism* (New York: International Publishers, 1975); Gus Hall, *Fighting Racism* (New York: International Publishers, 1985). Allen, *Black Awakening*; Miles, *Racism*.

75. See Stanley Elkins, *Slavery: A Problem in American Institutional and Cultural Life* (Chicago: University of Chicago Press, 1964); Winthrop D. Jordan, *White Over Black: American Attitudes Towards the Negro, 1550-1812* (Chapel Hill, NC: University of North Carolina, 1968); Carl Degler, *Neither Black Nor White* (New York: Macmillan, 1971).

76. See Kenneth Leech, "Diverse Reports and the Meaning of Racism," *Race and Class* 28, no. 2 (Autumn 1988), pp. 82-88.

77. These do not exhaust the referents of racism. For racism as prejudice, see Gordon Allport, *The Nature of Prejudice* (New York: Doubleday, 1958). For a distinction between racism and prejudice, see James M. Jones, *Prejudice and Racism* (London: Addison-Wesley, 1972), chapter 5. For racism as beliefs, see Anne Wortham, *The Other Side of Racism: A Philosophical Study of Black Race Consciousness* (Columbus: Ohio State University Press, 1977); Gary E. McCuen (ed.), *The Racist Reader: Analyzing Primary Source Readings by American Race Supremacists* (Anoka, MN:

Greenhaven Press, 1974); Reid Luhman and Stuart Gilman, *Race and Ethnic Relations: The Social and Political Experiences of Minority Groups* (San Francisco: Wadsworth, 1980). For racism as theory, see Cox, *Caste, Class and Race.* Racism is also conceived as an ideology. See Miles, *Racism.* For racism as a "doctrine," see C. Van Woodward, *The Strange Career of Jim Crow* (London: Oxford University Press, 1974); Hirsch, *The Riddle*; van den Berghe, *Race and Racism.* For racism as specific conditions of racial inequality, see Raymond Franklin and Solomon Resnick, *The Political Economy of Racism* (New York: Holt, Rinehart and Winston, 1973); Michael Reich, *Racial Inequality* (Princeton, NJ: Princeton University Press, 1981). Nor is the term racism restricted to relations between whites and nonwhites. For arguments to the effect that the American response to white ethnics was fundamentally racial and racist, see Ronald M. Pawalko, "Racism and the New Immigration: A Reinterpretation of the Assimilation of White Ethnics in American Society," *Sociology and Social Research* 65, no. 1 (October 1980), pp. 56-77.

78. Miles, *Racism*, p. 10.

79. Ibid., p. 6.

80. Ibid., p. 132.

81. Gerald Pine and Asa Hilliard III, "Rx for Racism: Imperative for America's Schools," *Phi Delta Kappan* (April 1990), p. 595.

82. Howard Schuman, "Sociological Racism," *Trans Action* 7, no. 2 (December 1969), p. 44.

2

The Racialization of Experiences

Chapter 1 dealt with the development, structure, functions, and variants of the racial theory. Some of the aspects of its adoption by governmental, educational, and research institutions can now be examined. As the plethora of texts and courses on racial and ethnic relations indicate, social scientists are at the forefront in the racial classification of the population. Courses on race and ethnic relations abound in educational institutions. Library shelves are also replete with texts on the experiences of racial and ethnic minorities. A critical reader, however, would note that human experiences are not, in themselves, racial; they are conceived as such through the racial classification of persons. On this basis, events in people's lives are also described racially to become "real" racial experiences, that is, experiences that are merely observed by social scientists.

In racial and ethnic relations texts as well as official documents, the population is divided into white and nonwhite categories. The white category is often subdivided into white Anglo-Saxon Protestants (WASPs) and white ethnics, or WETs. The nonwhite category refers to blacks, Hispanics, Asian Pacific Americans, and Native Americans; they are also referred to as racial minorities. Their historic, demographic, economic, political, and cultural conditions are generally presented as *the* social reality, not as a conceptualization of social relations from within a particular social theory. Each racial minority is said to have had specific experiences of victimization, but the experiences of blacks, or African Americans, stand out as a primary object of analysis. In social scientific texts as well as in official publications on a black experience, certain events are selected, measured in moral terms, and compared to that of other races, especially whites. The general conclusion is that U.S. society is plagued with racial discrimination, oppression, exploitation, and poverty. Descriptions of these conditions are presented as evidence that nonwhites are victims of racism.

This chapter develops a series of criticisms of this racialization of persons and their experiences. First, the color coding of the population derives from a thesis that color prejudice is operative in society. "Persons of color" are placed in a minority category, a category which is not commensurate with numbers but suggestive of experiences of racial and cultural discrimination. However, "persons not of color" can also be said to be victims of such discrimination. A focus on "racial minorities" is, at best, arbitrary.

Second, racial and ethnic descriptions of poverty and deprivation do not contribute to the development of solutions. The descriptions merely imply that biological and cultural attributes are responsible for these socioeconomic conditions. In order to avoid relapsing into biological causation, scholars must develop protracted denials of the biological implications of their racial descriptions. This explains why the race relations literature is overweight in terms of descriptions and lean on solutions to the discovered problem of racial inequality.

Third, in racial and ethnic relations texts, the terms inequality, oppression, and exploitation are rarely defined and when defined, reflect partisan ethical judgments. Thus, any depiction of any minority's oppression can be accused of omission and falsification.

Fourth, racial and ethnic descriptions are replete with arbitrariness and inconsistencies. Hispanics, for example, are presented as both a racial group, which is defined by (brown) skin, and an ethnic group, defined by language. They are part of the white race in FBI crime statistics, but are nonwhites in other official counts of the population. In effect, there is no consistency in the usages of racial and ethnic classifications.

Fifth, studies of racial and ethnic experiences repudiate their own racial and ethnic descriptions, for they produce a wide variety of different experiences within any single racial or ethnic group. This explains why these descriptions are often implicitly shelved. For example, discussions of racial experiences reach into analyses of U.S. foreign and immigration policies, capitalism, and third world underdevelopment.

Finally, racial and ethnic relations texts maintain a race-culture equation that was initiated by early classifiers such as Georges Cuvier, François Bernier, and Arthur de Gobineau. "Culture" is added on to "race" to develop studies of racial *and* ethnic experiences. Thus, biologically defined entities can be studied as social actors. However, by this token, such studies cannot refute sociobiological references to the genetic deficiencies of nonwhites and to genetically based kinship as explanations of discrimination. These explanations are implicit in racial and ethnic descriptions; they further imply that social policies to eradicate or ameliorate racial deprivation, poverty, and discrimination are bound to fail. Thus, racial and ethnic studies are comparative exercises in self-perpetuation.

RACIAL DEMOGRAPHY AND RACIAL DISCRIMINATION

In official compilations of demographic data by race and ethnicity, it is stated that African Americans, Hispanics, Asian Pacific Americans, and Native Americans comprised about 23 percent of the U.S. population of approximately 250 million in 1990.[1] Persons classified as blacks are the largest racial minority, some 30 million, or 12 percent of the total U.S. population. In virtually the whole race relations literature, each racial minority experience is deemed unique, but all minorities are said to be victims of discrimination generated by the actions of the majority, white people. These people are collectively accused of perpetrating a variety of depredations against nonwhites, and it is concluded that they are negatively racially motivated in their dealings with nonwhites.

The preliminary procedures in analyses of racial-ethnic experiences are classification, quantification, and comparison, not conceptual specification and logical justification. Definitions of Hispanics, for example, are glossed over; they are simply counted as the country's second largest minority, numbering approximately 20 million persons in 1990. Their nonwhite status is generally said to be not based on skin color, hair type, and facial form. If it were, many Hispanics could be called Caucasians. "Nonwhite" is related only marginally to color. It is a political economic categorization indicating that those so classified are victims of discrimination.

Hispanic socioeconomic circumstances are described as similar to those of persons classified as blacks. Mexican Americans and Puerto Ricans are regarded as the most disadvantaged among the Hispanic population. In some comparisons, Asian Pacific Americans are conceived as a model minority. Their achievements are said to belie the thesis of a pervasive white racism and to testify to the possibility of minority social mobility through adequate value orientations. This model minority has been lauded for having attained socioeconomic parity with whites, despite racist opposition. Its presence is said to prove racism's comparative insignificance and the importance of cultural capital. Thus, it has been suggested that certain cultural legacies in the African- and Mexican-American communities are at least partly responsible for their economic deprivation. These references to culture are analyzed in Chapter 3.

Racial minority experiences feature prominently in textbooks on racial and ethnic relations. References are made to a variety of historical and contemporary factors in order to explain their comparatively low level of socioeconomic achievements. But, given different modes of entry into the United States and varying patterns of settlement, the socioeconomic situation of these minorities is far from homogeneous. Comparisons indicate that Native Americans, Hispanics, and African Americans are the lesser-achieving groups.[2] Thus, it is admitted that rates and levels of achievement vary within each minority population. There are minorities within minorities.

In comparing the conditions of racial minorities in American society, it is often argued that overall black achievements suggest internal, organizational, and cultural inadequacies. Black culture is said to foster not adjustment and progress but defeatism, deviance, and deprivation. Persons classified as blacks, however, are not the poorest minority. Poverty is said to afflict Native Americans more chronically than any other minority. But overall, because of racially skewed opportunity structures, racial minorities are said to be getting a raw deal. A critically-thinking reader would recognize that the racial and ethnic identification of poverty and socioeconomic deprivation derives from the use of racial and ethnic theories of society. This recognition does not imply a denial or a confirmation of the existence of this deprivation. Rather, it implies that these theories guide the observer to the race and ethnicity of the deprived.

A thesis of racial discrimination underlies the racial counting of the population and its division into majority and minority. The underlying proposition is that white people are racist and use their positions of power to favor fellow whites and to oppress nonwhites. It is announced that, with some marginal exceptions, racial minority populations have been left out of the American dream. America's multidimensional patterns of racial inequality derive from past and present racial discrimination. Indeed, it is claimed that racial discrimination defines the nonwhite experience. This claim can be shown to be ambiguous through an analysis of various usages of the term racial discrimination.

Discrimination, in the sense of *discriminating action,* can be said to be an omnipresent feature of social relations, for human behavior necessarily involves making a choice between alternatives. Discriminating action, however, is different from *racial discrimination,* which pertains to actions having negative effects on persons who are racially classified. For example, if unemployment is an effect of employers' decisions, and if the unemployed are racially counted to discover a disproportionate number of "blacks," employers' decisions are called *racial discrimination.* The idea of *racially motivated discrimination* goes beyond racial discrimination; it identifies choices whose purposes are to injure or deprive persons classified as belonging to a race. Thus, a potential employer's rejection of equally qualified black applicants in preference for white applicants is said to represent racial discrimination, understood as racially motivated discrimination. Finally, *racially justified* discrimination refers to choices that are accompanied by references to the racial attributes of the persons being chosen.

The term racial discrimination is generally used to mean racially *motivated* discrimination. Nevertheless, the means of discovering racial motives, or intentions, remain deficient, so that the employer who is accused of racial discrimination can claim an innocence of racist motives and emphasize market influences on his or her decisions. Thus, sociologist Robert Merton distinguishes among the unprejudiced non-discriminator, the unprejudiced discriminator, the prejudiced non-discriminator, and the prejudiced discriminator.[3] Nonracial motives may be involved in an act of choice between persons classified as members of different races. Motives are not proven racial simply by virtue of racial descriptions of the effects of choices, or by pointing to the different racial membership of the discriminator and the discrimi-nated. Indeed, motives are ascribed to persons, depending on how they are classified.[4] If whites are deemed inveterate racists, their every action is suspiciously discriminatory. But in that case, the idea of racially motivated discrimination boils down to a suspicion that white people have evil intentions toward nonwhite people.

A BLACK EXPERIENCE

A black experience is generally presented as one of exceptional racial victimization. Such a presentation derives from the liberationist variant of the racial theory, which portrays society as white supremacist and redolent with racism and racial oppression. Most race relations texts claim that, although all nonwhites are historical victims of racially motivated discrimination, the ancestors of African Americans were particularly subjected to the most extreme form of exploitation—slavery. Thus, they were not voluntary immigrants. This forced migra-tion is said to be a unique feature of the black experience. However, the reference to involuntariness raises the philosophical issue of free will and determinism. The early English settlers who were fleeing persecution, the conquered Mexicans and Native Americans, the Chi-nese contract laborers, and the Vietnamese "boat people" can also be described as involuntary immigrants. They were either uprooted by violence or subjected to it once settled in America. What is unique about the Africans' entrance into the U.S is *their status as war prisoners and captives.* As captives and war prisoners, they could not request the status of indentured laborers. Their enslavement should be analyzed in conjunction with the dissolution of the indentured labor system that prevailed up to the mid-seventeenth century.

Africans entered the United States as captives and war prisoners; the overwhelming majority became human commodities and were sold into slavery. In his scholarly and illuminating analysis of slavery, sociologist Orlando Patterson writes: "slavery is the permanent, violent domination of natally alienated and generally dishonored persons."[5] U.S. slavery was no exception; it was a system of labor organization based on violence and the threat of violence for noncompliance with commands. It replaced a system of indentured or contract labor, which included both Europeans and Africans as servants. By the mid-seventeenth century, this indentured system was being dissolved. It was not commercially viable for wealthy farmers and did not solve the problem of a chronic labor shortage. Former servants became competitors, and the increased competition depressed prices and profits. Some of the more wealthy farmers must have reasoned: If only we could make farms into plantation prison camps, in which the inmates were at the complete disposal of the owners of the farm and had no chance of ever being freed. Slavery was the answer. It was not new to either human society or the Americas. But who was to be enslaved?

The supply of slave labor has to be perpetually replenished through violence. In seventeenth-century America, large numbers of slaves could not be garnered from the Native American population. Most of them were unaccustomed to settled agriculture and would not have survived the system of forced labor. Because Native Americans were in their natural habitat, the cost of recapturing runaway Native American slaves was prohibitive. Even so, approximately 10 percent of this population was enslaved. The European indentured servants could not be made into slaves without causing a cessation of the flow of European settlers. Conditions in the West African coastal states were ideal, however, for the replenishment of slaves. Indeed, Spanish, Dutch, Portuguese, and African merchants were already doing brisk business in procuring war prisoners and captives for West Indian plantations. This confluence of circumstances led to Africans becoming the most likely candidates for forced labor on plantations in the United States.

As property, slaves were denied contractual rights as well as the right to negotiate over working conditions, mobility, recreation, payment, and family formation. As rightless persons, they were stripped of all legal responsibilities. However, they were held accountable for their actions and punished accordingly. This accountability implies a recognition that slaves had a human personality. Slave laws of ownership, then, denied the human personality of the slave but required that "it" be accountable as a human being. The historian David Brion Davis, author of *The Problem of Slavery in Western Culture*, seizes on this contradiction to suggest that the ownership of a human being presents a series of moral and legal dilemmas.[6] Can a being that is held responsible for its actions and can own things be itself owned? By implication, a definition of slavery as ownership of a person is problematic. Indeed, as Orlando Patterson demonstrates, ownership of a person cannot be the defining feature of slavery. It is the slave owner who has to be acutely aware of that juridical aspect of the relationship. But slavery connotes total domination — an absence of any limits on violence against slaves and a related lack of negotiating capacities.

The overall traffic in African captives lasted three and a half centuries, and there are various estimates of the number of Africans captured and transported to European colonies. However, historian Philip Curtin presents a generally accepted figure of 9 to 10 million Africans reaching the Americas.[7] About 500,000 were brought to the English colonies in North America. According to historians, the first twenty African captives arrived on a Dutch ship in Jamestown, Virginia in 1619. They were exchanged for provisions but their status on the farms to which they were assigned was as indentured servants or contract laborers. After a specified period, indentured servants were released from servitude.

Subsequent groups of Africans also became indentured servants. However, from the mid-seventeenth century various Southern states passed laws that decreed that all incoming Africans were to be in perpetual servitude. This condition was made inheritable so that generations of "blacks" were prenatally enslaved. By the end of the seventeenth century, so-called Negro slavery was well entrenched in the colonies. In 1787, 90 percent of all slaves lived in five states — North Carolina, South Carolina, Virginia, Maryland, and Georgia.

Why were Africans chosen? This issue has generated longstanding controversies among historians.[8] Was enslavement a racially motivated decision? Were the slave traders, planters, and farmers economically motivated? Or did racial preconceptions as well as economic exigencies combine to produce the decision to enslave Africans? Was enslavement a reflection of the absence of powerful maritime African states that could have threatened military reprisals against the British government and the colonists? How should slavery be explained? Was it, indeed, racial so that it is part of a black experience? Here the relationship between classification and explanation should be recalled.

The conception of slavery as a racial phenomenon indicates usage of a racial classification of slaves. This racial conception requires also that slave owners, farmers, colonists, and traders be classified as whites and that racial statements be cited as evidence of racial motives. In other words, the idea of Negro slavery represents the application of the concept of racial discrimination to a particular event. However, the racial justifications voiced by planters, traders, and farmers do not constitute evidence of decisive racial motivations in enslavement. African merchants participated in the capturing, buying, and selling of other Africans. Some freed African indentured servants themselves became slave owners. Enslavement was also accompanied by nonracial justifications, especially theological and cultural kinds.[9]

Patterns and periods of enslavement varied within the Southern colonies and among regions in particular territories. This testifies to the presence of a variety of considerations other than race in the decision to enslave. The extent of slave ownership also does not justify the designation of slavery as a case of white over black. In 1860 the population classified as black numbered about 4 million, while those classified as whites amounted to 28 million. There were 400,000 slaveholding families out of a total of 1,500,000 farmers; hence, approximately 27 percent, of them held slaves. As historian James Oakes calculates: "In 1860 perhaps a third of all southern whites owned little more than the clothing they wore, while fewer than four percent of the adult white males owned the majority of black slaves. The majority of slaves were held by the one-fifth of slaveholders who owned twenty or more bondsmen."[10] Whiteness was not synonymous with slave ownership. The racial conception of slavery advanced in, for example, Winthrop D. Jordan's *White over Black*, is but testimony to the use of the racial theory in studies of the past.

Texts on American history generally claim that the last quarter of the nineteenth century witnessed an imposition of debt peonage on the South's black population and a substantial revocation of its civil rights.[11] Repressive legislation, vigilante violence, and political manipulation combined to hold the former slaves in virtual slavery, without the benefits of the master's welfare responsibilities. Southern legislatures enacted a variety of laws that effectively disfranchised the so-called black population and legalized racial segregation. These conditions of socioeconomic and legal subordination carried through into the 1950s. The Supreme Court ruled against segregated schools in 1954, but it was not until the passing of the Civil Rights Act of 1964 and the Voting Rights Act of 1965 that constitutional rights for blacks were enshrined in law. Two critical comments must be offered. First, these descriptions utilize the racial theory to portray violence and economic deprivation in black-and-white terms. Second, the fact that some legislators and planters did make references to race in justifying their policies indicates their usage of the racial theory, but this does not oblige social scientists to follow suit.

Race relations texts also present evidence of continuing racial exclusion and disadvantage. Some key claims are as follows: In the 1950s, persons classified as blacks earned 50 to 55 percent of the average white income. A quarter of a century later, the figure was approximately 60 percent. In the 1980's, more than 30 percent of all black families lived below the poverty line, calculated at $11,000 per year for a family of four. Twenty-seven percent earned less than $4,000 a year. Only 2 percent earned an income of over $25,000 a year.[12] These figures are presented as part of the picture of the state of black America. On the other hand, data are produced which suggest that in the 1980s, blacks experienced an unprecedented improvement in their standard of living and social welfare generally. By 1990 one-third of all black families were middle class, compared to one-tenth in 1965. Young, educated, black Americans now earn as much as similarly qualified whites. Black females entered the labor market on a mass scale, with a higher level of labor force participation than white females. The median income of black female professionals exceeds that of their white counterparts. In 1980 there were five times as many blacks in higher education as in 1960. These figures are also said to represent an empirical picture of the state of black America, one of progress and continuous social mobility. But of course it is possible to produce figures that point to a black underclass being decimated by racist economic and social policies. In effect, analyses of the comparative economic situation of so-called blacks are caught up in chronic patterns of statistical juggling.

Descriptions of black hyperunemployment — an extremely high level of unemployment — as well as overrepresentation in poverty and prisons permeate the race relations literature, where they are presented as proof of racial oppression. However, these descriptions may be criticized on the following grounds. First, conceptually, what is oppression? Definitions of oppression involve a similar moral thrust, as in conceptions of racism. Philosopher John L. Hodge offers this definition:

> Oppression occurs when the members of a group are restricted by others so that the group's members typically have fewer rights or less power than those who restrict them. Those who restrict the group are its oppressors . . . The oppressed are kept down, for example, by reduced access to education, job training, and political power.[13]

This definition is much too inclusive. Powerlessness, lack of rights, and denial of access to educational resources would need to be further specified. For example, access to which education is being restricted? Primary and most phases of secondary education are not only "free" but compulsory. The definition depicts a status of "members of a group," not generalized conditions. But individuals from all social strata periodically have their civil rights denied. Most struggles against group denial have been successful. What these situations suggest is that government's implementation of the Bill of Rights is assured only by mass vigilance. Hodge's definition of oppression would encompass the situation of potential airline passengers caught in a traffic jam as well as the relationship between teachers and students in a classroom. However, the claim of a specific black oppression expresses a fundamental moral concern for the deprived, and no doubt this human suffering is inexcusable, especially in a nation of comparatively vast economic and technological resources whose political representatives aspire to world leadership.

Second, the data on black youth overrepresentation in prisons are not proof of racial oppression. But it is not blacks who are overrepresented in prisons but representatives of a specific life-style, age group, and patterns of educational deprivation. The incarcerated may be said to be victims of irrational educational and social economic policies. The system of educational organization regularly generates pools of young illiterates, functional illiterates, and the ineducable, some of whom gravitate toward violence and "criminal" activities. They are of all skin colors, and bearers of legacies of parental neglect and abuse are chronically overrepresented among them. This overrepresentation in prisons, then, is traceable to a variety of individual failings; regional residues of unpreparedness for urban-industrial life; a punitive rather than a rehabilitative system of justice; labor markets that reject the untrained, unskilled, and uneducated; and patterns of recessions that permanently discourage some job-seekers. Illiteracy, lack of industrial skills, ineducability, unemployment, and unemployability underlie the holocaust in the so-called inner cities. At one analytical level, it is possible to focus on specific individual behaviors that contribute to these conditions. At another level, attention could be directed at overall social and economic policies. References to the skin colors of the persons involved lead to a pursuit of white racial motives, which, in turn, evokes mention of black biological/cultural attributes, which leads to an increased focus on racism, which is, in turn, challenged by charges of individual irresponsibility and racial-cultural deficiencies. Aspiring political representatives are particularly well poised to profit from this endless game of blaming victims and victimizers.

It may be argued that so-called black (male) unemployment is high primarily because of lack of education, social capital, and industrial skills. These conditions cannot be traced to white racism. For example, all-black school boards, local politicians, and teachers dispense education in black communities, and parents play a critical role in students' attitudes toward teachers, learning, and authority. If it is argued that white people control black school boards, teachers, and parents, then, a case is being made for an extraordinary white omnipotence.

The case for a worsening black situation can be supported statistically as persuasively as the case that there has been continued black progress over the last two decades. In response to the question "Are black Americans better off than they were four years ago?" J. A. Parker writes:

> Black-owned industrial enterprises increased in value from $473 million in 1973 to $2.2 billion a decade later. The number of blacks in the civilian work force rose by 31 per cent and income for black families increased to $19,620. The number of blacks moving to the suburbs has steadily increased. In 1950, there were 1.7 million. In 1960, 2.5 million. In 1970, 3.6 million and in 1980, 6.2 million. By 1984, more than 23 per cent of blacks were living in suburbs.[14]

However, compare those remarks with an extract from the U.S. Bureau of the Census: "In 1983, 47.2 percent of all black children under the age of sixteen were living below the poverty level. The median income of a white family in 1983 was $25,757 and for a black family $14,506."[15] While, according to the U.S. Department of Commerce:

> About 1 million Black students 18 to 34 years old were enrolled in college in 1981, double the number enrolled in 1970. . . . In 1982, the proportion of Blacks who had completed 4 years or more of college was about one-half the proportion of Whites who completed the same level, 13 percent and 25 percent, respectively. In 1970, the proportion for Blacks was about one-third the proportion for whites (6 percent compared to 17 percent).[16]

What these conflicting claims demonstrate is that black and white are not useful categories for socioeconomic research. As Charles Murray writes:

In 1980, for example, there were 1.4 million black households with a money income of $25,000, the members of which are surely exasperated at the impressions left by constant invidious statistical comparisons of blacks with whites. By the same token, large numbers of whites are poor, ignorant, and vulnerable to exploitation. In 1980, 19.7 million whites were living beneath the poverty line (about 2.3 times the number of blacks) many of whom are surely exasperated at the comparisons that make "white" interchangeable with "doing fine."[17]

Black-white income comparisons are "contaminated" by a variety of other variables such as age, regional background, gender, and educational levels. Thus, contrary conclusions are reached, depending on whether black individual income, black female income, or black family income is calculated. An overall racial economic situation is as elusive as the amount of melanin that makes a person white or black. The black experience turns out to be composed of many different experiences. Indeed, only the premise that white racism is a pervasive influence on the lives of all blacks sustains the idea of a black experience. Abandon this premise and the racial nature of experiences is dissolved.

AN HISPANIC EXPERIENCE

The presence of Hispanics in the United States constitutes a reminder that the Americas were first an object of competing north and south European interests. These interests culminated in a phenomenal migration to the "New World." Various regions of the Americas became part of individual European empires. Out of the British loss of North American colonies in 1776 emerged the United States of America, which by the beginning of the nineteenth century was claiming eminent domain over the Americas. The Spanish imperial presence in America and the Pacific was effectively destroyed by the Spanish-American War of 1898. The United States gained control over Spain's possessions such as Cuba, Puerto Rico, the Philippine Islands, and Guam. The United States thereby came of age as an imperial power itself. Its subsequent interventionist and immigration policies effectively created the conditions for Hispanic immigration.

Who are Hispanics? The term Hispanic represents classification by language and art forms, and according to demographers Rafael Valdivieso and Cary Davis:

> The very term "Hispanic" is a label with a nebulous meaning, applied by the general population to an ever-changing group of U.S. residents. The terms Hispanic or Latino generally refer to persons whose cultural heritage traces back to a Spanish-speaking country in Latin America, but also include those persons with links to Spain, or from the southwestern region of the U.S., once under Spanish or Mexican control.[18]

In 1989 this category of persons amounted to approximately 20 million, or 8 percent of the U.S. population. The four largest aggregates were Mexican American, 12,110,000; Puerto Rican, 2,500,000; and Cuban, 1,035,000. The "other Hispanic" category and Central and South Americans numbered over 4,000,000 persons.[19]

Hispanics are said to be the second largest minority in the United States; they comprise a variety of nationalities from Central and South America. The circumstances surrounding their entry into the United States encourage the use of an immigrant-assimilation model. Indeed, the designation Hispanic experience suggests a broad focus on an immigrant group unified by a common language. However, the suggestion of homogeneity is unwarranted. Modes of entry into the United States, occupational location and distribution, social intercourse, and even the Spanish spoken by Cuban Americans, Mexican Americans, and Puerto Ricans deny the thesis of an Hispanic identity or community. The term Hispanic, then, identifies a linguistic commonalty, not a mobilized collectivity, a group identity, a regionally concentrated population, or a population with a uniform socioeconomic condition. These configurations suggest that persons represented in the category Hispanic are not only culturally discrete but also significantly differentiated at socioeconomic levels.[20] Indeed, there are wide socioeconomic disparities within each Hispanic subgroup.

In comparisons of the Mexican and Cuban-American experiences, certain differences are highlighted. For example, mass Cuban immigration to the United States followed the dramatic political developments in Cuba in the early 1960s.[21] Cuban migrants were more political refugees than settlers. This migration is generally divided into three waves of populations, which were of different socioeconomic origins and profiles. Joan Moore and Harry Pachon write: "the first wave was 94 percent white, averaged 34 years of age, and was well educated (14 years of school). The second wave was less white (80 percent), younger, and poorer. And the third wave (Marielitos) was only 60 percent white, much younger, and even poorer."[22] These observations on the racial composition of Cuban immigrants follow a race relations tradition of racially classifying immigrants. However, white skin should not be taken as the source of the socioeconomic successes of some early Cuban Americans. The authors mention two other significant determinants, age and income distribution, and ignore a third, the level of U.S. government involvement in the settlement of the first wave of Cuban refugees who harbored hopes of returning to a free Cuba. The third wave of Cuban immigrants arrived in 1980, by which time the first group's hopes of a return were dashed. This group manifested low levels of education, proficiency in English, and industrial skills. More significantly, its official reception was not part of the grand scheme of liberating Cuba from Castroism. It is the members of the second and third waves who generally inhabit the lower echelons of the Cuban-American socioeconomic hierarchy.

The first wave of Cuban immigrants received the largest amount of per capita federal assistance given to immigrants in the history of the United States. Population scientist Paul R. Ehrlich and his associates write:

> The United States government made public assistance available to the Cuban refugees on a lavish scale, but available only in Miami. These programs were run with federal money but administered by Florida or Dade county. This effort was so successful that as late as 1976 almost half of all Cuban aliens reporting their residence were still in Florida. The impact and magnitude of this contrived immigration is something that is seldom discussed.[23]

In keeping with the spirit of collaboration, the Cubans' right of entry was unrestricted; their media-cultivated image was that of a beleaguered group victimized by Castro's communism, a group that would return to their homeland once Castro was overthrown. These immigrants would assist the U.S. government in this publicly declared objective. These declarations lessened the hostile public response generally meted out to immigrants. The officially encouraged regional concentration of Cuban immigrants fostered the development of a Cuban-American economic enclave and networking financial centers. This success in the business sector has led to the suggestion that the Cuban-American experience stands in sharp contrast to that of other Hispanics. The standard of living of early Cuban immigrants is superior to that of the later immigrants, most Puerto Ricans in New York, and undocumented Mexican workers in California and Texas. In terms of federal policies, there are Hispanics, and Hispanics.

Some social scientists challenge the accuracy of the designations Hispanics and even Latinos. The persons included in these categories represent a mass of behaviorally distinct and diverse nationalities. Sociologist Felix Padilla writes:

> To date, social scientists have failed to make a conceptual distinction between behavior that is Latino-or-Hispanic related and behavior that is the expression of individual and separate Spanish-speaking ethnics. In other words, there is little conceptual precision on the meaning of the concept of Latino or Hispanic when used as an expression of a particular form of group identity and behavior.[24]

To Padilla the category Hispanics is misleading, insofar as it purports to denote a group with a common ancestry, culture, and life situation. On the other hand, other scholars justify the collective designation on grounds that a common cultural heritage characterizes those who are identified as Hispanics and Latinos.

There is a more important issue to be addressed in the continuing saga of to see, or not to see, differences and similarities. A principle should be established that any such observation must be justified. In other words, the observer must clarify why an observed difference, or similarity, is significant enough to warrant attention. Otherwise, social studies can become caught up in endless rounds of observations of differences and similarities. The dominant pattern in social studies is one of identifying differences or identifying similarities in order to stress differences at another level. For example, a common Spanish heritage is discovered to denote that Hispanics are different from Anglos, African Americans, and Asian Pacific Americans. The principle of finding similarities to claim differences can be reversed. It could be argued that the differences within the Mexican-American population are subversive of the idea of either a Mexican-American or an Hispanic ethnic group.

Varying periods and modes of entry of Mexicans into the United States render Mexican Americans a most diverse population. Attempts to identify a general Mexican-American identity merely uncover more differentiation. Objective, subjective, legal, biological, regional, and cultural criteria crisscross and intersect to generate multiple layers of identities — Novos Mexicanos, Hispanos, Tejanos, Chicanos, and Americanized Mexicans. The Census Bureau proposes that Hispanics are classified "regardless of race." However, in studies of racial and ethnic relations, Mexican Americans have been designated a nonwhite race, foreigners, and a conquered, or colonized nation within the United States.[25] Some Mexican Americans, the descendants of Spanish Southwest residents, however, may also claim to be a white ethnic group within U.S. society; their traditional rights of residence are much stronger than descendants of some European settlers.

Some residents of the state of New Mexico prefer to be perceived as descendants of Hispanics of north-central Mexico, who are ancestrally different from the mestizos of the Southwest. Indeed, New Mexico has the highest number of Hispanos compared to other states. But why are they Hispanics? Given their generations of residency in North America, it could be argued that they are as American as Bostonian Puritans and should not be called Mexican Americans. As the use of Spanish in the home decreases through intermarriage with so-called Anglos, not all "Hispanic-looking" or Spanish-surnamed persons necessarily speak Spanish fluently, or even as a second language.[26] Hence, even the idea of Hispanics as a linguistic community is untenable. The term Hispanics, then, settles uneasily within assessments of Hispanic appearance, nature of surname, country of origin, knowledge of Spanish, and self-identification.

The use of the classification Hispanics to include Mexican Americans has been deemed "discriminatory."[27] As a research category, it obscures critical variations in socioeconomic achievements. Objections have also been raised against the classification Mexican Americans. Alfredo Mirandé writes:

> The pervasive use of "Mexican American" fails to recognize that "Chicanos" is a word self-consciously selected by many persons as a symbolic positive identification with a unique cultural heritage. Many have not realized that Mexican American is analogous to Negro, or colored, whereas Chicano is analogous to black.[28]

Mirandé's protests against sociological-assimilationist analyses of the Mexican-American experience are supplemented with an alternative perspective that emphasizes a distinct political-cultural formation among Mexican Americans. This group is designated Chicanos, which is deemed preferable to Mexican American. It is claimed that Chicanos and Mexican Americans are not interchangeable. Chicanos emerged out of the crucible of U.S. annexationist and colonial policies in the Southwest. The name functions as a clarion call for political struggles against this historical U.S. imperialist oppression.

As with African American and black, some persons still retain a preference for Mexican American, disdaining the radical political implications of Chicano. Nevertheless, the claim that Mexican American is synonymous with the now-discredited "Negro" hints at the possibility that the shifting nature of racial and ethnic designations diminishes their utility for social studies, except as barometers of changing political appraisals. Whichever name is chosen can be deemed politically incorrect and unacceptable. Thus, research on Hispanics, as with African Americans, continues to be politically rather than logically evaluated.

Racial and ethnic evaluations of persons who "look Mexican American" create paradoxical social situations in social intercourse and interpersonal relations. Such persons are assumed to be Spanish speaking, an assumption that is often not justified. Some so-called

Mexican Americans will be caught up in an ethnic exclusion and racial inclusion syndrome, which can lead to an identity conflict. Some are anatomically white, but non-Protestant and Spanish-speaking. They can be rejected by WASPs for being Catholic and Spanish-speaking, but be more socially acceptable than African Americans or even mestizos. These "white" Mexican Americans could also be rejected by blacks, while black-skinned Hispanics could resent being allocated to the black category. For the anatomically white Hispanics, identifying as, or with, Caucasians is socially hazardous, and made difficult by religious and language differences from WASPs.

Some features of the so-called Mexican-American experiences are similar to those of Puerto Ricans — forced incorporation into the United States, anatomical variety, and political economic ties with the United States that produce compelling push-pull factors. These result in perpetual streams of migration and reverse migration and marginalization in terms of a national identity. Mexican Americans and Puerto Ricans necessarily face difficulties in the acculturation process. Puerto Ricans share the Mexican American's relatively easy adaptation to U.S society. However, this comparatively effortless adaptation constitutes an obstacle to a clean break with the mother country. Indeed, it is not clear which country is the mother country. For many generations of Mexican Americans and Puerto Ricans, identification with Mexico and Puerto Rico and identification with the United States are mutually exclusive. But neither country can be discarded easily. For some Puerto Ricans and Mexican Americans, Americanization — disappearance as an immigrant minority and assimilation into U.S. society — is arduous. This social psychological limbo may be a factor in their comparatively lower levels of socioeconomic achievements.

Since 1952, Puerto Ricans have been citizens of the United States. Neither they nor the descendants of nineteenth century Mexican citizens of the United States can be legitimately deemed "immigrants." The refugee and sojourner status of some contemporary Central American immigrants also diverges from traditional patterns of Mexican migration. They are better referred to as "migrants." Hispanic experiences, then, do not lend themselves to an all-inclusive, immigrant analysis. On the other hand, a racial analysis is severely limited, given that most so-called Hispanics "look white." In keeping with the racial minority focus, however, they are frequently called a "brown population" — they are not to be classified as whites for purposes of socioeconomic comparisons and political evaluations of Anglo policies.

Whether Hispanics are considered nonwhite or white depends on which anatomical attributes are considered decisive for racial classification. Indeed, the use of racial criteria in the classifying of U.S. citizens points to a certain arbitrariness in the Hispanic classification. In 1960 the Bureau of the Census identified the Hispanic-American population as white persons of Spanish surname.[29] Both the anatomical characteristics and economic status of later migrants forced an official redefinition of Hispanics.[30] They were regarded as mestizos, a combination of Caucasoid, Mongoloid, and Negroid characteristics. It is not clear whether this means that groups of Hispanics are white, brown, and black, or that they are all racially mixed. If the former, some Hispanics should certainly be classified as white. In the latter case, they would all be considered black in the U.S. but not necessarily so in Latin America.

White Hispanics could legitimately protest against being lumped together with black Hispanics. Black Hispanics could make a coherent case for being included in the black population. Most Hispanics, however, could claim Native American and European status, if bloodlines were to be traced back to 1492. An unwillingness to measure the amount of whites and white blood in the Hispanic population leads to the utilization of language, last names, and self-classification as official means of identification. In effect, different patterns of racial and ethnic evaluation produce a free-floating population called Hispanics. They are black-skinned, white-skinned, olive-skinned, and brown-skinned. Their Spanish is regionally and nationally differentiated. By no stretch of the sociological imagination can they be called a group. Hispanics survive in academic research and official demographic statistics by virtue of a commitment to racial and ethnic theories of society.

The regional concentration of the three major so-called Hispanic categories is considered significantly related to U.S.-Latin American relations. Persons classified as Mexican Americans reside mainly in the five southwestern states. The concentration of Puerto Ricans in New York and Cubans in Miami reflects both an initial sojourner orientation and entrapment by kinship and communal ties. In recent years the flow of other Central Americans to the United States has increased dramatically. They now number some one and a half million persons. The immediate push factor in this new migration was the civil wars in Central America. The involvement of U.S. interests in these wars and the striking disparities in North and Latin American living standards ensure a continual flow of these migrants and refugees. Each of these nationalities, then, enters the United States under particular circumstances and follows traditional processes of isolation in enclaves followed by dispersion.

Dissertations on racial minority experiences are organized around a thesis of victimization by whites. In radical political economic writings, the Mexican-American experience is conceptualized as patterns of race-class exploitation and internal colonial domination.[31] These features are said to be manifest in the fact that some 50 percent of the Mexican-origin population live in "barrios," a concentration of residential and business dwellings occupied by Spanish-speaking people. In the internal colonial model, the barrio is the Mexican-American ghetto, a colonized enclave. However, distinctions must be made among a slum — which can have both Mexican-American and other residents — a substandard area with overwhelmingly Mexican-American inhabitants, a Mexican-American community comprising both poor and well-to-do homes, and a rundown housing stock whose inhabitants apparently are immobilized by political, economic, and social barriers.

In *Race and Class in the Southwest*, sociologist Mario Barrera summarizes a radical/Marxist reading of Mexican-American history:

> In the nineteenth century the area that is now the Southwest was incorporated into the United States through a war of conquest. With the Southwest came a population of former Mexican citizens who were now

granted American citizenship by the Treaty of Guadalupe Hidalgo. These were the original Chicanos. During the remainder of the century a social and economic structure crystallized in the Southwest in which Chicanos and other racial minorities were established in a subordinate status. It is into this structure that succeeding generations of Chicanos have been fitted during the twentieth century, with some modifications.[32]

The period 1819 to 1848 marks the colonization of northern Mexico by Anglos. The Mexican government's toleration and encouragement of U.S. settlement on Mexican territory led to conflicts with some settlers. These escalated into violent confrontations, the dissolution of the region's feudal-pastoral economic structure, the incorporation of its residents as U.S. citizens, and the political-economic demotion of Mexican landholders to lower-echelon ranchers and landless laborers. The Treaty of Guadalupe Hidalgo (1848) specified that Mexican property and cultural practices would be respected and maintained by U.S. government administrators and settlers. Both, however, were ultimately encroached upon and invalidated. Together with the Gadsden Purchase (1853), the treaty established the Mexican-U.S. border, which is often regarded as an obstacle to evolving processes of U.S.-Mexican economic interdependence and integration.

In the radical political economic analysis of the Chicano experience, it is argued that mid-nineteenth-century northern Mexicans lived through progressive encroachments on their lands by U.S. settlers, violent confrontations, and ultimately war between Mexico and the United States. The U.S. annexation of Mexico's northern provinces created a Mexican population within the borders of the United States. They and their descendants became Mexican Americans primarily as a result of conquest and territorial amalgamation by the United States. The burgeoning industrialization of the Southwest in the 1880's led to a steady increase of this population. The demand for labor "pulled" streams of Mexican immigrants away from dictatorial repression and impoverishment in Mexico, while in the early twentieth century the social upheavals of the Mexican revolution "pushed" hundreds of thousands of Mexicans into the Southwest. Push-pull factors continue to contribute to a mushrooming maquiladora or runaway industry in

U. S. and Mexican border towns as well as problems of illegal immigration and undocumented workers.[33]

Some analysts of these problems marginally touch on the racial and ethnic features of the populations. Others emphasize political and economic factors in the oppression of Chicanos. Sociologist Joan Moore makes an appeal for the inclusion of the Chicano experience within studies of intergroup relations. She writes: "Academic social scientists have been extraordinarily blind to Chicanos, Puerto Ricans, Native Americans, and other nonblacks. Generations of textbooks on intergroup relations have discussed only blacks."[34] This accusation is formulated inaccurately, however. Textbooks on the relations between persons classified as blacks and whites define their field as race relations. To include Mexican Americans under race relations could draw the wrath of those who argue that Mexican Americans are mostly Caucasian and mestizos. As sociologist Edward Murguia suggests:

> The Mexican American people, a mixed Indian-Spanish racial group, are neither clearly Caucasian nor non-Caucasian, and here once again we see the ambiguity in the variable of race that we have observed in the variables of mode of entry, size and distribution with reference to the Mexican-American people.[35]

However, to claim that Mexican Americans are not clearly Caucasian is to legitimize an incoherent racial classification. Who is clearly Caucasian? No particular Caucasian can be selected as the model of a Caucasian, without raising the ghosts of de Gobineau and Hitler. Indeed, no particular Mexican can be chosen as the racial representative of the Mexican-American people.

The request that Chicano replace Mexican American should not come as a surprise. If Mexican American is an imposed label, an inferior social class constructed by Anglos, opposition to this stigmatization must forge a new classification. The idea of a Chicano experience is meant to suggest a revolutionary opposition to the various forms of oppression of Mexican origin people and their alienation from the land of their ancestors. Chicanos are said to be a distinct cultural entity, a colonized group, whose unity is reflected in the idea of La Raza. Barrera writes: "The concept of La Raza, probably the most generally accepted self-designation (and properly understood as "the people" rather than "the race") best expresses this feeling of unity."[36] However, Barrera himself elsewhere refers to Chicanos as a racial minority. These diverse depictions of Chicanos imply that the Chicano experience does not easily fall under racial, ethnic, or class relations. Not racism, ethnocentrism, or capitalism represents an adequate explanation of this experience.

As with the African-American experience, the study of the Chicano experience illustrates a major difficulty in the analysis of human society. Events must be selected and analyzed through some theoretical prism. This prism generates a classification of the protagonists. If a human-centered theory is not chosen, the analysis becomes open to charges of arbitrariness. Such objections have been raised to both the "Mexican-American" and the "Chicano" experience. Should these designations of multiple meanings not be abandoned? The Mexican-American population is said to comprise different racial admixtures, different social strata and different cultures derived from varying modes and periods of entry into the United States. This amounts to different degrees of acculturation and assimilation, standards of living, and levels of identification with either the United States or Mexico. Who is the Mexican American?

Should the Chicano experience be designated "ethnic," "class," "colonial," or "third world"? A combinational compromise, expressed in the conclusion that all these elements are involved, is unsatisfactory because arguably, a class analysis subsumes the economic referents in ethnic, colonial, and third world focuses. A racial analysis would be on its own terms objectionable. Some Mexican Americans cannot be deemed nonwhite. Their minority status derives from not racial but cultural and class differences from Anglos. Hence, the inclusion of the Mexican-American experience under race relations is permissible only if being a biological race is not considered a necessary condition for a population's inclusion. However, if racial attributes play no part in the decision to include a population, whose experiences do not belong in racial studies? The complications generated by the retention of race should be taken as an opportunity to move the analysis of social relations away from racial experiences. The problem is not that non-black nonwhites have been left out of racial studies. They do not belong there in the first place. Racial studies were developed to chart the place and fate of the Negro in white society.

The abandoning of the racial focus is particularly relevant to the analysis of the Mexican-American experience, for this experience has been powerfully shaped by U.S. foreign and immigration policies. For example, the U.S. government's appropriation of one-half of Mexico's territory in the mid-nineteenth century cannot be analyzed as a racially motivated decision. Although some U.S. settlers used racial terms to describe the residents of what is now the Southwest, mid-nineteenth-century U.S.-Mexican relations involve political, philosophical, and economic considerations. Sociologist Edward Orozco emphasizes a clash of cultures: "In truth, the clash is between two cultures, religions: Christian Mexicanism with its God-centered, three dimensional Catholic focus, and republican protestantism with its secular, one-dimensional man centered emphasis."[37] However, so dominant has been the racial theory that even the admission that Mexican Americans are not a racial group does not prevent references to Anglos in the race-class and internal colonial perspectives.

The analysis of the Mexican-American experience through race-class and internal colonial models stands opposed to the neoclassical economic analysis that emphasizes push-pull factors in migration and the eventual assimilation of those migrants through their own individual efforts. In the internal colonial analysis, it is argued that the comparatively inferior economic circumstances, residential isolation, and marginalized political status of Mexican Americans in the Southwest mark them as an internally colonized people. As migrants, they enter a secondary labor market that condemns them to low wages, substandard education, inadequate health and welfare services, and political invisibility. The explanation of these conditions necessitates an analysis of Spanish colonialism and continuing U.S. imperialism against the Mexican people.

In analyses presented by the internal colonial model, the early U.S. settlers' mid-nineteenth century push to capture the whole North American continent involved the displacement of Mexicans from their lands through violence, "legal" edicts, broken promises, and deceitful

Figure 2.1

	Migratory	Immigrant	Permanent
Legal	Commuters	"Bracero" type	Permanent residents
Illegal	"Traditional" male migrants	Illegal, cyclical	Illegal, permanent

commercial arrangements. Mexicans are immigrants to the Southwest only by virtue of superior Anglo firepower and willingness to acquire wealth by any means necessary. Indeed, hidden within Anglo references to Mexicans as "immigrants" is a history of violence, dispossession, political subordination, and relegation to second-class citizens in a region that traditionally belongs to their forebearers. In effect, Chicanos are an internally colonized people, segregated in barrios and periodically subjected to expedient patterns of importation and deportation. However, these arguments are in need of considerable modifications, given the admission of socioeconomic stratification and diversity of life-styles among those classified as Chicanos. Does Chicano refer to an immigrant, a migrant worker, a citizen whose immediate ancestors emigrated from Mexico, or a citizen whose ancestors have resided in the Southwest since the sixteenth century? Various patterns of migration and residency may have rendered the term "Mexican American" incoherent, but "Chicano" is no more logically sound.

Some analyses of illegal immigration highlight the relationships among Mexico's domestic economic policies, its dependency on political and economic developments in the United States, U.S. corporations' involvement in Mexican agriculture, and patterns of Mexican emigration.[38] Mexican-origin migration may be categorized according to immigrants' legal status and period of entry into the United States. In a recent study, two researchers at the Rand Corporation, Kevin McCarthy and Robert Valdez, depict three major categories — migratory, immigrant, and permanent resident populations — which may be further subdivided as illustrated in Figure 2.1.[39]

According to McCarthy and Valdez, there are six legally distinct sets of Mexican-American residents in the United States. Some can hardly be said to have experienced processes of Americanization. Others are Mexican only by stretching the concept of ancestry to its outer limit. Each of these residents has a different socioeconomic-economic profile. Hence, data on Mexican Americans in relation to health, welfare, crime, poverty, unemployment, education, and immigration need to be carefully qualified. Indeed, the classification Mexican Americans provides a poor foundation for ameliorative public policies.

It may be argued that some of the conditions that affect most migrant Mexican workers — English-language deprivation, undocumented status and harassment, entrapment in the secondary labor market — are rooted in structural weaknesses in the Mexican economy. These weaknesses "push" hundreds of thousands of educationally and vocationally deprived workers into the U.S. In analyzing their fate, the maldistribution of land in Mexico, the debt problems of the Mexican government, the operations of U.S. manufacturing corporations and agribusinesses, and chronic, rural hyperunemployment must be treated as more significant than any racial and ethnic composition.

The state of the border economy and the structure of the demand for labor in the primary receiving states of California, Arizona, New Mexico, and Texas are key elements shaping the life situation of Mexican-origin migrant workers. They are entering regions beset with fiscal imbalances, technological retrenchment, and slow economic growth. Difficulties in the settlement of migrants and immigrants are compounded by an inadequately developed infrastructure of social services, such as low-cost housing, vocational training schemes, medical and welfare facilities, language programs for migrant workers, and ineffective trade union organization. Given these circumstances, migrant workers periodically become economically unnecessary and deportable "aliens." Thus, the harassment of Latino-looking persons by law enforcement agencies and the electoral utilization of the illegal immigration issue reflect related conditions of a demand for "cheap" labor, runaway infrastructural degeneration, and inexorable push factors in the Mexican economy.

In responding to pull factors, migrant workers can quantitatively and qualitatively oversupply the labor market. Their legal status, levels of education, skills, proficiency in English, and industrial experience can also relegate them to the tertiary, low-paying sectors of the economy. This relegation results in comparatively low incomes and the search for "cheap" residences. Substandard incomes restrict migrant works to substandard housing and living conditions. The overall effect is a hard core of slum dwellings, which are transformed into barrios by other socioeconomic-political forces. The sources of barrios, then, cannot be explained in terms of racism or internal colonialism, but in terms of the mismanagement of Mexico's economy, capital movements in the Southwest, human capital endowments, and a low level of social-political mobilization and participation from the Mexican origin population.

AN ASIAN PACIFIC-AMERICAN EXPERIENCE

The borders of U.S. society have been described as "the golden door." Indeed, the comparatively high standard of living in the United States represents a magnet for multitudes of migrants, both settlers and sojourners, from all the other continents. Moreover, U.S. foreign policies often generate compelling push conditions. State and local responses to immigrants, however, frequently negate the objective of welcoming "huddled masses" to a land of freedom and opportunity. They have often not allocated the economic and educational resources necessary for the smooth integration of immigrants into the host society. Employers have utilized the immigrants' disorientation and disorganization to pursue labor policies that minimize labor costs. These are some of the conclusions reached by scholars who favor an analysis of immigrant experiences in the context of (global) capitalist development and immigration.

This approach is developed in *Asian Immigrant Workers in the United States Before WW II: Labor Immigration under Capitalism*. The editors, Lucie Cheng and Edna Bonacich, claim that aspects of the Asian Pacific-American experience can be analyzed through the combined operations of shifting U.S. foreign, immigration, and social policies, including the peculiarities of state and local politics, as they dovetail or conflict with federal edicts. Recent U.S. foreign policy concerns influenced the relaxation of immigration and citizenship policies as they apply to Asians and increased the pull of the magnet of economic opportunities. Pull factors, then, are not a mere reflex of neutral economic conditions. Rather, Cheng and Bonacich suggest that immigration policies reflect the force of naked economic interests and the operation of systemic processes of exploitation. In their words, immigrants are "cut off from the mainstream of the working class movement and are forced into enclaves that are like 'internal colonies.' Thus the treatment of immigrant workers, including the prejudice and discrimination they face, must also be seen as part of the world capitalist system."[40] The push factors that generate immigration to the United States are not separable from global developments, especially the economic underdevelopment of the third world through conquest, enslavement, colonialism, and the operations of multinational corporations.

The motivational dynamics of migration are similar, whether it is Mexican peasants fleeing economic deprivation in northern Mexico or Cambodians seeking to escape the ravages of civil war. All immigrants are in search of a "better life." However, once in the United States, they are confronted by policies of neglect and exploitation that result in familiar patterns of deprivation. In many cases, so wretched are conditions in their native countries that even chronic socioeconomic deprivation in the United States is considered a better life.

Like Mexican migration, Asian immigration into the United States followed the contours of U.S. internal economic developments as well as foreign and immigration policies. These policies are global enough to create both push and pull factors in Asia. For example, civil wars in Southeast Asia constitute one of the push factors in the most recent wave of Southeast Asian migration into the United States. This modern migration, then, is not unrelated to U.S. military involvement in that region. However, large-scale Asian immigration into the United States began in the mid-nineteenth century.[41] Starting in 1849 Chinese migrants entered the United States as part of the gold-inspired migration into California. Three years later, thousands of Chinese migrants entered the United States as contract laborers and were employed mainly in the construction of the Central Pacific railroad.

Chinese immigration was curtailed in the late nineteenth century and accelerated into a "normal" pattern only after the 1965 liberalization of immigration procedures. The post-1965 immigrants include a variety of Southeast Asian nationals, who had not previously entered the United States in significant numbers. The 1970s signaled their unprecedented entrance into the United States.[42] Their refugee status illustrates the relationship between foreign and immigration policies: U.S. corporate and military involvement in the domestic affairs of Asian countries is a "triggering variable" of migration.

References to racial attributes have accompanied the restrictive immigration policies toward Asians in the nineteenth century. Chinese immigrants, although qualifying as "poor and huddled masses," were subjected to official exclusion and defined in Californian courts as Negroes, who therfore could not testify against a white man. Between 1882 and 1929 various congressional acts prohibited them from "freely" entering the United States.[43] These acts created a climate that tolerated further persecution, segregation, vigilante violence, forced labor, deportations, and pogroms. Until 1952 Asian Americans were considered ineligible for citizenship through naturalization. For over a century comparative quotas on Asian immigration reflected a preference for northern Europeans. Some authors claim that a virtual "yellow phobia" dominated immigration policies toward Asians throughout the nineteenth and the first half of the twentieth century.[44] The post-Vietnam War objective of improving relations with Asian countries prompted a relaxation and, ultimately, the removal of restrictions on admission, naturalization, and civil rights. Thus, since 1975 thousands of Indochinese have been admitted and resettled through government, corporate, and private programs.

The U.S. government has had considerable difficulty establishing consistency among foreign, immigration, and social policies. It exercises its right to regulate the movement of people across its borders. This regulation has often served a variety of foreign policy goals and domestic interests. Indeed, many immigration problems, whether that of undocumented workers or refugees, are generated by the U.S.

government's often imprudent involvements in the politics of the sending countries. There are also omnipresent racial and ethnic classifications in the United States that encourage various patterns of differentiation and segregation and even foster the denial of civil rights. Federal and local government policies are unavoidably in lockstep with the experiences of immigrants. Seventeenth-century African and British indentured servants, nineteenth-century Asian contract laborers, twentieth-century Hispanic immigrants, and Asian and Central American refugees were slotted into U.S. society through different levels of government intervention. This fact belies the contention of a historically free market economy and has obvious implications for the dispute over the legitimacy of contemporary government intervention.

The category Asian American and Pacific Islanders is a comparatively novel classification of persons. In 1990 this population was estimated at approximately seven and a half million, or just over 2 percent of the U.S. population. Some 50 percent are indigenous with grandparents and great grandparents born in the United States. This is one reason why the most appropriate designation still eludes identification. Asian Americans and Pacific Islanders is but one of a series of designations, which includes Orientals, Asians, and Asian Pacific Americans, and objections have been raised against each of these categories. This population is said to comprise Americans of various national origins, including Chinese, Japanese, Filipino, Middle Eastern, Indian, Laotian, Korean, Vietnamese, Hawaiian, Samoan, and Guamanian. Thus, the geographic base of Asian Pacific migration spans over six thousand miles.

A similar diversity pertains to the degree of acculturation among those of citizen, migrant, and refugee status. Some persons who "look Asian" could be third- or fourth-generation American citizens. To describe them as Asian carries an illegitimate suggestion of not belonging or of being new to the United States. Others may be of the first Asian-American generation, while still others may be recent refugees from the civil wars in Southeast Asia. These national, intranational, and generational differences limit the usefulness of the classification Asian Americans. In the 1980 U.S. Census, the term was abandoned in favor of Asian Americans and Pacific Islanders.

Different types of experiences are bound to permeate the lives of the so-called Asian Pacific-American population. However, the thesis of a white supremacist society leads to the idea of a collective racial experience of victimization. Thus, certain internal socioeconomic and cultural differences are ignored in order to develop a collective contrast with whites and other racial minorities. As Don S. Nakanishi writes: "Like blacks, Asian Pacific Americans are rarely viewed as a highly heterogeneous population with a myriad of real and symbolic levels of internal differentiation of social classes, generations, religions, gender, countries of origin, languages, and cultural norms."[45] The term Asian Pacific Americans may itself be a stereotype, in that it lumps heterogeneous populations into one category on the basis of apparent similarities in skin color, hair type, and eye shape.

In fact, the classification Asian Pacific American incorporates over two dozen different nationalities. It does not imply either racial homogeneity or an Asian identity. Indeed, there is no logical justification for aligning Pacific Islanders such as Filipinos, Guamanians, and Samoans with Southeast Asian nationals. The influence of the threefold classification of the human species into Negroes (Africa), Mongoloids (Asia), and whites (Europe) on immigration and public policies is immediately obvious. The underlying reasoning appears to be that some Filipinos, Guamanians, and Samoans look like Asians, and are, therefore, classifiable with Asians. Nevertheless, the anatomical heterogeneity of Pacific Islanders does not fit any of the three racial classifications. They do not constitute a race within the terms of reference advanced by the threefold division of the human species.

Each of the different Asian Pacific nationalities comprises populations that may be further differentiated by language and dialects, customs, and traditions. Chinese Americans, for example, speak Mandarin or Cantonese. These languages coexist with hundreds of dialects in different provinces in South China, Taiwan, Hong Kong, and Vietnam. Like Japanese Americans, Chinese Americans represent over four generations of residence in the United States. Hence, early Chinese and Japanese immigrants may be distinguished from contemporary Southeast Asian refugees. The latter themselves vary, and include the Hmong who come from mountainous regions in Laos, the Khmer from Cambodia, and both Vietnamese and "ethnic Chinese" from Vietnam. Moreover, the refugee status of Indochinese is radically different from nineteenth-century Chinese and Japanese sojourners and settlers. What is especially significant, then, about the Asian Pacific-American experience is its breadth and impreciseness.

It follows that the classification Asian Pacific is more a geographic convenience than a denotation of a group. The varying patterns of Asian and Pacific Island immigration ensure that the socioeconomic conditions of this population are highly differentiated. Asian and Pacific Island immigrants came at different periods of U.S. history, for different reasons, and with varying results. Yet the proposition that the overwhelming number of nineteenth-century Asian immigrants represented a brawn, as opposed to the brain, drain of the twentieth century is not accurate. Contemporary Vietnamese, Cambodian, Filipino, and Korean immigrants and refugees represent both unskilled and semi-skilled labor, as did some pioneer Chinese immigrants. It was the contract labor system and intense indigenous opposition to free competition that forced many Chinese and Japanese immigrants into railroad construction, farming, and the service sectors. Both their descendants and later immigrants can now be found in administrative, managerial, and technical occupations. Unlike the pioneers, many are not sojourners but highly qualified immigrants in pursuit permanent residency in the United States.

Differences in push-pull factors are expressed in different rates of success for various Asian-Pacific immigrants. The "pioneers" were confronted with a variety of legal and violent restrictions that limited their economic advancement and occupational dispersion. Reports of opposition to Vietnamese and Korean business enterprises suggest that contemporary Asian-Pacific immigrants also face barriers to their socioeconomic mobility. Although this population is the most suburban of racial minorities, residential patterns suggest some isolation, or self-isolation. Chinatowns, Koreatowns, Little Tokyos, Manilatowns, or heavy urban concentrations of Asian Pacific Americans indicate that residential dispersion is either undesirable or difficult. There are reports of chronic and unattended illnesses in certain sections of the Asian Pacific-American population and difficulties in access to employment and social services. However, the study of these social problems and the development of solutions are stymied by an exaggerated emphasis on the successes of some Asian Pacific-Americans.

THE MODEL MINORITY THESIS

The racial theory emphasizes the victimization of nonwhites by whites, and the uniqueness of each race's immigrant experiences. However, some aspects of immigrant experiences are comparable. Consider the issue of voluntary/involuntary migration. Contemporary Asian-Pacific immigrants do not leave their homelands as captives, or as a result of foreign conquest and dispossession, although Indo-China's civil wars derive in no small measure from the dislocations caused by U.S. military interventions. However, insofar as military occupation and life-threatening political persecution led to migration, it is not voluntary. The African migration between the seventeenth and nineteenth centuries was explicitly coerced. Most Africans entered the United States as commercial objects within a slave labor market. In the post-Civil War period, violence was used to relegate so-called Negroes to the bottom of the occupational pyramid. Patterns of violence also ensured that some European indentured servants and early Chinese, Japanese, and Mexican workers entered the United States stripped of certain crucial civil rights. This facilitated their protracted confinement in the lower rungs of the occupational ladder. Common threads of deprivation, physical threats, and violence run through all patterns of large-scale migration.

Most immigrants tend to gravitate toward lower-level agricultural, infrastructural, and service sectors of the economy. However, given their widely different levels of education and training, a noticeable feature of the labor market situation of Asian Pacific Americans is an overrepresentation in both the lowest and the uppermost categories within the occupational pyramid.[46] A proportional dispersion throughout the major occupational categories has not occurred. A small percentage of this population can be found in highly desirable occupations such as computer technology, engineering, and accounting. This condition is referred to as a bipolar skewing of occupational distribution. The fact that Asian Pacific Americans are overrepresented at both the top and the bottom of the occupational hierarchy is cited as evidence that they experience discrimination in obtaining positions commensurate with their education and training and are not promoted according to their qualifications. A focus on the Asian-American presence in the upper level of the occupational pyramid provides the basis for the success stories that emerge from all immigrant experiences. Asian Pacific Americans are frequently deemed a "model minority" due to the successes of *some* Asian Americans.[47]

It is reported that Asian-American students surpass whites in median school years completed and score higher on various academic tests and that Asian-American workers are disproportionately represented in professional, managerial, administrative, and technical occupations. Overall, Asian Americans are said to have lower rates of unemployment, welfare dependency, crime, divorce and deviant behavior, and higher levels of family income. These achievements are said to add up to a comparatively exemplary performance; they are suggestive of cultural and personality endowments compatible with industrial efficiency and progress. In intraminority comparisons, the thinly veiled question is: Why can't the other minorities be like the Asians?

The model minority thesis has been subjected to caustic criticisms, however.[48] The criticisms expose a particular ambiguity in the thesis, for it is not clear whether Asian Americans are a model for other minorities or a model of immigrant success. The former interpretation is analyzed in Chapter 3, which addresses comparisons of ethnic achievements. Regarding the latter meaning, both the purposes and methods of measuring Asian-American successes have been challenged. One critic warns against "the masked negativity of positive stereotypes." However, the most frequently voiced criticism is that the model minority thesis is based on incomplete research and, therefore, represents an overgeneralization. For example, the low Asian Pacific-American unemployment rate reflects a widespread practice of holding multiple jobs to make ends meet and the practice of preferring underemployment to unemployment. Many Asian Pacific Americans are confined to occupations far below their education, talents, and aptitudes. The assertion of an absence of poverty among Asian Americans has also been challenged. In the words of demographers William P. O'Hare and Judy Felt:

> Poverty among the Asian-American community tends to be over-shadowed by high-income Asian Americans. Yet, a large segment of the Asian-American population lives in poverty. The poverty rate for Asians in the late 1980's (17 percent in 1988, and 14 percent in 1989) was roughly twice that of non-Hispanic whites (8 percent).[49]

While the observation that some Asian Americans avoid welfare services may be accurate, it must be added that this avoidance probably derives from a fear of officialdom and an ignorance of rights and entitlements by the older generation of Asian immigrants who may have experienced some bureaucratic harassment earlier. However, O'Hare and Felt also dispute the claim that Asian Americans are not involved in welfare delivery processes.

> Because of increasing poverty rates and rapid population growth, Asians have become a much larger share of the poverty population. In 1979, Asians made up 1.7 percent of the poverty population, by 1989 they comprised 3.0 percent. Contrary to popular wisdom, poor Asian Americans are more likely than non-Hispanic whites in poverty to participate in government welfare services.[50]

These observations support other claims that many of the older and current immigrants have serious mental health problems deriving from self-isolation, neglect of their veteran experiences, a traumatic adjustment to urban American life, and memories of victimization from the civil wars in their homelands. Their invisibility reflects the general inadequacy of outreach welfare and health care services.

The above-average *family* income of Asian Pacific Americans does not justify a model minority thesis. These incomes reflect more a demographic than a comparative economic index. Over 75 percent of the Asian Pacific-American population is concentrated in three states: New York, Hawaii, and California. The comparatively superior median income in these states cannot but be reflected in data on Asian

Pacific-American incomes. Asian Pacific-American family incomes are above average also because of a high rate of family participation in economic activities. For these and other reasons Asian Pacific Americans need not be considered a success story. They have "made it" only in the sense of consistently struggling to overcome residual, indigenous fears of a yellow peril, and indeed may be beginning to pay the price of this "success" in the form of hostile responses to the entrepreneurial activities of Koreans, Vietnamese, and Japanese, and the limiting of Asian enrollment in higher education. The model minority thesis, insofar as it arouses apprehensions about an Asian takeover of "our turf," may well be a journalistic kiss of death.

Certain Asian Pacific-American achievements may be said to be remarkable, given the anti-Asian nature of immigration policies and the violence to which the early immigrants had been subjected. Some entrepreneurial and educated South Vietnamese refugees earn above-average income and are only minimally acculturated.[51] Some Chinese American senior citizens speak little or no English and are in desperate need of social services and welfare assistance. The Chinatowns and Little Tokyos of New York and Los Angeles are neither seed beds of deviance and deprivation nor unqualified success stories. Rather, they represent patterns of highly concentrated urban immigrant enclaves, comprising "sweatshop" manufacturing; service enterprises, mainly catering and cleaning; middlemen operations; and extraordinary individual commercial, banking, and professional accomplishments. What this demonstrates is that some individual enterprises are models of achievement, not "Asian Americans."

Interminority comparisons have proceeded side by side with a focus on intraminority differences in socioeconomic mobility. Explanations of these differences generally address length of urban residency, extent of acculturation, push factors, government intervention, internal social organization, and community-specific values. Not a racial but an acculturation factor is applied to Japanese Americans to generate categories such as Issei, Nisei, Sansei, and Yonsei — the first to fourth generation of Japanese Americans. Rates of socioeconomic mobility vary among them. The focus on these factors should include analysis of the different educational attributes of the immigrants, their

plans and predispositions — seeking permanent residency or sojourn-
ing — as well as their individual entrepreneurial skills. In this context,
the answer to the question of why some Asian Pacific immigrants have
been more successful than others must involve analysis of immigrants'
original endowments, motivations to succeed, and the definition of
success.

As if as evidence that differences are in the eyes of the beholder,
sociologist Rodolfo Alvarez has developed a chronological, fourfold
classification of social psychological processes among the Mexican-
origin population.[52] These processes produce the creation generation,
the migrant generation, the Mexican-American generation, and the
Chicanos, categories that correspond to the four generations identified
among Japanese Americans. Economist Thomas Sowell has charted
different experiences of three ethnic groups among blacks in the United
States — descendants of the free colored population, descendants of
the Southern slave population, and West Indian immigrants.[53] Each is
said to have a distinct socioeconomic profile. A similar type of distinction may be made regarding the Asian American and Pacific Island
population. Some are immigrants only recently domiciled in the United
States. Others are Americans of Asian Pacific ancestry. Many are
necessarily caught up in the ambivalence of hyphenated identities.
Finally, there is an isolated, older generation still immersed in the
language and customs of its countries of origin. For research purposes,
there is no Mongoloid race or homogeneous Asian Pacific Americans.
Classification of persons by their skin color — whites, blacks, browns,
and yellows — is of limited usefulness and grossly misleading in social
studies.

A NATIVE AMERICAN EXPERIENCE

The successes of some Asian American and Pacific Islanders may be
contrasted with the absence of any extensive Native American socioeconomic mobility. According to some analysts, Native Americans are
the most disadvantaged minority in U.S. society.[54] In virtually all texts
on racial and ethnic relations, the post-Columbus period of Native
American history is presented as a tale of genocide. A common claim

is that by the end of the nineteenth century, a population of between 3 to 12 million was reduced to 250,000. Native Americans were the first victims of the twin juggernauts of mercantilism and the Calvinist notion of predestination. The precepts and perceptions of the early English settlers generated attempts at religious conversion, protection of "a primitive and childlike race," dispossession, and destruction of "savages."

Seventeenth- and eighteenth-century settlers were primed by commitments to piety and profit. Their zealous pursuit of wealth was manifest in processes of Indian enslavement, relocation, decimation through so-called Indian Wars, and segregation. In *Democracy in America*, a work published in 1832, Alexis de Tocqueville identified three popular views about Native Americans that stood out in nineteenth-century congressional records, local legislative documents, and media comments. These are: Indians are of a different, if not inferior, race and civilization, they are non-Christian, and their way of life is an obstacle to progress. It was popularly believed that Indians were "savages" obstructing the realization of Puritan destiny to build "the city on the hill" and the goal of conquering a continent. The settlers' perceptions of Indians, however, were not uniformly expressed throughout all periods of contact — the founding of settlements, their transformation into English colonies, the formation of states, and post-Revolutionary developments into nationhood. Because these perceptions of Native Americans varied regionally and chronologically, no simple identification of racism suffices as an explanation of policies toward them. What seems certain is that English settlers generally accepted an equation of *different* and *unequal*.

With the establishing of settlements in North America, Native Americans were confronted with a diverse settler population — colonial authorities, various types of traders, farmers, and Christian missionaries. The nature of the conflicts between settlers and Native Americans varied by settlement, political changes in the colonies, and characteristics of the given tribe. Nevertheless, between 1607 and 1754 settlers' encroachments on tribally held land were the principal source of conflict. The British crown intervened in the mid-eighteenth century to protect Native Americans from the settlers' hunger for land. The

American Revolution, then, left Native Americans — some of whom fought with the British — at the mercy of manifest destiny. Between the sixteenth and nineteenth centuries, the dispossession of Native Americans was a principal objective of the settlers. This dispossession involved the destruction of Native American forms of social organization through congressional dissolution of tribal independence in 1871 and the Dawes Severality Act of 1887 that dismantled tribes as legal entities that can own land. Attempts at the physical extermination of Native Americans were intensified after the Civil War to the extent that, according to historians Thomas A. Bailey and David M. Kennedy, "from 1868 to about 1890, almost incessant warfare raged in various parts of the West between Indians and whites. A printed list of the names of the engagements alone covers over 100 pages."[55] Raids, skirmishes, wars, and massacres defined the relations between settlers and Native Americans. The significant feature of these relations, then, was a state of mutual enmity. Generally, not only were their interests considered mutually exclusive, but both parties considered violence a natural means of conflict resolution.

After dispossession and the failure of extermination, a second objective, the assimilation of Indians, began to acquire prominence by the end of the nineteenth century. Indians were to be molded into a single ethnic group through "Pan-Indian" education, the destruction of tribal social organization, the encouragement of urban migration, and the granting of citizenship to "civilized tribes." However, the administration of Indian life from above and beyond, as it were, was plagued with problems of bureaucratic inefficiency, corruption, and neglect, as in earlier pacification policies. The Indian Reorganization Act of 1934 reflects a modification or reversal of assimilationist objectives. The tribal structure and autonomy of particular societies were to be restored and preserved through the refurbishing of reservations.

The colonization of North America was costly in terms of loss of human life. The contact between the early settlers and Native Americans resulted in policies of both deliberate and inadvertent mass slaughter. As noted, estimates of the number of Native Americans occupying North America at the time of contact vary from 3 to 12 million. They comprised hundreds of different tribes with specific forms of social organization and behavioral attributes. Despite the popular perception of "savages," some tribes were considered easily assimilable and were duly induced to abandon their traditional way of life. Others resisted the new "civilization" to the death. Indeed, it is generally conceded that Native Americans, not any other racial minority, are the principal victims of the introduction of "Western civilization" in the Americas.[56]

According to sociolgists Winona LaDuke and Ward Churchill, the pacification of Native Americans was part of policies of dispossession and extermination. Native Americans now occupy about 3 percent of their original areas of habitation. As these authors depict the comparative socioeconomic conditions of Native Americans:

> Theirs is the highest rate of infant mortality on the continent, the shortest life expectancy, the greatest incidence of malnutrition, the highest rate of death by exposure, the highest unemployment, the lowest per capita income, the highest rate of communicable or "plague" diseases, and the lowest level of formal educational attainment.[57]

LaDuke and Churchill argue that a modern "radioactive colonialism" completes the destruction not accomplished by hundreds of military assaults. Most of the urbanized Native Americans — approximately 45 percent of the population — vegetate on the periphery of urban labor markets. Reservation residents are trapped between the "exploitative" operations of uranium mining companies and inefficiently administered welfare programs. Significantly, radical/Marxist analyses of the Native American experience place greater emphasis on political economic than on racial interests.[58] But why identify persons racially or culturally then offer nonracial and noncultural explanations of their experiences? Consistency demands racial causation, which means either white racism or nonwhite genetic deficiencies.

Despite the popular presentation of the past as a story of confrontation between white men and Indians, it is generally recognized that the different Native American tribes were by no means harmoniously related and did not regard themselves as a race or family of Indians. Indeed, the collective classification "Indians" contradicts the recognition of their anatomical, cultural, and social organizational diversity.

Similarly, the term whites does not reflect the mercantilist concerns, Christian zeal, commitments to a manifest destiny, laissez-faire capitalism, and individual pursuits of economic security through land ownership that shaped the settlers' perceptions and policies. The nomenclature whites engenders a search for racial motives, but unless these motives are going to be attributed to the nature of white people, their doctrinal roots deserve analysis.

The mutually hostile policies of most settlers and Native Americans may be said to represent a clash of societies committed to nonverbal means of conflict resolution. Native Americans endorsed a violent defense of their land and way of life, to the death, if need be. The settlers were also committed to violence as an instrument of progress, for their intellectual environment harbored a Judeo-Christian emphasis on violence for a just cause. These doctrinal aspects of so-called Indian Wars bear investigation. Other relevant aspects pertain to the equation of different and inferior, the racial theory being developed in the seventeenth and eighteenth centuries, and Calvinist notions of predestination and identification of poverty as sinful. An exclusive focus on the racial attributes of the victors and victims merely reflects the continued influence of the racial theory.

A racial identification of Native Americans breaks a principle of consistency. Originally deemed a separate "red race," Native Americans defy the threefold classification into Negroids, Caucasoids, and Mongoloids. As with blacks, Hispanics, and Asian Pacific Americans, their anatomical variety is striking. Centuries of so-called miscegenation with successive waves of European and African settlers further complicate a racial identification. For example, most Hispanics have some Native American ancestry. Similar admixtures prevail in the white and black populations. If Indians or Native Americans are the descendants of an original Asian migration over the Bering Straits into North America, surely they are kin to Asian Pacific Americans. Given the centuries of European-Indian-Negro cohabitation, it may be argued that Native Americans are systematically and enormously undercounted. If consistency is to prevail, a separate category for persons of Mongoloid ancestry is needed. Arguably, this category would cover at least 80 percent of the U.S. population.

According to 1960 to 1980 census figures, there were 523,591, 792,730, and 1,418,195 American Indians in 1960, 1970, and 1980, respectively.[59] The 68,000 increase (14 percent) between 1960 and 1970 and the almost 100 percent increase between 1970 and 1980 illustrate the arbitrary nature of racial identification. As Alexandra Harmon writes: "In the United States, whether a person has identified himself or been identified by others as an Indian has varied with the historical period, the social and political setting, and the purpose of the identification."[60] Not surprisingly, some commentators detect chronic patterns of arbitrariness and undercounting/overcounting in the census identification of racial groups.[61] Races cannot be accurately counted, and, indeed, the census allocation of blacks to the nonwhite category is questionable. Professor Albert Murray writes:

> As for U.S. Negroes being non-white, nothing could be further from scientific accuracy. Indeed no classification was ever less accurate. By any definition of race, even the most makeshift legal one, most native-born U.S. Negroes far from being nonwhite, are in fact part white. They are also by any meaningful definition of culture, part Anglo-Saxon, and they are overwhelmingly Protestant.[62]

The government's racial-ethnic breakdown of the population cannot be said to be helping nonwhites, given the liberationist claims of persistent racial oppression and socioeconomic deprivation. But race relations scholars tolerate and even applaud the official disregard for logic and consistency. Conservative, liberal, and radical/Marxist writings display an equally sacred commitment to the racial and ethnic labeling of persons. The weight of political-electoral considerations blocks consideration of an alternative system of population classification.

The official identification of persons as African Americans, Hispanics, Asian Pacific Americans, and Native Americans derives from the use of anatomical and cultural characteristics to categorize citizens. These characteristics have been selected by federal, state, and local authorities and presented as a basis for the allocation of rights and resources. They are used in the formulation of social policies as well as to shape identities and experiences. Racial experiences are, therefore, not separable from academic investigations and government interventions. However, government's selection of the racial theory for the purpose of classification lacks both rhyme and reason. If the continuation of this type of classification derives from the conviction that it would be electorally unprofitable to desist, then a case can be made for a redefinition of democratic politics. While particular legislators may profit from the conservation of races, the society itself is certainly the worse for wear. Both Republican and Democratic political strategists may well rue the day voters were divided into blacks and whites.

Given the politics (postelection government interventions to help its constituencies) and the moralistic thrust of social studies (America is a white racist society), social scientists are bound to seek out disadvantaged racial minorities. The problem with this collective racial analysis is that any identification of a racial group overlooks both internal socioeconomic and cultural differentiation and across-group similarities. Thus, it has been argued that there are different ethnic groups and classes *among* Caucasians, African Americans, Hispanics, Asian Pacific Americans, and Native Americans. "Empirical" research can be directed at any of the subgroups in order to repudiate general propositions on racial well-being and deprivation. The portrayal of nonwhites as disadvantaged and deprived in terms of employment, income, education, housing, health care, the administration of justice, and media images only serves to intensify controversies over racial genes, culture, racism, and government intervention. Racial blame is shifted backward and forward, without any analysis of the question whether the racial classification of persons was valid in the first place. Each piece of research claims to be rooted in concrete experiences. However, opponents claim that its results are *empirically* flawed and present divergent empirically data that are in turn rejected. This condition of continual reciprocal invalidation cannot generate solutions to the problems discovered. America's so-called racial and ethnic problems remain as ineradicable today as on the day human beings were deemed whites and nonwhites.

NOTES

1. See U.S. Bureau of the Census, *Current Population Reports, Series P-25, No. 1053, Projection of the Population of States by Age, Sex, and Race 1989-2010* (Washington, DC: U.S. Government Printing Office, 1990); William P. O'Hare, Kevin Pollard, Taynia L. Mann, and Mary Kent, "African Americans in the 1990's," *Population Bulletin* 46, no. 1 (July 1991), p. 6.

2. Depictions of these trends are longstanding. See Robert M. Jiobu, "Earnings Differentials Between Whites and Ethnic Minorities: The Case of Asians, Blacks and Chicanos," *Sociology and Social Research* 61, no. 1 (October 1976), pp. 24-38; Joan Moore, "Minorities in the American Class System," in Norman Yetman (ed.), *Majority and Minority: The Dynamics of Race and Ethnicity in American Life* (London: Allyn and Bacon, 1985), pp. 502-522; Gail E. Thomas (ed.), *U.S. Race Relations in the 1980's and 1990's: Challenges and Alternatives* (New York: Hemisphere Publishing Corp., 1990); Martin Marger, *Race and Ethnic Relations* (San Francisco: Wadsworth, 1991).

3. Robert Merton, "Discrimination and the American Creed," in Norman Yetman (ed.), *Majority and Minority*, pp. 40-53.

4. See Alan Blum and P. Mc Hugh, "The Social Ascription of Motives," *American Sociological Review* 36, no. 1 (February 1971), pp. 98-109.

5. Orlando Patterson, *Slavery and Social Death: A Comparative Study* (Cambridge, MA: Harvard University Press, 1982), p. 13.

6. See D. Brion Davis, *The Problem of Slavery in Western Culture* (New York: Cornell University Press, 1966).

7. See P. D. Curtin, *The Atlantic Slave Trade: A Census* (London: University of Wisconsin Press, 1969). But see also Patterson, *Slavery*, pp. 159-164.

8. See Laura Foner and Eugene Genovese (eds.), *Slavery in the New World: A Reader in Comparative History* (Englewood Cliffs, NJ: Prentice-Hall, 1969); Robin Winks (ed.), *Slavery: A Comparative Perspective* (New York: New York University Press, 1972); Winthrop D. Jordan, *White Over Black: American Attitudes Towards the Negro, 1550-1812* (Chapel Hill, NC: University of North Carolina Press, 1968).

9. See Thomas Gossett, *Race: The History of an Idea in America* (New York: Schocken Books, 1965); Forrest G. Wood, *The Arrogance of Faith: Christianity and Race in America from the Colonial Era to the Twentieth Century*

(New York: Knopf, 1990); George Fredrickson, *The Black Image in the White Mind* (New York: Harper and Row, 1972).

10. James Oakes, *The Ruling Race: A History of American Slaveholders* (New York: Knopf, 1982), p. 38.

11. See Mary Frances Berry, *Black Resistance/White Law: A History of Constitutional Racism in America* (New York: Appleton-Century-Crofts, 1971); Donald G. Newman, *Promises to Keep: African-Americans and the Constitutional Order, 1776 to the Present* (New York: Oxford University Press, 1991).

12. See Raymond Franklin and Solomon Resnick, *The Political Economy of Racism* (New York: Holt, Rinehart and Winston, 1973), chapter 4; Manning Marable, *How Capitalism Underdeveloped Black America: Problems in Race, Political Economy and Society* (Boston: South End Press, 1983). For grim pictures of the contemporary "black economy," see O'Hare et al., "African Americans in the 1990's,"; pp. 16-35; Ken Auletta, *The Underclass* (New York: Random House, 1983); Christopher Jencks and Paul E. Peterson, *The Urban Underclass* (Washington, DC: The Brookings Institution, 1991).

13. John L. Hodge, "Equality: Beyond Dualism and Oppression," in David Goldberg (ed.), *Anatomy of Racism* (Minneapolis, MN: University of Minnesota Press, 1990), p. 90.

14. J. A. Parker, "Black America Under the Reagan Administration," *Policy Review*, no. 34 (Fall 1983), p. 30.

15. U.S. Bureau of the Census, *Statistical Abstract of the United States*, 105th ed. (Washington, DC: U.S. Government Printing Office, 1985), p. 63. See also Charles V. Willie (ed.), *The Caste and Class Controversy* (Bayside, NY: General Hall, 1979); Walter Williams, *The State Against Blacks* (New York: McGraw-Hill, 1982), chapter 4.

16. U.S. Department of Commerce, *Bureau of the Census, America's Black Population: 1970 to 1982, A Statistical View* (Washington, DC: U.S. Government Printing Office, 1983), p. 16.

17. Charles Murray, *Losing Ground: American Social Policy 1950-1980* (New York: Basic Books, 1984), p. 55.

18. Rafael Valdivieso and Cary Davis, "U.S. Hispanics: Challenging Issues for the 1990's," *Population Trends and Public Policy*, no. 17 (December 1988), p. 2.

19. U.S. Bureau of the Census, *Current Population Reports: The Hispanic Population of the United States Series P. 20, No. 446* (Washington DC, U. S. Government Printing Office, 1990).

20. There is a wealth of studies of the differences within the so-called Hispanic population. See A. J. Jaffe, Ruth M. Cullen, and Thomas D. Boswell, *The Changing Demography of Spanish Americans* (New York: Academic Press, 1980); Joan Moore and Harry Pachon, *Hispanics in the United States* (Englewood Cliffs, NJ: Prentice-Hall, 1985); Alejandro Portes and Robert L. Bach, *Latin Journey: Cuban and Mexican Immigrants in the United States* (Berkeley, CA: University of California Press, 1985).

21. Thomas D. Boswell and James R. Curtis, *The Cuban American Experience: Cultures, Images, and Perspectives* (Totowa, NJ: Rowman and Allanheld, 1984); and Paul R. Ehrlich, Loy Bilderback, and Anne H. Ehrlich, *The Golden Door: International Migration, Mexico, and the United States* (New York: Wideview Books, 1981).

22. Moore and Pachon, *Hispanics in the United States*, p. 36.

23. Ehrlich, Bilderback, and Ehrlich, *The Golden Door*, p. 83.

24. Felix Padilla, "Latino Ethnicity in the City of Chicago," in Susan Olzak and Joane Nagel (eds.), *Competitive Ethnic Relations* (New York: Academic Press, 1986), p. 153.

25. See David J. Weber (ed.), *Foreigners in Their Native Land: Historical Roots of the Mexican Americans* (Alburquerque, NM: University of New Mexico Press, 1973); Rodolfo De La Garza, Frank D. Bean, Charles M. Bonjean, Ricardo Romo, and Rodolfo Alvarez (eds.), *The Mexican American Experience: An Interdisciplinary Anthology* (Austin, TX: University of Texas Press, 1985).

26. See H. Manuel, Spanish Speaking Children of the Southwest (Austin, TX: University of Texas Press, 1965); Gilles Grenier, "Shifts to English as Usual Language by Americans of Spanish Mother Tongue," in De La Garza, et al. (eds.), *Mexican American Experience*, pp. 346-358.

27. See Halford Fairchild, "Chicano, Hispanic, or Mexican American: What's in a Name?" *Hispanic Journal of Behavioral Sciences* 3, no. 2, (1981), pp. 191-198.

28. Alfredo Mirandé, *The Chicano Experience: An Alternative Perspective* (Notre Dame, IN: University of Notre Dame Press, 1985), pp. 2-3.

29. See U.S. Bureau of the Census, *Nonwhite Population, 1960* (Washington, DC: U.S. Government Printing Office, 1963).

30. See U.S. Bureau of the Census, *Census of Population and Housing* (Washington, DC: U.S. Government Printing Office, 1970).

31. See Mario Barrera, *Race and Class in the Southwest: A History of Racial Inequality* (London: University of Notre Dame Press, 1979); Joan Moore, "Internal Colonialism: The Case of the Mexican Americans," *Social Prob-*

lems 17 (Spring 1970), pp. 463-478; Rodolfo Acuna, *Occupied America: A History of Chicanos* (New York: Harper and Row, 1981); Tomas Almaguer, "Toward the Study of Chicano Colonialism," *Aztlan: Chicano Journal of the Social Sciences and the Arts* 2, no. 1 (Spring 1971), pp. 7-21; Tomas Almaguer, "Race, Class and Chicano Oppression," *Socialist Revolution* 5 (July-September, 1975), pp. 71-99; Tomas Almaguer, "Historical Notes on Chicano Oppression: The Dialectics of Racial and Class Domination in North America," *Aztlan: Chicano Journal of the Social Sciences and the Arts* 5, nos. 1 and 2 (Spring and Fall 1974), pp. 27-56; Richard Romo, *East Los Angeles: History of a Barrio* (Austin, TX: University of Texas, 1986).

32. Barrera, *Race and Class*, p. 7.

33. Miles Hansen, *The Border Economy* (Austin, TX: University of Texas Press, 1986); David S. North and Marion F. Houston, *The Characteristics and Role of Illegal Immigration on the U.S. Labor Market: An Exploratory Study* (Washington, DC: U.S. Department of Labor, 1976); Vernon M. Briggs, Jr., *Immigration Policy and the American Labor Force* (Baltimore: John Hopkins University Press, 1984).

34. Joan W. Moore, "Minorities in the American Class System," in Yetman (ed.), *Majority and Minority*, p. 503.

35. Edward Murguia, *Assimilation, Colonialism, and the Mexican American People* (New York: University Press of America, 1989), p. 49.

36. Barrera, *Race and Class*, p. 1.

37. Edward Orozco, *Republican Protestantism in Aztlan* (New York: Petereins Press, 1980), p. 12.

38. See Daniel Levy and Gabriel Szekely, *Mexico: Paradoxes of Stability and Change* (Boulder, CO: Westview Press, 1983). Arthur F. Corwin, "Mexican Policy and Ambivalence Toward Labor Emigration to the United States," in Arthur F. Corwin (ed.), *Immigrants — and Immigrants: Perspectives on Mexican Labor Migration to the United States* (London: Greenwood Press, 1978), pp. 25-37; Wayne A. Cornelius, *Mexican Migration to the United States: Causes, Consequences and U.S. Responses* (Cambridge, MA: Center for International Studies, 1978).

39. Kevin F. McCarthy and Robert Valdez, *Current and Future Effects of Mexican Immigration in California* (Santa Monica, CA: Rand, 1985), p. 6.

40. Lucie Cheng and Edna Bonacich (eds.), *Asian Immigrant Workers in the United States Before WW II: Labor Immigration under Capitalism* (Los Angeles, CA: University of California Press, 1984), p. 2.

41. See Lemuel F. Ignacio, *Asian Americans and Pacific Islanders: Is There Such an Ethnic Group?* (San Jose, CA: Philipino Development Associates, 1976); Ronald Takaki, *Strangers from a Different Shore: A History of Asian Americans* (New York: Penguin, 1990).

42. See Donald Hohl, "The Indochinese Refugees: The Evolution of United States Policy," *International Migration Review* 12 (Spring 1978), pp. 128-132; Dinker I. Patel, "Asian Americans: A Growing Force," in John A. Kromowski (ed.), *Racial and Ethnic Relations 91/92* (Guildford, CT: Duskhin Publishing Group, 1991), pp. 86-91.

43. See U.S. Commission on Civil Rights, *The Tarnished Golden Door: Civil Rights Issues in Immigration* (Washington, DC: U.S. Government Printing Office, 1980), pp. 7-12, cited in John A. Kromowski (ed.), *Racial and Ethnic Relations 91/92* (Guildford, CT: Duskhin Publishing Group, 1991), pp. 40-44.

44. See Ehrlich, Bilderback, and Ehrlich, *Golden Door*, chapter 2; Stanford Lyman, *Chinese Americans* (New York: Random House, 1974); H. Brett Melendy, *Chinese and Japanese Americans* (New York: Hippocrene Books, 1984); Takaki, *Strangers.*

45. Don S. Nakanishi, "Seeking Convergence in Race Relations Research: Japanese-Americans and the Resurrection of Internment," in Phyllis Katz and Dalmas A. Taylor (eds.), *Eliminating Racism: Profiles in Controversy* (New York: Plenum Press, 1988), p. 161.

46. See William P. O'Hare and Judy C. Felt, "Asian Americans: America's Fastest Growing Minority," *Population Trends and Policy*, no. 19 (February 1991), pp. 2-16.

47. See William Petersen, "Success Story, Japanese-American Style," *New York Times Magazine*, January 9, 1966; Harry L. Kitano and Stanley Sue, "The Model Minorities," *Journal of Social Issues* 29, no. 2 (1973), pp. 1-9; L. Ling-chi Wang detects an unwarranted self-righteousness in President Carter's words: "We have succeeded in removing the barriers to full participation in American life . . . Their successful integration into American society and their positive and active participation in our national life demonstrates the soundness of America's policy of continued openness to peoples from Asia and the Pacific." Cited in "Statement," in U.S. Commission on Civil Rights, *Civil Rights Issues of Asian and Pacific Americans: Myths and Realities*, (Washington, DC: U.S. Commission on Civil Rights, 1979), p. 43; "Asian Americans: A Model Minority," *Newsweek*, December 6, 1982, pp. 39-51.

48. See Eugene F. Wong, "Asian American Middleman Minority Theory," *Journal of Ethnic Studies* 13, no. 1 (Spring 1985), pp. 38-51. Kwang Ghing Kim and Won Moo Hurh, "Korean Americans and the Success Image: A Critique," *Amerasia* 10, no. 2 (1983), pp. 3-22. U.S. Commission on Civil Rights, *Civil Rights Issues*, pp. 389-566; United Way, *Executive Summary: Asian Pacific Needs Assessment* (Los Angeles, CA: United Way of Los Angeles, 1988); Thea Lee, "Trapped on a Pedestal: Asian Americans Confront Model-Minority Stereotype," in Kromowski (ed.), *Racial*, pp. 95-98.

49. William P. O'Hare and Judy C. Felt, "Asian Americans," p. 12.

50. Ibid.

51. See Daniel Montero, *Vietnamese Americans: Patterns of Resettlement and Socioeconomic Adaptation in the United States* (Boulder, CO: Westview Press, 1979); Kenneth A. Skinner, "Vietnamese in America: Diversity in Adaptation," *California Sociologist* 3, no. 2 (Summer 1980), pp. 103-124.

52. Rodolfo Alvarez, "The Psycho-Historical and Socioeconomic Development of the Chicano Community in the United States," in De La Garza et al. (eds.), *Mexican American Experience*, pp. 33-56.

53. See Thomas Sowell, "Three Black Histories," in Thomas Sowell (ed.), *Essays and Data on American Ethnic Groups* (Washington, DC: Urban Institute, 1978), pp. 7-64.

54. Steve Talbot, *Roots of Oppression: The American Indian Question* (New York: International Publishers, 1985); Winona LaDuke and Ward Churchill, "The Political Economy of Radioactive Colonialism," *Journal of Ethnic Studies* 13, no. 3 (Fall 1985), pp. 107-132.

55. Thomas A. Bailey and David M. Kennedy, *The American Pageant*, vol. 11, 7th ed. (Lexington, MA: D. C. Heath, 1983), p. 524.

56. See Paul Radin, *The Story of the American Indian* (New York: Liverwright, 1944); William Brody and Sophie Brody, *The Indian: America's Unfinished Business* (Norman, OK: University of Oklahoma Press, 1966); Murray Wax, *Indian-Americans: Unity and Diversity* (Englewood Cliffs, NJ: Prentice Hall, 1971); Thomas (ed.), *U.S. Race Relations*, part 3; Joseph E. Trimble, "Stereotypical Images, American Indians, and Prejudice," in Phyllis Katz and Dalmas Taylor (eds.), *Eliminating Racism: Profiles in Controversy* (New York: Plenum Press, 1986), pp. 181-201.

57. LaDuke and Churchill, *Political Economy*, p. 111.

58. For discussions of the applicability of Marxism to the Native American experience, see Ward Churchill (ed.), *Marxism and Native Americans* (Boston: South End Press, 1983).

59. Norman Yetman, "Statistical Appendix," in Norman Yetman (ed.), *Majority and Minority*, p. 532.
60. Alexandra Harmon, "When Is an Indian Not an Indian? 'The Friends of the Indian' and the Problems of Indian Identity," *Journal of Ethnic Studies* 18, no. 2 (1990), p. 95.
61. See U.S. Congress, House Committee on Post Office and Civil Service, *Decennial Census Improvement Act of 1991* (Washington, DC: U.S. Government Printing Office, 1991); Review Progress of Coverage Evaluation and Adjustment Procedures of the 1990 Census (Washington, DC: U.S. Government Printing Office, 1991).
62. Albert Murray, *The Omni Americans: New Perspectives on Black Experiences and American Culture* (New York: Outerbridge and Dienstfrey, 1970), pp. 79-80.

3

The Racialization of Culture and Achievements

Three centuries of debates over race have demonstrated convincingly that racial differences are not natural in the sense of having an existence beyond criteria of racial classification. There are anatomical differences among human beings, innumerable anatomical differences, because the conceptual possibilities of variations are infinite. Specific differences have been selected to allocate persons to races. Hence, more precisely, races are the product of the racial classification employed by human beings. Insofar as it is this classification that is erroneous, race cannot be deemed a problem in intellectual, political, or economic life, or a social formation. It is the illegitimate practice of racial classification that requires critical analysis, especially when its illegitimacy is compounded by an alignment of race and culture. For example, sociologist Edward Murguia writes: "Culture is related to race because when the different races originally made contact with one another their cultures were very different."[1] By implication, each race has its own culture. This is a most popular proposition, which sidesteps the issue of racial classification. Because culture is an omnipresent social phenomenon, this remark also implies that race cannot be abandoned. No demonstration of its arbitrariness can shake connotations of cultural differences. But whether a race can be said to have a culture depends on how culture is specified.

The term culture has a wide variety of definitions. In anthropological and sociological writings, it is used to refer to mores, values, and beliefs that guide individual and group conduct. Anthropologist Edward

Tylor's century-old definition is much cited: "Culture or civilization, taken in its wide ethnographic sense, is that complex whole, which includes knowledge, belief, art, law, morals, custom, and any other capabilities and habits acquired by man as a member of society."[2] Culture may, therefore, be identified through values and artifacts possessed and the behaviors expressed by groups as they interact among themselves and with the environment. In a modification of Tylor's definition, attention is drawn to the attributes of not human beings, but groups. For anthropologists Alfred Kroeber and Clyde Kluckhohn, culture

> consists in patterned ways of thinking, feeling, and reacting, acquired and transmitted mainly by symbols, constituting the distinctive achievements of human groups, including their embodiments in artifacts; the essential core of culture consists of traditional (i.e., historically derived and selected) ideas and especially their attached values.[3]

Culture may be defined universalistically, that is, through symbol construction and utilization, or particularistically — in terms of specific material objects, beliefs, achievements, and behavioral patterns.[4] It is the latter conception of culture that has been appropriated, especially by sociologists, to construct ethnic groups and racial cultures. If the essence of culture is ideational symbols that are transmuted into values, and if only human beings possess this capacity for symbol manipulation, then culture is exclusive to human beings. It is a *species*-unique process of symbol construction and subordination to symbols (values). No human *group* can be said to have a culture.

The combining of anatomical and cultural criteria results in a certain symmetry between racial and ethnic groups. In effect, it strengthens racial classification, suggesting that blacks, browns, yellows, reds, and whites can also be culturally demarcated. Socioeconomic inequalities among these racial-cultural groups are singled out for analysis so that studies of racial-ethnic inequalities are organized around four significant premises: (1) a causal relationship pertains between skin color and socioeconomic situations; (2) races are socioeconomically homogeneous groups; (3) racial and ethnic (in)equality is recognizable and (un)desirable; and (4) races possess their different cultures. In the development of these arguments, terms such as Euro-Americans, African Americans, Hispanics, Asian Pacific Americans, and Native Americans are utilized. The last four are depicted as disadvantaged nonwhites, racial minorities, and ethnic groups.

As indicated in preceding chapters, racial classification violates a rule of consistency. The races produced are phenotypically distinct within one set of criteria, but not another, and are often genetically indistinguishable. However, the classification survives as an engineered and enforced tradition that serves accession to political offices. It informs government policies seeking to maintain overall social control through the creation and manipulation of "groups" and activists' attempts to conserve, or liberate certain races from, a perceived racial status quo. Social scientists also promote a subservience to racial classification by asserting that there are cultural differences that have a corresponding relationship to race. In the process, culture becomes a racial phenomenon. The racialized career of the culture concept is expressed in:

1. an equation of race and culture,
2. the development of an ethnic theory of social relations that examines cultural divisions within the white race,
3. attempts to maintain racial classification through reference to cultural differences that are said to produce different ethnic groups, and references to these differences to explain racial-ethnic achievements and underachievements, and
4. the culture-structure distinction that underlies disputes over the causes of racial and ethnic inequality.

If race is to survive in social studies, it must be married to a behavioral category such as culture. The ethnic group is the offspring of this union, but it retains its autonomy from race by virtue of the discreteness of culture. An ethnic group is defined with reference to culture, while a race is identified anatomically. However, a race can also be an ethnic group because, given the marriage, each race can be said to have its own culture. Thus, the distinction between ethnicity and race collapses. However, it must be maintained, if racial groups and ethnic groups are to be differentiated. This contradiction is compounded by references to racial *and* ethnic groups. The ambiguity is significant. Are racial and ethnic groups one and the same, or are some groups of race, and others of ethnicity?

In the equation of race and culture, a racial group is also an ethnic group. As sociologists Reid Luhman and Stuart Gilman write: "we find that groups of people who are said to differ racially invariably also differ ethnically. . . . The racial groups are also ethnic groups."[5] By implication, blacks and whites are simultaneously distinct races and separate ethnic groups by virtue of their cultural differences. The identification of cultural differences serves to maintain racial classification. As Harvard's Professor Henry L. Gates writes: "And indeed, the trojan horse of culture has today become a favored means of transport for the ideologies of race."[6] The wheels of the horse are made of ethnicity. An ethnic group has a distinct culture and represents a group irrespective of its anatomical heterogeneity. But then a race, an anatomically homogeneous group, is also an ethnic group by virtue of possessing its own culture. The "politics of difference," to use Shelby Steele's phrase, triumphs. Racial differences may be ambiguous, but no one can deny the "reality" of cultural differences. However, once this is accepted, it becomes possible to "blame" the race's culture for socioeconomic inequalities and to compare different racial-ethnic experiences.

The transition from racial studies to racial and ethnic studies retains the category of race. Blacks, a racial designation, is used interchangeably with African American, a classification that has no anatomical implication. Three of the four so-called nonwhite races are ethnically addressed as Hispanics, Native Americans, and Asian Americans, respectively, not as browns, reds, and yellows. The term blacks, however, has been maintained throughout the various name changes that this population has gone through; its triumph over its competitors — Negroes, coloreds, Afro-Americans, and African Americans — indicates certain functions of the racial theory: the demonstration of polar and unbridgeable differences between black people and white people and the rooting of socioeconomic inequalities in natural attributes. If these attributes are no longer blameworthy, look to "culture."

From its inception, the development of the racial theory involved the culture concept.[7] Language and often religion played a part in racial demarcation. More significantly, an observed, cultural inferiority was the basis of the construction of a hierarchy of white and nonwhite races. Nineteenth-century, especially late-nineteenth-century, writings on comparative history and social relations are replete with arguments suggesting racial-cultural hierarchies and a biological determination of culture differences. Most of these writings state that given the genetic superiority of the white race, its culture must also be most advanced. Indeed, the discovery of permanent biological differences between Negroes and whites was intended to demonstrate white cultural superiority. European civilization, personality, and physical features are not only placed at the apex of human achievements but also correlated with Caucasian genes. Culture is itself a racial phenomenon. This thesis continues to permeate social studies.

RACIAL CLASSIFICATION, CULTURE, AND THE BOAS REVOLUTION

In the naturalist variant of the racial theory, the cultural achievements of the white race, or Europeans, are the measure of history and all things human. Other societies, their inhabitants and practices are judged according to European standards. "Western civilization" and "Western culture" were used as if they were tautologies. By the late nineteenth century, Herbert Spencer's writings and the "science" of eugenics had created an influential tradition of biological determinism or, as some would have it, racist thinking. Its most pungent criticisms came from the Boas school of cultural anthropology in the early twentieth century.[8] Franz Boas' rejection of biological determinism rests on a conception of culture as adaptive processes. If a race survives in its environment, then, it is any other race's equal. Boas endorsed racial classification, but considered racial behavior to be culturally malleable. He and his associates suggested that it would be more prudent to analyze race relations through reference to cultural characteristics, development, and change, not natural or biological attributes.

A principal thesis of Boasian cultural anthropology is that, whatever the genetic elements in the human constitution, human behavior goes beyond biology by virtue of the capacity for learning and the reshaping of both natural drives and the environment. Culture is visible in patterns of adaptation to and mastery of the social and natural environments. And just as different natural environments produce different anatomical attributes in human beings to form races, so these different races possess different cultures. However, all cultures are relatively equal, that is, in relation to their ecological context. Hence, races are also equal to one another. Boas' retention of the race-culture equation carries the possibility that culture may come to be used in the same deterministic manner in which race is used.[9] It does, however, serve the purpose of repudiating hierarchical and polar conceptualizations of races and civilizations. Boas' writings may be said to constitute the most powerful early twentieth-century challenge to the naturalist variant of the racial theory. They proclaim that insofar as different races survive in their habitat, their culture is coherent and viable. Their belief systems and artifacts enhance their adaptation to their environment and, therefore, should be judged in this context. By implication, cultures as forms of social organization are relatively equal. There are no "primitive cultures." All human beings express the capacity to adapt to and, ultimately, master the environment. Hence, there is no inequality among cultures, only relative variations. These variations are themselves changed through social contact. Indeed, not only cultural but also anatomical changes may themselves take place through environmental relocation. For example, the descendants of Polish and African immigrants, now Polish Americans and African Americans, are culturally and even anatomically distinct from indigenous Poles and Africans.

Writings of the Boas school of cultural anthropology utilized three divergent conceptions of culture — culture as objects possessed, adaptive mechanisms, and symboling processes. Culture as objects possessed pertains to tangible and intangible entities such as values, beliefs, artifacts and skills. This conception of culture underlies the discovery of different ethnic groups as well as recommendations of pluralism and multicultural celebration. Discrete cultures may be discovered, if culture is defined with reference to objects. It can then be allocated to previously specified groups, for example, races, generations, genders, classes, and nations. Group anatomical differences can be correlated with different cultural objects to produce the idea of different races having their different cultures.

If races are inferior and superior, then so are their cultures. But how are cultures being evaluated, by which criteria, and by whom? With these questions the Boas school launched an attack on ethnocentrism. What was made significant is that the process of examining cultures is fraught with methodological difficulties. The examiners bring their own value systems to bear on the cultures being examined. In constructing cultural comparisons, investigators need a context-sensitive methodology in order to avoid ethnocentrism. Cultures must be seen through the eyes of their participants and practitioners. Otherwise, ethnocentric distortions occur and any group can claim its culture to be superior, or *the* culture. Anthropologist Alfred Kroeber writes:

> The principle of cultural relativism has long been standard anthropological doctrine. It holds that any cultural phenomenon must be understood and evaluated in terms of the culture of which it forms a part. We the students of culture, live in our culture, are attached to its values, and have a natural human inclination to become ethnocentric over it with the result that, if unchecked, we would perceive, describe, and evaluate other cultures by the forms, standards, and values of our own thus preventing fruitful comparison and classification.[10]

Cultural relativism is the answer to the ethnocentrism of scholars who examine other cultures through the prism of European or Western culture.

The third conception of culture, as symboling processes, has universalist implications that are damaging for both the race-culture equation and the idea of a racial-cultural hierarchy. As Boas writes: "It is our task to discover among all the varieties of human behavior those that are common to all humanity. By a study of the universality and variety of cultures anthropology may help us to shape the future of mankind."[11] Anthropology should seek out cultural similarities even as it discovers differences. But there may be a conflict between these simultaneous discoveries of universality *and* variety, unless the term culture is being equivocally used. Anthropologist Walter Jackson discerns a contradiction rather than an equivocation in Boas' analysis of culture. He writes: "Boas never confronted the contradiction between his universalism and his commitment to respect minority cultures."[12] Boas' antiracism begs the question; it presumes the existence of the humanity that it is attempting to discover in cultural universalism.

There is no need to impute a cultural essence to human beings in order to demonstrate the irrelevance of racial differences and the oneness of humanity despite cultural and behavioral variations. These issues can be resolved definitionally. All definitions of culture refer to symboling processes and, insofar as these processes are unique to human society, they make culture synonymous with "human." The symbolic rituals of other animals are learned, but animals are programmed to follow their rituals. As Alfred L. Kroeber suggested, culture is limited to human beings.[13] They may be said to be the only beings of culture. Human society is defined not just by the construction of symbols but by a chosen subservience to symbols. Human beings are subservient to symbols by choice. Atheists emerge in even the most religious communities. As culture is the symboling behavior of the human species, it is unique, unitary, and universal. The idea of racial, gender, generational, national, class, and other group cultures is specific to the conception of cultures as objects possessed.

In conceiving culture as adaptive mechanisms, the Boas school was able to argue that cultures cannot be unequal. Every surviving race demonstrates its cultural resilience, adaptability, and mastery over the environment. Hence, "patterns of culture" are to be placed along a continuum, not a hierarchy. Moreover, cultures are essentially pliable so that any race can adopt new cultural patterns. The evaluation of European (white) culture as superior to the non-European and, on this basis, the demonstration of racial superiority are methodologically flawed. Indeed, race is of limited usefulness in explaining behavior and social change. It is culture that tells the human story.

The writings of Boas and his students effectively displaced the earlier emphasis on unequal biological endowments as the factor responsible for alleged unequal cultural achievements and rebutted the notion of unequal cultures. However, the suggestion of the pliability of culture itself generated further controversies. As Walter Jackson notes, up to the mid-twentieth century, anthropological and sociological discussions of race relations are dominated by analyses of the relationships between: culture and race (W.E.B. Du Bois), African and Negro cultures (Melville Herskovits), culture and American democracy (Horace Kallen), and culture and social behavior (E. Franklin Frazier). One of the most portentous questions posed in these writings is: Do persons classified as Negroes possess their own African culture? If so, it may be thought that they are not fully Americanized and are not entitled to America's blessings. On the other hand, if Negroes have lost their African heritage, as sociologist E. Franklin Frazier insists, then they are a culturally dependent and subjugated people. Thus, one of Harold Cruse's propositions in *The Crisis of the Negro Intellectual* is that black cultural regeneration and autonomy is an indispensable condition of political mobilization and liberation. This proposition constitutes the basis of the contemporary Afrocentric thrust.

The repercussions of the Boas revolution were far-flung. Discussions of culture moved from a recognition of black cultural autonomy to the relevance of culture as a means of political mobilization. They fueled the development of pride in African residues, African-American artistic and literary expressions, the Harlem Renaissance, a militant African consciousness manifest in the popularity of Marcus Garvey's repatriation project, and, ultimately, the intensification of desegregationist struggles. These struggles evolved into the civil rights movement of the 1950s. This organization, in turn, influenced the rise of the women's, ethnic, Chicano, Native American, and student movements and accelerated the pursuit of nonwhite political power. Public policy responses were expressed in government affirmative action, welfare, and antipoverty programs. However, the affirmative action and antidiscrimination legislation of the 1960s fueled a white ethnic resurgence in the 1970s and intensified the intraracial stratification that became the focus of class analyses in the late 1970s and 1980s.[14] These developments, then, represent a long play on race, culture, and class. More precisely, racial, ethnic, and class theories of society are continually and unwittingly being merged in studies of American society. The merger, however, is geared to the retention of racial classification, because racial conditions are taken as a reality to which "culture" and "class" are applied.

THE RESURGENCE OF CULTURE AND ETHNICITY

A separate and distinct ethnic theory of society may be constructed out of the analyses of the relationship among racial classification, culture, and social change (see Figure 1.1, column 3). Its object of study is ethnic groups, which are constructed through references to differences in religious beliefs and practices, languages, culinary, musical and sartorial tastes, art forms, communicative customs, and moral traditions.[15] In the ethnic theory, values and beliefs, especially ethnocentrism, are deemed causally significant in explaining relations among ethnic groups. In *Red, White, and Black: The Peoples of Early America*, historian Gary Nash announces a self-consciously revisionist use of the ethnic theory, suggesting that:

> to cure the historical amnesia that has blotted out so much of our past we must reexamine American history as the interaction of many peoples from a wide range of cultural backgrounds over a period of many centuries. . . . Africans, Indians, and Europeans all had developed societies that functioned successfully in their respective environments. None thought of themselves as inferior people.[16]

In this "cultural approach," the past is to be interpreted through a prism of ethnicity but not ethnocentricity. The Boasian project is continued. But this ethnic or cultural focus is not a novelty in the study of social relations. As indicated, a similar development had emerged in the 1920s. There are some differences, however, in that the modern cultural thrust is rooted in:

1. the discrediting of racial classification in anthropological and, less so, sociological studies;

2. the identification of different white *experiences*, through comparisons between WASP and south/central European immigrants;
3. the perception of intraracial socioeconomic differences, and;
4. a recognition of the limitations of the racial theory in relation to Euro-ethnic concerns about victimization as well as the new Hispanic and post-Vietnam Asian-Pacific immigration.

What emerges from discussions of the role of cultural attributes in social mobility is that African-American achievements are the standard basis for inter- and intra-ethnic comparisons. A "black condition" is used to measure the socioeconomic progress of late-nineteenth-century European, Hispanic, and Asian immigrants. It provides the benchmark for charting the progress of so-called Euro-ethnics and twentieth-century Hispanic, Asian, and Caribbean immigrants. This comparative focus on blacks or African Americans will not be easily terminated.

The last two decades of racial and ethnic studies contain such conclusions as: African Americans are a highly differentiated social group; the socioeconomic mobility of Asian Pacific Americans outstrips all other racial minorities and even some whites; rates of social mobility vary between white Protestants and Roman catholics. The general observation is that racial and ethnic groups are internally culturally diverse and economically stratified. Thus, the diverse and radical implications of the culture concept have not led to an abandoning of racial classification in social studies. Instead, the conception of culture as objects is utilized to give races their cultural history. Ethnic relations are simply added on to studies of race relations. While textbooks and college courses in the 1950s and 1960s were titled "Race Relations," the 1970s witnessed a shift into "Racial and Ethnic Relations." Two decades later the experiences of different races and ethnic groups are still the point of departure for the study of social processes in U.S. society.

In the combining of anatomical and cultural criteria of classification, ethnic subdivisions are drawn among whites and nonwhites. Religion, a cultural element, and race are merged as criteria of demarcation in the acronym WASPs, or White Anglo-Saxon Protestants, while WETs identifies "white ethnics" — non-Protestants such as Jews and Roman catholics. Ethnic demarcation gained increasing prominence during the 1970s, as if in reaction against an earlier emphasis on a bipolar racial specificity. Sociologist Stephen Steinberg writes:

> The late 1960s witnesses an outbreak of what might be called "ethnic fever." One after another, the nation's racial and ethnic minorities sought to discover their waning ethnicity and to reaffirm their ties to the cultural past. Ethnic fever had its origins in the black community, where black nationalism, after a long period of quiescence, emerged with renewed force. The contagion rapidly spread to other racial minorities — Chicanos, Puerto Ricans, Asians, Native Americans — who formed a loosely organized coalition under the banner of the Third World. Eventually ethnic fever reached the "white ethnics" — Jews, Irish, Italians, Poles, and others of European ancestry.[17]

The idea of U.S. society as a cluster of different cultures continues to be revived in discussions of multiculturalism.[18] However, some of Steinberg's formulations can be challenged. It is not at all certain that the nation's racial and ethnic minorities were pursuing their cultural roots and not slices of economic and political pies. Beneath the ethnic fever, then, may have been a malaise of competition and economic discontent.

In the resurgence of ethnicity in the 1970s, certain scholars questioned the legitimacy of placing the white ethnics alongside WASPs as collective racial sinners.[19] It was argued that not all white-skinned persons are psychologically white, and racist. And, by the same token, not all racists are WASPs, just as all WASPs are not racist. It is testimony to the insoluble nature of racial disputes that Murray Friedman's remarks, voiced two decades ago, echo and reecho in contemporary discussions:

> It is perhaps understandable that blacks should take phrases like white racism and a White America as adequate reflections of reality. Nevertheless, these phrases drastically obscure the true complexities of our social situation. For the truth is that there is no such entity as white America. America is and always has been a nation of diverse ethnic, religious and racial groups with widely varying characteristics and

qualities; and conflict among these groups has been (one might say) 'as American as cherry pie.'[20]

Racism is a state of mind that is not determined by skin color; its victims are not always black. Not all blacks are poor and disadvantaged. All whites are not rich and powerful. The successful white ethnic had made it by dint of hard work. As Michael Novak writes:

> The ethnics believe that they chose one route to moderate success in America; namely, loyalty, hard work, family discipline, and gradual self-development. They tend to believe that some blacks, admittedly more deeply injured and penalized in America, want to jump, via revolutionary militance, from a largely rural base of skills and habits over the heads of lower-class whites.[21]

Novak argued further that persons classified as whites represent internally differentiated social categories. White ethnics — who are themselves internally differentiated as Poles, Italians, Jews, and Irish — are economically and culturally distinct from WASPs and have been victimized by them.

In the body of writings depicting the cultural uniqueness and historical patterns of victimization and deprivation among white ethnics, racial and ethnic oppression is conceived as two sides of a single coin of racism/nativism. It is claimed that Euro-ethnics, or immigrants from East and southern Europe and their descendants, are a historically disadvantaged group within the white population. Social scientists and civil rights organizations should not continue to make light of the trials and tribulations of these "unmeltable ethnics." Jews, too, had been lynched, placed in concentration camps, denied entry into America while fleeing from Hitler, and barred from higher educational institutions. Italian, Greek, Polish, and Irish immigrants experienced considerable discrimination, oppression, poverty, and stereotyping. America is a nation of incompletely Americanized settlers. If it is a melting pot, white ethnics have certainly not risen to the top, and whatever successes they have had are attributable to their internal fortitude. Blacks should not try to jump the historical queue by enlisting the government to impose racial quotas to redress grievances that white ethnics had not perpetrated.

Urban America has been a graveyard of both white ethnic and nonwhite attempts to realize the American dream. However, the entrenched concentration on race has led to Euro-ethnics becoming a forgotten and officially ignored minority. To be sure, they have not experienced the unique and manifold devastations of enslavement, but like the migrating Southern blacks they endured the pathologies of early American industrialization and urbanization. The most immediate experience of the new immigrants was ghettoization, or confinement to "ethnic neighborhoods." Their contemporary experiences are of benign neglect and statistical invisibility. Injudicious and insensitive racially based federal interventions not only deny Euro-ethnics the resources necessary to correct serious structural imbalance in education, employment, welfare, and social services, but also tolerate discrimination against these persons. These assertions surface particularly in criticisms of affirmative action.[22]

The development of racial-ethnic comparisons proceeded simultaneously with the proliferation of radical political economic and class analyses of racial inequality. These analyses focused on racism and capitalism as the combined cause of racial deprivation and inequality, and suggested the need for tougher civil rights laws and affirmative action programs. By contrast, ethnic analyses drew attention to cultural proclivities and increasing *intraracial* socioeconomic disparities to mount a sustained opposition to affirmative action. Blacks were redefined as an ethnic group, and if America was to remain a culturally plural society, no ethnic group must be shown governmental favors.

Over the last two decades, opposition to affirmative action and welfare programs has become a standard feature of ethnic writings. As civil rights and other radical activists responded in defense, key propositions were developed:

1. Nonwhites are not the only victims of racism.
2. African-American cultural deficiencies may be the root cause of black deprivation.
3. Judgments based on overall comparisons between whites and blacks were inconclusive, because generational rates of social

mobility, period of entrance into the city, and educational-indus-
trial endowments ensure differences in levels of socioeconomic
achievement.

4. There is no standard white success rate. Rates of socioeconomic
mobility varied among successive waves of white immigrants to
the city. The already urbanized Jews, Italians, and Greeks fared
much better than their rural counterparts.

5. The ascent of the rural-origin African Americans is comparable
to that of the rural-origin Euro-ethnics. They are both "newcomers" to the urban environment. African-American progress should,
therefore, be compared not to white social mobility generally but
to the immigrant experiences of various ethnic groups *within* the
white population.

6. African Americans have resided in North America since the
seventeenth century. However, they are rural-origin newcomers
to the city. The presence of a growing African-American middle
class suggests that their rate of socioeconomic advancement is
much quicker than that of some earlier white immigrants.

7. Those African Americans who are still in trapped in poverty need
only to reorganize their value system in order to experience a
takeoff into sustained social mobility.

8. Ultimately, slowly, and sometimes painfully, U.S. society will
absorb all its different racial and ethnic groups into the mainstream.

The ethnic-immigrant analysis challenges the proposition that, by
the twentieth century, African Americans should have achieved more
than white immigrants because of their longer stay in America. While
African Americans are among America's oldest immigrants, *they are
some of its youngest urban immigrants*. Their isolation in the rural
South had made them incomplete U.S citizens prior to their migration
to the cities. This justified both the designation "newcomers" and the
comparison with later ethnic immigrants. If the special circumstances
of black urban migration are taken into account, the immigrant-assimilation model is eminently applicable to African Americans. These
circumstances are: their level of industrial skills and education, their
mode of entry into the labor market (as "strikebreakers" or unionized

labor), the state of the economy, the level of white trade union organization, the housing situation in the given city, and most important, internal variations in rates of social mobility. The fundamental flaw within the radical political economic analysis of inequality lies in its assumption that all blacks remained in ghettoes, generation after generation. Some black families had moved on and up, while others remained, trapped by a variety of individual and social structural circumstances. But this is a normal phenomenon in a capitalist society.

Core features of this ethnic-immigrant comparison are, first, the perception of ubiquitous but varied structural constraints on all immigrant achievements; second, the identification of different rates of success *among* both whites and blacks; third, the suggestion that there are internal, culturally specific sources of group inequality; and fourth, a denial of the necessity, viability, and even the legality of affirmative action egalitarianism. Andrew Greeley summarizes aspects of the white ethnic experience:

> There were no quotas, no affirmative action, no elaborate system of social services, and, heaven knows, no ethnic militancy (although it need not follow that there should not be these things for the more recent immigrants to the big cities of the United States). There was no talk of reparation, no sense of guilt, no feelings of compassion for these immigrants.[23]

These expressions of historical pain are not an exaggeration. Stanley Lieberson catalogues a series of official defamations of Slavs and Mediterranean peoples. These "races" were perceived as biologically and morally inferior to white Americans. Lieberson writes: "These racial notions received official government support through the Immigration Commission formed by Congress in the first decade of the century."[24] It wasn't only Madison Grant who regarded the new European immigrants as a pollutant of "the great American race."

According to the ethnic theory, southern and East European immigrants had been confronted with similar structural obstacles to their social mobility. They elevated themselves by tugging at their own bootstraps. It was nothing short of an "ethnic miracle." Blacks could do likewise, and some did. However, the counterclaim is that if this miracle is to be taken as evidence of internal cultural fortitude, it must be demonstrated that white ethnics did not profit from discrimination against blacks — from anti-Negro laws, political disfranchisement, and occupational and residential segregation. As claimed in some liberationist writings, every act of racial exclusion increased the pool of resources available to all those defined as white. Therefore, the notion that there were no quotas for whites needs to be reexamined. Policies of exclusion against blacks created an informal quota system for all whites. White ethnics, then, did not confront an identical social ecology and do not bear comparable legacies from past victimization.

Sociologist Nathan Glazer's remarks suggest that the African Americans' survival is also a miracle:

> If one takes the national view, the view that includes Negro enslavement, the legally inferior position of Negroes set forth in the Constitution and in state and local law for centuries, the disfranchisement of Negroes after the Civil War, and the heroic and not yet completed struggle to achieve full legal equality in the South, then it is indeed enraging to be answered with the ethnic comparison.[25]

This rage is expressed in fundamentalist claims that the South's edicts of exclusion compare to the workings of a caste system, or an apartheid state, and that whiteness has always been ruthlessly prioritized in American society.[26] African Americans, then, are not like other immigrants; they have been subjected to a level of destruction from white people that is unequalled in the annals of human history.

In radical/Marxist and fundamentalist analyses, comparisons between African-American and ethnic experiences are considered to be ahistorical, because they ignore the racist dynamics of American history. Throughout African Americans' stay in America, racist pressures have been applied to them in the form of a systematic exclusion from economic and educational resources as well as political representation. African-American males are especially economically excluded and destroyed in America's streets by a combination of miseducation, poverty, and law enforcement. They are then accused of genetic and cultural failings, despite outstanding individual successes when racist repression is relaxed or eliminated as a result of protest and struggles.

How much does past discrimination account for the so-called overrepresentation of African Americans in poverty? No plausible answer can be constructed. The underlying methodological difficulty concerns the measuring of past socioeconomic processes and human responses. No adequate theoretical instruments can be developed to capture past evaluations of political economic deprivation and physical destruction of a population. Thus, the analysis of the experiences of the descendants of slaves and new European immigrants must be speculative regarding which group *felt* the hardships more, even if it is agreed that legacies of enslavement and jim crowism generated radically different starting points for African Americans and ethnics.

The analytical difficulties in the comparison of racial and ethnic group experiences are formidable. What, after all, is an ethnic group? Certainly some Irish immigrants were more successful than others. Rates of social mobility also varied among Sephardic, Ashkenazic, German, and East European Jews. To which group and subgroups among the WETs are African Americans being compared? What is culturally specific to so-called white ethnics, apart from an imputed absence of WASP advantages? Some anthropologists have as vigorously challenged the reference to culture as the core of ethnicity. As Frederik Barth writes:

> It is important to recognize that although ethnic categories take cultural difference into account, we can assume no simple one-to-one relationship between ethnic units and cultural similarities and differences. The features that are taken into account are not the sum of "objective" differences but only those which the actors themselves regard as significant.[27]

In other words, objectively identified cultural differences do not in themselves constitute a separate ethnicity. Indeed, the culture concept is diversified enough to raise questions about the viability of an equation of culture and ethnicity.[28] A cultural group is not necessarily an ethnic group. Cultural peculiarities do not imply distinct ethnicities. In any case, whether there are cultures, or only *one* culture, depends on how inclusively culture is defined.

The significance of these conceptual issues may be expressed in the following questions: Should social relations be studied through references to biological attributes (race) or cultural elements such as values, beliefs, identities, and ethnicity? Should these categories be defined subjectively or objectively? Are conceptualizations of biologically and culturally defined groups identical, supplementary, or mutually exclusive? If they are mutually exclusive, how are issues of weighting racial and cultural factors and multiple causation to be resolved? If they are not mutually exclusive, the procedures for their combination must be established. The facts presented in support of the ethnic theory, for example, are irrelevant to a racial analysis. Indeed, insofar as "facts" are part of the descriptions generated by a theory, they cannot serve as proof of the incoherence of another theory.

This issue of coherence is not a mere philosophical aside, for it is involved in the identification of social problems and the direction of public policy solutions. If a particular theory is discredited, so too are its problems and policy recommendations. Recognizing this distinction among theories throws light on the nature of the disagreements over affirmative action. Affirmative action is a solution to *racial* problems; it is specific to a racial theory of social relations in which racism is said to be operative. In an ethnic theory of society, problems are not racial but ethnic, and solutions must address cultural stereotyping and ethnocentrism. Ethnic theorists would proclaim that affirmative action not only leaves the victimization of ethnics unresolved, it also further victimizes them by conceiving of them as privileged whites and denying them access to resources that they need to counter their victimization. In a cruelly practical fashion, affirmative action punishes the victims of nativism, ethnocentrism and antisemitism.

The liberationist variant of the racial theory focuses on the victimization of nonwhites, and especially blacks. Each strand except the meritocratic endorses affirmative action for blacks as a necessary redress for past victimization. By contrast, the ethnic analysis suggests that affirmative action should be applied to Asian Pacific Americans and Euro-ethnics as well, or be condemned as reverse discrimination. In this analysis, it is not white racism as such that plagues society but a general xenophobia and cultural intolerance. The focus on ethnicity, then, involves descriptions of the victimization of non-WASPs and implies different public policies to resolve ethnic problems. Racial and ethnic theories of social relations are mutually irreducible analytical systems. Therefore, the "black experience" cannot be compared to that of ethnic groups such as Jews, Poles, or Italians. Such comparisons cannot but prove what was known in advance, that the experiences are separate and distinct.

RACIAL AND ETHNIC INEQUALITIES: CONSERVATIVE, LIBERAL, RADICAL, AND FUNDAMENTALIST EXCHANGES

Radical political economists, as well as fundamentalist, conservative, and liberal social scientists, express a notable concern with the disadvantaged status of African Americans. Their analyses of racial inequality represent elements of the liberationist variant of the racial theory. Its earlier exponents include: Pan-Africanist, Marxist, cultural nationalist or Afrocentric, and separatist writings. These modalities are embodied in earlier disputes among W.E.B. Du Bois, Booker T. Washington, and Marcus Garvey. Du Bois argued intensely against the conservative accommodationism of Washington and the militant separatism of Garvey. But they shared a vision of an economically liberated Negro race that was proud of its history and culture. These themes are manifest in the radical, liberal, and conservative positions that have recently emerged. Their exponents are divided over issues of the role of racism in the black experience, the extent of black progress, the significance of class distinctions in the black community, the relevance of culture to the analysis of racial-ethnic inequalities, and the place of government interventions in the amelioration of black poverty.

From the late 1970s, the writings of William J. Wilson, Thomas Sowell, Glenn Loury, Walter Williams, and Shelby Steele, among others, emerged as "liberal" and "conservative" challenges to those analyses that identify white racism as the direct or sole cause of black deprivation.[29] The crux of the conservative-liberal rebuttals comprises: a denial of the centrality of racism in the black experience, a rejection of most forms of government intervention, an explanatory focus on individual values, and an affirmation of black progress, said to be discernible in critical class cleavages. Glenn Loury writes:

> This observation of widening differences among Blacks has been fiercely resisted by many in the black community. Numerous tracts have been written "proving" that things have been getting worse for Blacks as a whole, denouncing the "myth of black progress," showing that talk of an emerging black middle class is premature, and insisting that the role of racism as the fundamental cause of the problems of Blacks has not diminished.[30]

Thomas Sowell's writings in particular claim that radical political economic and fundamentalist writings are sterilized of critical cultural and public policy influences on behavior. Since the 1960s, a civil rights elite has monopolized the ears of Congress and the media with shopworn, self-serving solutions that simply mired blacks deeper in despair and deprivation. The suggested alternative analysis would focus on the effects of government intervention, whether intentionally benign or malevolent, comparative ethnic experiences, socioeconomic differentiation in the black population, and the role of internal community values in social mobility.

Bygone Du Bois-Washington disagreements have reemerged as conservative, liberal, and radical scholars dispute the significance of economic and cultural factors in racial experiences, particularly "black poverty." However, what has not been recognized is that the disagreements reflect traditional conflicts in philosophical, sociological, and macroeconomic theories. For example, do empirical data suffice to invalidate another set of data? Should cultural or structural variables be emphasized in the explanation of behavior? These questions are relevant to the claims and counterclaims about black progress. However, in the exchanges among these scholars, certain conceptual issues have been overlooked, such as the implications of racial and ethnic group classification and the related absence of consensual definitions of culture and racial discrimination. Without such a consensus, it cannot be determined when race relations are economically or culturally determined processes. Even if a definition is agreed upon, a second difficulty emerges. If experiences are economically and culturally conditioned, why are they *racial* experiences? The invocation of culture implies that all black-skinned persons are not black. The assertion of profound socioeconomic disparities among persons classified as blacks indicates not "a black experience" but separate experiences that are not necessarily credible as "black" experiences.

"Black community," "black poverty," and "ethnic inequality" are not innocent descriptions, and their implications ought to be addressed. Indeed, the disputes have shown the racial descriptions to be an obstacle to conclusiveness. Consider the question of black unemployment. In so-called conservative writings, the condition of virtual unemployability among black youth is attributed to cultural peculiarities within the black population as well as minimum wage laws that artificially maintain a high price for unskilled labor. It is argued that the pursuit of educational achievement demands sacrifice, the capacity for deferred gratification, self-discipline, commitment to long-term objectives, family cohesiveness, and respect for knowledge. The absence of these attributes results in low educational aspirations among contemporary blacks, however much historical white opposition may have curtailed educational opportunities.

These assertions are bolstered with reference to other ethnic experience. Comparisons of African-American and other ethnic lifestyles suggest a cultural endowment of perseverance and self-discipline that results in superior Jewish and Asian-American educational achievements. It is argued that these traits had surmounted a similar history of WASP opposition. Jewish and Asian Americans possess a particular respect for knowledge and stable family structures that translate into educational and, ultimately, socioeconomic progress. Examination of ethnic, especially Asian-American, social mobility demonstrates that it is indigenous cultural factors rather than exogenous structural constraints that are responsible for differences in socioeconomic achievements.

The conservative label on these arguments should not prevent attention from being drawn to a particular effect of the focus on internal values and traits. It implicitly repudiates (1) the usefulness of racial classification in social studies, (2) the naturalist variant that emphasizes biological deficiencies, and (3) the emphasis on racism favored by the radical/Marxist and fundamentalist wings of the liberationist variant. Racial classification has been made redundant by increasing intra-ethnic socioeconomic inequalities which indicate that American society reflects more than a bipolar racial stratification. Indeed, profound social and economic polarities permeate all racial and ethnic communities. Thus, neither genetic racial deficiencies nor white racism can be related causally to racial inequality. A new direction of studies of international comparisons of ethnic experiences must be initiated. The so-called black conservative scholarship, then, like the liberal, is suggesting a break with race and a refocus on culture in order to explain the experiences of racial minorities. Its generally pejorative characterization testifies to the popularity of the more militant wings of the liberationist variant.

What explains the apparent stagnation of over one-third of the so-called black population in poverty? Why are Asian Americans more socioeconomically mobile than Africans? Are cultural or structural conditions responsible for seemingly chronic patterns of racial-ethnic inequalities? It is a tribute to the politically fertile role "blacks" play in social studies that their life situation and behaviors are compared to Hispanics and Asian Americans to discover whether internal or external, racial or cultural, factors account for different rates of success among these groups. Stanley Lieberson raises the questions:

> If blacks did have greater obstacles, to what degree were these due to race? Second, if race did play an important role, how does one reconcile this interpretation with the fact that such other non-white groups as the Chinese and Japanese have done so well in the United States (to be sure only after a rocky start)?[31]

Sociologists generally discuss these aspects of the black experience with reference to either structural or cultural factors. The culture-structure dichotomy, however, is relevant to not only the black experience, but also to the experiences of white ethnics and of both Central American and Asian-Pacific immigrants.

Conservative, liberal, radical political economic, and fundamentalist writings manifest two competitive explanatory frameworks. The first identifies society's institutional patterns, historical

Figure 3.1
RACIAL / ETHNIC INEQUALITIES

Structural Factors	Cultural Factors
Class Structure	Socio-Personal Values
Historical Opportunity Structure	Attitudes toward Education
Attitudinal Racism	Family Relationships
Institutional Racism	Psychological Inclinations
Urban Economics	
Public Policies	

group control over resources, and the distribution of power as the determinant of persistent racial inequalities. The second locates the source of inequality in the motivational, organizational, and cultural attributes of the less-achieving population. However, the writings of individual authors do not fit neatly within a structure-culture dichotomy. Rather, their analyses move randomly across a landscape of explanatory variables. For example, Thomas Sowell's writings on racial and ethnic deprivation include *causal* references to government affirmative action and welfare programs, racism, African-American culture and family organization, civil rights agitation, and trade union monopoly.

Figure 3.1 depicts some of the commonly cited structural and cultural factors.

A conception of culture as tangible and intangible objects facilitates the identification of the culture possessed by a race. Only within such a conception are white and black cultures and ethnic groups constructed. While Boas used this conception of culture to demonstrate the relative equality of all cultures and races, some modern conservative writings suggest that black cultural deficiencies could explain the entrapment in poverty. This "cultural deficiency model" stresses disruptive black attitudes to family, education, work, and consumption.

Black males especially are said to hold certain values of thriftlessness, instant gratification, and promiscuity that militate against socioeconomic mobility. These values are often described as cultural legacies from the slave past. In effect, an enemy within may be far more destructive of black progress than racism.

References to black cultural deficiencies are reminiscent of "a family deficit model" that was advanced in Congressman Daniel P. Moynihan's *Negro Family: The Case for National Action*, in 1965. Moynihan suggested that the matriarchal black family disfigured the black male's attitudes to work and authority: "At the heart of the deterioration of the fabric of Negro society is the deterioration of the Negro family."[32] So-called conservative and liberal scholars draw on certain themes from Moynihan as well as the ethnic-immigrant analogy. In this analogy, it is claimed that white ethnics managed to make significant gains, despite experiencing nativist discrimination. From the mid-1970s ethnic theorists also opposed affirmative action for racial minorities and developed cultural deficiency models to explain racial disadvantages. Indeed, the notion of racially motivated discrimination as an explanation was rejected. Blacks, as such, were not victims of white racism. Rather, some blacks were trapped in inner city poverty because of certain cultural legacies and attitudes and government connivance in the construction of a system of welfare dependency. Moreover, it was claimed that the postwar black rate of progress is faster than that experienced by non-WASP immigrants in the nineteenth century. As regards "the black underclass," its members can surely be like those early white ethnic immigrants who pulled themselves up from their own bootstraps. These arguments implicitly repudiate any emphasis on racism as a critical determinant of racial-ethnic inequality.

In *The Economics and Politics of Race*, Thomas Sowell echoes earlier-expressed observations on the liberating force of culture when he writes: "Groups that arrive in America financially destitute have rapidly risen to affluence, when their cultures stressed the values and behavior required in an industrial and commercial economy."[33] This statement highlights a critical difference between "liberal" and "con-

servative" analyses of race relations. William J. Wilson, a self-con-
fessed liberal, discounts the role of culture, suggesting:

> In short, cultural values do not determine behavior or success. Rather,
> cultural values grow out of specific circumstances and life changes and
> reflect one's position in the class structure. Thus, if lower class blacks
> have low aspirations or do not plan for the future, it is not ultimately the
> result of a different cultural norm but because they are responding to
> restricted opportunities, a bleak future and feelings of resignation origi-
> nating in bitter personal experiences.[34]

While critical of any reformulation of Oscar Lewis' "culture of poverty," Wilson does not entirely rule out the influence of values, but
advises that sociologists consider both cultural and structural elements
in explaining social behavior. In concrete research contexts, Wilson
gives primacy to structural conditions, especially job opportunities
whose absence is said to be the most potent source of the black
underclass.

In *The Truly Disadvantaged*, a work published nine years after
The Declining Significance of Race, Wilson takes up the issue of the
role of racism in ghetto underclass formation. He more emphatically
repudiates any use of racism to explain the contemporary urban crises.
The Truly Disadvantaged contains an examination of the life situation
of the ghetto underclass in the context of major urban-economic
displacements.

The underclass comprises people whose lives are replete with
cycles of illiteracy, abnormally high unemployment, poverty, crime,
illegitimacy, single parentage, welfare dependency, and drug addic-
tion. These people have not only not benefited from antipoverty and
affirmative action programs, but they are also victimized by techno-
structural changes in the U.S. economy. They constitute not so much
an urban segment of "the other America" as an increasingly alienated
other world. The underclass inhabits every major American city and
enclaves dot rural communities. Its condition suggests pathological
structural arrangements. The amelioration of the condition of this
group must now occupy the efforts of public policy makers, and their
problems cannot be just addressed racially. Despite the overrepresenta-

tion of blacks in the underclass, Wilson argues that their conditions are not to be explained only in terms of racism, institutional racism, or even an economic structure of racism. Indeed, racism's explanatory value is marginal. He writes:

> In other words, complex problems in the American and worldwide economy that ostensibly have little or nothing to do with race, problems that fall heavily on much of the black population but require solutions that confront the broader issues of economic organization, are not made more understandable by associating them directly or indirectly with racism. Indeed, because this term has been used so indiscriminately, has so many different definitions, and is often relied on to cover up lack of information or knowledge of complex issues, it frequently weakens rather than enhances arguments concerning race.[35]

Wilson admits that American history has, indeed, bequeathed a racial division of labor and that a racist ideology is active in the society. But coupled with this, technological transformations, cyclical regressions, and changing geographic configurations within the economy are also adversely impacting the black working class and the lowest segments of the population.

The displacement of some, especially young black workers from declining industries and their relegation to the ranks of the unemployed, the unemployable, and the underworld are compounded effects of "ghetto-specific cultural characteristics," industrialism, and urbanism. But the cultural characteristics of the underclass cannot be given any singular explanatory value. Wilson writes: "to emphasize the concept social isolation does not mean that cultural traits are irrelevant in understanding behavior in highly concentrated poverty areas; rather it highlights the fact that culture is a response to social structural constraints and opportunities."[36] Culture does not float around as an isolated incentive to action. Rather, it is an organic reflection of socioeconomic conditions. Hence, it cannot explain these conditions. The ghetto underclass needs macroeconomic policy solutions, not programs of cultural regeneration.

What the liberal analysis shares with that of Loury, Williams, and Sowell is the thesis that the black population is undergoing profound processes of socioeconomic polarization, differentiation and distress, and a deemphasis on racism. The substantial variations in life situations, life-styles, and behavior patterns among African Americans constitute evidence that the issue is not interracial inequality. Therefore, studies of race-specific social conditions are flawed, and race-specific solutions such as affirmative action will not alleviate the situation of those most in need. Wilson concludes that research should focus on the ghetto underclass that has not benefited from affirmative action programs and continues to languish in the depressed urban economy. Because this ghetto underclass is not black, remedies should present a universal agenda.

Descriptions of the pathologies of the inner city have been appearing in urban sociological writings for over half a century. As sociologist John Rex notes:

> Gunnar Myrdal had suggested that the position of the American urban poor and, particularly, the black American poor was that of an "underclass" who were continually unemployed and increasingly unemployable, who lived in a culture of poverty and a tangle of generationally transmitted pathologies.[37]

The "ghetto underclass" is not a recent phenomenon. Like "the poor," it is merely periodically rediscovered and reinterpreted in studies of social problems. The core question asked is: Who, or what, is responsible for this socioeconomic holocaust in the inner city? Conservative writings identify a ghetto culture cum liberal government interventions as the responsible factors. Liberal analysts stress structural elements, such as macroeconomic policies, unequal opportunities, and institutionalized discrimination. In radical political economic analyses, these problems are laid at the door of laissez-faire capitalism; educational organization; particular economic policies; processes in the world economy; and racism, which is heavily emphasized in fundamentalist writings.

Most sociologists would agree that victimization is a pervasive feature of U.S. society. What is not so easily agreed upon however, is that the conceptualization of victimization is influenced by specific social theories. Nevertheless it should be clear that in the ethnic theory, for example, ethnic, not racial, groups are said to have been victimized by other ethnic groups. The Marxian class theory of social relations presents workers as the principal victims of the ruling class. In a human-centered theory, human beings are presented as the victims of logically deficient government and corporate policies; they are self-made victims of an irrationally organized social formation. Sociologist Herbert Gans suggests then that social scientists terminate their excessive studies of the poor:

> Equally important, I wish that social scientists would decrease their study of the victims of poverty and devote more research to its causes — the economic, political, and other processes by which America has developed by far the highest rate of poverty in the "first world" of highly developed nations.[38]

Insofar as Gans' remarks were addressed to the research on poverty done at the University of Chicago by sociologist William J. Wilson, they are not accurate.

Wilson suggests that the disproportionate number of blacks in the lower echelons of the socioeconomic order is attributable to a historic racial division of labor, patterns of industrial urban development, processes of deindustrialization, public policies, group-specific cultural endowments, and social isolation. He also opposes race-specific solutions to poverty. But the data on racial disproportion in the underclass must be regarded as a product of a race-specific research. Although racial identifiers — skin color, hair type, and nose shape — appear to be merely neutral means of classification, their selection to identify a race implies some form of racial causation in the explanation of behavior. Members of "the underclass" could be categorized according to educational and vocational criteria. They would then appear as Triple U's — the unskilled, uneducated, and unqualified — and the cause of their unemployment would be identified in inadequate educational and vocational policies. Wilson's liberal analysis advances a pejorative classification, the underclass, and addresses black overrepresentation in this class but denies the significance of race and rejects race-specific solutions. Radical/Marxist and fundamentalist responses were suitably outraged.

In the radical/Marxist and fundamentalist literature, the relation-ship between values and social structure is interactive.[39] Black culture shapes and is shaped by structural conditions; it cannot be an obstacle to black progress. Without a positive black culture, black Americans would not have survived in racist white America. Black culture con-stitutes a rich and powerful tradition that expresses some of the finest elements of the human spirit. If it is deformed, it is because of the racist currents in American society and age-old patterns of educational and economic deprivation. However, the disfigurement of black culture — if indeed, that has occurred — is laid at the door of "a conspiracy to destroy black males." The destruction of the black family is regarded as a consequence of chronic racial discrimination. It is noted that, significantly, black male unemployment is well above that of black females. Stable employment and stable fatherhood are closely related. How can black males be good fathers, if the white males who control the economic system are so Negrophobic that they go to vast lengths to abort the presence of black males on the upper rungs of the corporate ladder, and so immune to black suffering that they tolerate a 40 to 50 percent level of black youth unemployment?

Radical/Marxist and fundamentalist responses are equally caustic in their rejection of any blaming of the structure of the black family. Inadequate parenting is a result of limited opportunities for gainful employment in certain sections of the black community. Insofar as good parenting and a cohesive family structure are missing from the lives of black youth, their educational and economic achievements become part of cycles of stagnation and regress. Blacks are being doubly victimized. Twin tragedies of educational and economic depri-vation constitute the defining feature of a large portion of the black community. Black culture and family organization are then labelled deficient, traced to slave legacies, and considered responsible for their economic deprivation. Thus, practical racist victimization is com-pounded with intellectual assaults on black culture, history, and social organization.

Radical political economic writings concentrate on racism *and* the economic structure in their explanations of the persistence of poverty among blacks. Capitalism and racial inequality go hand in hand. It is pointed out that despite a quarter century of overall socioeconomic progress, 30.9 percent of black families are living in poverty. About half of the black population live slightly above or on the poverty line, and the median black family income is about two-thirds of the median white income. The tenacity of this inequality is inexplicable, except with reference to external forces, namely, capitalism and institutional racism. Any reference to black culture and family structure as causally effective in the formation of racial inequality represents a case of "blaming the victim." A hostile white environment combined with laissez-faire economic policies irrepressibly limit black achievements.

According to the radical analysis, African-American and Asian-American achievements represent a case of chalk and cheese. So radically different are their size, distribution, mode of entry, physical appearance, and orientations that Asian Americans do not represent an adequate comparison for African Americans. First, Asian Americans may possess a "sojournering personality" that features distinct entrepreneurial and overachieving drives. Second, white responses to African Americans and Asian Americans are historically dissimilar. Third, being barely 3 percent of the population, Asian Americans do not so visibly compete with whites over economic resources. They are also anatomically closer to whites. Hence, they confront a less intense white xenophobia and defamation of their racial and cultural attributes. This latter point implies that Asian Americans may also have a critical social psychological advantage. Because they are not subjected to a constant defamation of their racial attributes, they possess greater racial pride and self-esteem. No other racial minority is subjected to such a systematic level of racial smears as blacks.

In *The Content of Our Character*, Shelby Steele criticizes these radical and fundamentalist arguments. Steele claims that blacks' self-image (as victims of white racism) aborts the feeling of being in control of their own destiny. It may even escalate into a racial paranoia that prevents blacks from believing in themselves and depletes their will to compete, overcome odds, and succeed. Thus, it is the radical emphasis on white racism's omnipresence and omnipotence that is ultimately most destructive of African American self-esteem and motivation. Glenn Loury, a professor in the John F. Kennedy School of Government at Harvard University, also takes issue with the radical and fundamentalist emphasis on white racism. He suggests that the identification of white racism should not lead to blacks abandoning their responsibility for their own destiny and becoming wards of government affirmative action and welfare programs.

The characterization of Steele, Loury, and other critics of the militant liberationist perspectives as conservatives who are hostile to the black community needs to be reexamined. Their propositions are neither antiblack nor divisive, unless any criticism of radical and fundamentalist writings is to be regarded as politically incorrect. Indeed, elements of the conservative analysis implicitly efface the distinction between culture and structure and may even be empowering. This is so because they assert that cultural deficiencies are engendered by the belief that one is not the architect of one's fate. This conviction is self-fulfilling. Black demotivation, disempowerment, and underachievement are fostered by explanations which emphasize that the society is controlled by racist whites who hate blacks. By identifying the counterproductive effects of this belief one is not blaming the victim. Rather, this identification could halt further self-victimization. Such propositions tread a political precipice, however. Because they are not accompanied by a ritual condemnation of white racism, they are interpreted as "dangerous to the black cause." Nevertheless, "conservatives" may further claim that it is necessary, possible, and perhaps even mandatory to instill a sense of self-responsibility in "the black underclass," without denying the force of either white racism or the juggernauts of technology, industrialism, and "global drift." The real conservatives are those whose analyses disempower blacks by perpetually offering them definitions of themselves as victims. This is but a short step to self-pity, loss of hope, and a plunge into despair and self-destructive activities. At one level the comparing of African Americans and Asian Americans is valid. Asian American activists are not on the "white man's media" pumping and priming Asian-American youth with notions of being hated by the white majority and potentially crippled by racist forces that are beyond their control. The secret of their comparative overachievement is what is not being done to Asian-American minds by the politics of antiracism.

Some of Thomas Sowell's remarks may also be regarded as an attempt to restore the sense of responsibility and power that radical analyses deny blacks. He writes:

> The history of black Americans has been a history of a rise from a position lower than that of any other minority in America. That rise was so painfully slow as to be almost imperceptible at various times, but over the decades the socioeconomic rise of black Americans has been consistent and has finally accelerated to a level approaching that of others with far more initial advantages.[40]

By implication, blacks are neither nonachievers nor underachievers. If time scales and trends in social mobility are analyzed, it would be discovered that blacks are by no means permanent pariahs of U.S. society. Hence, there is no peculiar or significant pattern of black economic underdevelopment or underachievement. The ghetto underclass contains shifting elements of all races. *Some* blacks are failing to enter the mainstream rapidly, just as some nineteenth-century white immigrants languished in poverty for generations. Even so, not all blacks, just as not all whites, should be expected to become rich or attain middle class status. All the trees in a forest do not grow equally tall. The termination of government intervention, which was initiated ostensibly to help blacks, is the first step toward an overall structural rehabilitation. It is this intervention, itself a function of periodic electoral considerations, that stymies the efforts of African Americans to change their socieconomic conditions.

All liberationist writings may be deemed "conservative" of racial and ethnic relations. But what would be the significance of this designation? Conservatism is by no means equatable with "reactionary." Sowell, Loury, Williams, Steele, and others have been labeled black conservatives. However, this designation serves no useful purpose. The elusiveness of "whiteness" and "blackness" is legendary, and if "conservatism" means satisfaction with the status quo, it does not fit these authors. The larger and related question is: Can studies of racial and ethnic experiences move beyond the political and moral denunciation evinced in accusations against civil rights moralists, liberals, and "the light-skinned elite"?[41] References to authors as white liberal, black conservative, black liberal, and black Marxist represent exercises in political evaluation and analytical obfuscation; they should have no place in intellectual exchanges.

COMMONALTIES, CONVERGENCE AND CONTRADICTIONS

The divisions among meritocratic, liberal, and radical/Marxist analysts of race relations reflect, inter alia, the unfolding of three particular social theories — racial, ethnic, and class — and attempts at combinations. Fundamentalist and radical Marxist writings construct descriptions of the stifling effects of racism and capitalism on black underachievements. Meritocratic and liberal writings seek to integrate racial, ethnic, and Weberian class theories in their references to cultural traits and income (read class) differences among blacks. They continue a Frazierian tradition of focusing on economic and cultural differentiation within the so-called African-American population. Their claim is that this community, like other ethnic communities, is characterized by multidimensional patterns of differentiation. Hence, its members share color more than class and culture. However, its socioeconomic heterogeneity remains comparatively underinvestigated because social studies retain racial classification.

There are some areas of agreement that derive from a collective allegiance to racial classification. First, racism's explanatory value is not totally rejected, only marginalized, in meritocratic and liberal analyses. Second, given the causal references to both structure and culture, these writings covertly efface the culture-structure dichotomy. For example, if it was the enslavement of Africans that generated peculiar white attitudes and values, then structural conditions could themselves produce a deformed white culture that, in turn, underdevelops the black economy. All liberationist writings concede that centuries of slavery, jim crowism, segregation, and media derogation of the African-American image must have some negative social psychological effects on African Americans and, subsequently, on their values and behavior. What some would insist, however, is that the individual must take responsibility for the retention of values that lead to deprivation and destruction. Culture and structure are interactive.

A third area of analysis that indicates a glimmer of convergence among the various liberationist perspectives is the need for educational reform. In the pursuit of the means of life, education is a preeminent facilitator of success. In consequence, educational opportunities and attitudes toward education enjoy some prominence in explanations of both initial and current ethnic disadvantages and inequality. All liberationist writings stress that "black education" is a tragedy and a travesty. Prescribed remedies range from schools of choice to greater black parental involvement in schooling, black self-help in educational reform, and multiculturalism. Attitudinal changes are also recommended, on the grounds that Jewish and Asian-American successes are undergirded by a strong commitment to education. This claim has been disputed on two counts. First, critics contend that the comparison with Asian-American attitudes to education is flawed, unless Asian immigrants can be shown to have experienced the centuries of school segregation and racially justified inferior education. Second, educational success is more often than not a function of having achieved middle-class status.

In fundamentalist and radical/Marxist analyses, a history of unequal racial educational opportunities is said to be the major source of black underachievement and a reflection of the durability of white opposition to racial equality. Blacks, by law and customary policies, have been systematically denied access to educational institutions. "Compulsory ignorance laws" and segregated and unequally endowed schools resonate throughout the history of black education. As historians Mary Frances Berry and John W. Blassingame note:

> Beginning in the colonial period, whites insisted on the compulsory ignorance of blacks to insure the continuation of slavery and caste distinctions. South Carolina early instituted the pattern of deprivation when it enacted a law in 1740. "That all and every person and persons whatsoever who shall hereafter teach, or cause any slave or slaves to be taught to write, or shall use or employ any slave as a scribe in any manner of writing whatsoever, hereafter taught to write; every such person or persons shall, for every offense, forfeit the sum of one hundred pounds current money."[42]

Southern planters and legislators connived to maintain those defined as blacks as a laboring class. When the need for black education was grudgingly conceded, it was not to be education but limited training.

In keeping with its stress on the operation of white racism in virtually every aspect of American life, the fundamentalist and radical/Marxist perspectives point to centuries of educational neglect and the lack of commensurate rewards for educated blacks as negative influences on the level of learning and the motivation to learn among blacks. White America is said to be still not reformed. In 1966 the famous report by James S. Coleman and his associates unearthed chronic educational deprivation among blacks.[43] A quarter of a century later, studies indicate that blacks still receive fewer years of formal schooling and a lower quality education than whites. Despite the *Brown* v. *the Board of Education* decision in 1954, in the 1990s the separation of black and white students is said to be still rampant in the nation's public schools.[44] Fundamentalist and radical/Marxist writings point to a plethora of local, state, and federal policies that continue to deny blacks access to quality education. The overall result is that approximately 50 percent of young black urban residents remain Triple U's. This makes them virtually unemployable in an economy undergoing rapid structural changes. The liberal perspectives takes these conditions as an indictment of not capitalism and racism but social policies in a deindustrializing economy beleaguered by globally engendered dislocations.

Unemployment, unemployability, and induction into the underworld necessarily follow from the Triple U status. Therefore, overall educational and industrial policies should be examined. No amount of punitive and/or welfare measures will eradicate the underclass. However, what the liberal analysis should add is that no educational and training programs will make a dent in the life circumstances of the so-called underclass if "full employment" continues to be a moving mirage and unemployment itself a means of combatting inflation. As sociologist Robert Green notes:

> The government has always accepted a certain jobless rate as constituting "full employment" in statistical terms. In the 1940's, the government

accepted a 2 percent jobless rate as full employment. In the 1950's, that became 3 percent; then it became 4 percent in the early 1960's, where it remained fairly static until the 1970's. In the mid-1970's, an apparent consensus among economists was that full employment actually meant a jobless rate of 5 to 6 percent.[45]

By the early 1990s, the official rate of unemployment is 7 to 8 percent, while black unemployment is twice the national average and urban, black youth unemployment reaches some 50 to 60 percent. These racial descriptions do not generate an outpouring of full employment policies. So complex and globally unmanageable are the causes of different types of unemployment that remedies can address only its symptoms — homelessness, hunger, school dropout, and entrance into the underworld economy. It follows that the unemployed should not be approached as blacks and whites. Such an approach merely perpetuates the implication of racial causation. As Wilson insists, remedial policies must be based on a "hidden agenda" of universalism. There is neither intellectual virtue nor political capital in racial descriptions of urban problems. Such descriptions are almost a guarantee of policies that will maintain the status quo.

As mentioned, the significance of four specific phenomena governs the intellectual exchanges within meritocratic, liberal, radical/Marxist, and fundamentalist perspectives: racism, culture, internal black socioeconomic stratification, and government intervention for the eradication of racial and ethnic inequalities. From the analysis of these variables certain conclusions may be drawn:

1. There is enough critical material to support the claim that the Asian-American success story is based on superficial analyses of economic indices. Persons classified as Asian Americans have not "made it" and cannot be held up as a model minority. The increase in income accruing to some Chinese, Korean, and Japanese Americans should be considered in conjunction with the descriptions of chronic problems of employment, welfare, and health care problems facing the new Asian immigrants.

2. Government responses are a critical factor in determining the fate of racial minorities. Economist Walter Williams states that much

of black history is a story of the government's reinforcement of the denial of blacks their constitutional rights as individuals.[46] Government interventions are not aimed at resolving racial problems. Indeed, the problems are not yet demonstrated to be racial.

3. Comparisons among African-American and ethnic American economic achievements do not provide a viable basis for generalizations on the role of culture in racial behaviors. Alleged Jewish and Asian-American respect for the value of education has been interpreted as a function, not a cause, of their social mobility.[47]

4. In admitting to internal racial socioeconomic heterogeneity, radical, meritocratic, and liberal scholars ambush their studies of the black experience. What is the socioeconomic referent of blacks or African Americans, if they are not identifiable as a socioeconomic aggregate? These terms have no theoretical content, except as an ambiguous denotation of skin color, hair type, and facial form. Racial and ethnic studies have not moved an inch away from eighteenth- and nineteenth-century measurements of the body.

5. Comparisons of racial minorities and development of cultural and economic configurations are interminable by virtue of the analytical emptiness of racial classification.

Persons classified as blacks are being placed in a Catch-22 situation. If they enter the corporate structure, they can be accused of selling out or acting white, or they are reminded of the presence of "corporate racism."[48] If they pursue government employment, they are deemed unsuccessful, because these occupations do not provide superior monetary rewards. If they enter the business world as entrepreneurs, they are held up as proof that all is well with blacks but often also denigrated as "a black bourgeoisie." What is not generally perceived is that since there are no blacks or whites as homogeneous socioeconomic groups, "black achievements" comprise a multitude of achievements that do not set well with the racial description.

Any observation about blacks can be met with the objection that these blacks are of a specific class, status group, region, age, or educational level. In other words, they are not representative of "blacks." But, then, if they are a class, or an underclass, why identify them through blackness? Wilson's analysis pays the price for attempting to divide blacks into classes in order to demonstrate the operation of structural factors in black poverty. Sociologist Charles V. Willie comments:

> Wilson's analysis, which emphasizes historical structural barriers as impediments to human fulfillment, eliminates psychological discomfort and denies social discrimination as a real problem. Wilson's analysis of poor blacks ignores some of their fundamental human experiences such as discomfort and discrimination. . . .[49]

Willie's comments can, in turn, be criticized for their moralistic emphasis and for ignoring the structural conditions that necessarily impinge on individuals in society. But the writings of both Wilson and Willie could be placed within a racial tradition that identifies persons according to their skin color, hair type, and facial form. What neither scholar recognizes is that racial referents are the single greatest contributory factor not only to their endless disputes but also to the continuation of the holocaust in urban and rural ghettoes.

Blacks and whites are not viable analytical categories. Indeed, any remark about the black experience may be considered controversial, or objectionable. For example: "Blacks have their own culture." One response could be: "It is racist to suggest that blacks, despite almost four centuries of residency, are not fully Americanized." If the contrary is voiced — "blacks do not have their own culture" — the reaction could be: "To deny the uniqueness of the black experience is racist." Studies of racial and ethnic relations are replete with accusations and counteraccusations of ignoring some facet of racial experiences, some empirical data, some subjective element, or some political imperative, and the development of more empirical studies of racial situations, without offering a logical justification of "racial." This is the state of the debate in meritocratic, liberal, radical, and antiracist writings. Each camp maintains "the black experience" as an object of study, without recognizing that the object of study itself is a phantom. Thus, proponents and opponents have to be politically classified and vilified. In the mist of mutual recriminations, it is rarely recognized that the suffering in the inner city is prolonged by these squabbles. Both policymakers and the public must stand immobilized by the repetition of elements of racial, ethnic, and class analyses that are, in turn, traceable to differences within social scientific traditions.

Disputes among meritocratic, liberal, radical/Marxist, and fundamentalist writings can also be traced to unresolved issues in the philosophy of social sciences. These disputes have become controversies — that is, insoluble intellectual differences — by virtue of social scientists' lack of acquaintance with the philosophical parameters that undergird social sciences. In consequence, philosophical categories, such as reality, truth, observation, and experience, are innocently and irresponsibly used. Political and personal evaluations of arguments prevail. The prospect for conclusive intellectual exchanges rests on an awareness of the need to stipulate discursive ground rules and an abandoning of what is almost an American tradition of tolerating fallacies and theoretical blind alleys.

BEYOND RACIAL-CULTURAL REFERENTS

The utilization of the concept of culture has come full circle. It was initially explored by the Boas school to combat racism. The Boas revolution precipitated protracted sociopsychological and political reevaluations of the black experience. A half century later, culture was being reclaimed as a barometer of black behavioral deficiencies. The career of the culture concept is, indeed, checkered, and because it is invoked to maintain racial classification, there is scant reference to its many definitions.

In racial studies, the term culture is rarely explicitly stipulated. Indeed, lack of attention to key concepts is a striking feature of discussions of racial and ethnic relations. Nonetheless, conclusive discussions of racial and ethnic relations must be based on consistent definitions of culture. This ground rule is not meant to split hairs. Conceptual clarity and consistency would provide a clear answer to questions such as: What is the relationship between racial and ethnic classifications? How valid is the reference to culture to explain racial and racial-ethnic relations, and to construct racial-ethnic comparisons given the admission of various subcultures within a given culture? A case can be made that contemporary social sciences have inherited ambiguous and confusing legacies of race and culture. Proponents of the meritocratic, liberal, radical, and fundamentalist perspectives do not consider an implicit possibility that racial classification might itself be a cultural input that affects structural conditions. It is conceivable that explanatory references to race and constant studies of blacks as *a problem* produce a problem personality, a self-doubting self-image. It follows, then, that an effective approach to black socioeconomic rehabilitation would be an abandoning of racial classification. Black liberation demands the negation of blackness. This is, indeed, a paradox of Hegelian proportions.

Racial-ethnic comparisons necessarily retain the collective classifications white, African American, Asian Pacific American, and Hispanic. These classifications may be useful for census enumerators. They fail, however, to do justice to the economic, cultural, and educational differences within each of these populations. However, given the definitional elusiveness of these categories as statistical blocs, each aggregate racial fact has a counterfactual. For example, it has been suggested that black educational achievements are lower because of their comparatively inferior genetic endowments.[50] However, some whites remain remarkably unassimilated into the mainstream. Some perform worse than Asian Americans on IQ tests and Scholastic Aptitude Tests (SATs). If these whites are genetically inferior to other whites, "poor" genes are not racially distributed and references to black genetic endowments fail as an explanation of their patterns of underachievement and overachievement.

Pierre L. Van den Berghe has charged that studies of race relations lack comparative focus.[51] However, particular racial achievements are necessarily studied in relation to others. Studies of race relations are intrinsically comparative. So-called black achievements are, by definition, constructed in relation to white or other achievements. These comparisons pursue but cannot deliver conclusive arguments about the attributes of whites or nonwhites. For example, the comparison between African-American and Asian-American achievements can be said to be odious on the grounds that these immigrants had entirely different starting points and faced different levels of opposition and political climates. This discussion necessarily leads into studies of changing economic conditions, the time scales of continental patterns of migration and adaptation, processes of industrialization, regional socioeconomic variations, educational policies, past public policies, cultural attributes, and group motivation. Each of these factors can be further decomposed and mutually counterposed. Hence, the investigation of racial and ethnic inequalities opens a Pandora's box of discussions of free will and determinism, idealism and materialism, and the use of the past to explain a present that defines the nature of the past. Whatever the outcome, more philosophically sensitive social studies are needed. Their first task would be to examine the logical structure of racial and ethnic classifications.

Constant discoveries of differentiations within racial and ethnic groups question the analytical usefulness of the terms blacks, whites, Asian Americans, Native Americans, non-whites, WASPs, white ethnics, new ethnics, and the black underclass. In other words, theories of race and ethnicity do not provide viable classifications of social relations. Any reference to a black situation can be controverted with the question: Which blacks? Evidence of racism as a formative force in black deprivation can be slighted by drawing attention to the complicity of some Africans in enslavement, or the victim's responsibility for ending his or her victimization. It follows that there can be no end to the disputes over the causes of the differential rates of success between racial and ethnic groups.

These strictures apply especially to the idea of black poverty, which represents a racial description of certain economic conditions. This description obscures the controversy surrounding the concept of poverty itself. Some of its weaknesses are analyzed in economist Charles Murray's *Losing Ground*.

1. As defined by economists in the early 1960s, a value judgment on a minimal, decent existence was the bottom line, which indicated absolute rather than relative poverty.
2. The proportion of a typical family's spending on food ignores variations in atypical families, which are precisely the families that the poverty line seeks to pinpoint.
3. The concept of poverty does not indicate quality of life but, by innuendo, moves from monetary and consumptive quantification

to an evaluation of life situation. Thus, measurement of poverty ignores the nonmonetary payments in households and communities as well as nonmonetary differences in life experiences.

4. The discovery of earnings by government and the Internal Revenue Service is notoriously unreliable.[52]

It may also be argued that poverty cannot be ameliorated or eradicated; it is a concomitant of capitalist commodity production. The poor are simply those whose labor is not highly valued or desired. Their condition represents a denial, through money, of access to the means of life. This denial derives from the mode of production, including the nature of goods produced. In capitalist commodity production, goods are produced through wage labor, and the wages paid to the laborers entitle them to the means of life, which are commodities. The defining feature of commodities is that access to them is dependent on purchasing power. Purchasing power, in turn, depends on the sale of labor power. Those who cannot sell their labor power, either because of violence (captives, prisoners of war, slaves) or feebleness (infants and the aged), are in greatest danger of being denied access to means of consumption; they are labeled "poor."

The notion of the "poor" merely traps social studies within relations of distribution, and the racial description of the poor necessarily runs into analytic difficulties because it hints at both distributive-organizational *and* racial causes. What is the cause of black poverty? Black genes, argues the naturalist. Capitalism and racism, suggests the radical and Marxist political economist. But the question no one asks is: Has poverty been conceptually identified such that it can be racially described?

Even more contentious is the claim that blacks are overrepresented among the poor, that is to say, there is a racial surplus of poverty. Given the general condition of poverty, some persons classified as blacks must be expected to be poor. However, according to official and unofficial quantifications, while approximately 13 to 20 percent of the population is poor, fully 30 percent of the black population experiences this condition. The term black poverty, then, can only refer to a surplus of persons classified as blacks who are in poverty. It is this surplus —

between 10 to 17 percent of the black poor — that is to be explained. The racial description can be omitted.

In radical political economic writings, it is claimed that the racial surplus of poverty is an effect of racism/capitalism. However, the racial nature of the surplus may be said to be only one of many ways of classifying the poor. The surplus could be categorized sexually, generationally, educationally, or regionally. A preponderance of young, uneducated, unskilled, single female parents and rural residents of "poor" Southern states pulls down the so-called black median income, just as surely as the residence of the majority of Asian Americans in Hawaii, New York, and California inflates the Asian-American median income. Any population that has a preponderance of persons in the eighteen-to-twenty-four-year age bracket, resides in low-income regions, and depends predominantly on a collapsing system of public education is bound to have a greater number of persons in the low-income category. The racial classification implies racial causation, but low income is a consequence of a multiplicity of socioeconomic conditions.

"Black poverty" is a metaphor, and a misnomer and, if taken literally, a case of premature racial labeling. What are the common attributes of the black poor, other than their skin color, hair type, and facial form? In any case, some of the black poor are poorer, or less rich, than others. They are stratified by other attributes such as age, regional origin, gender, educational level, and work experience. Because these attributes may be significant in the generation of low income, these persons should not be all lumped together as the "black poor," unless it can be demonstrated that their blackness is somehow responsible for their poverty. This signals a return to either black genes or white racism.

The toleration of the regressive nature of racial studies reflects a divestment of philosophy from social sciences, a disregard for logical rules, and a commitment to empirical means of proof. Philosophically sensitive social research would recognize that racial comparative statistics on consumption and employment/unemployment do not depict a racial reality. Rather, they are the data produced by the racial theory. A racial comparative count of the unemployed that demonstrates an overrepresentation of black workers implies that the disparity has been racially produced. Hence, racial solutions must be advanced. However, because an infinite number of institutional, cultural, systemic, and historical processes may be said to affect human experiences, no racial solution can be considered optimum. The multiplicity of solutions to racial problems, then, is not accidental.

On the other hand, racial solutions are impossible to implement. For example, a racial analysis of the labor market discovers a surplus of black unemployment. Even the most extreme solution to the racial disparity — removing white workers and giving their positions to black workers — must consider the comparative qualifications, skills, and education of white and black workers. Thus, it will not be white workers as such who will be removed but specific categories of workers. If the racial surplus of unemployment comprises unskilled workers, then, ameliorative policies should be directed to the structure of the demand for and supply of labor. An economic analysis of the labor market finds a surplus of unemployment among unskilled, uneducated, and untrained workers. This surplus is explained in terms of wage rates, human capital endowment, and the rigors of capitalist exploitation. The racial features of the unemployed population must be deemed irrelevant. If they are to be considered significant, then, why not other features, such as gender, generational, regional, and cultural attributes?

The omnipresent possibility of discovering other human attributes or social factors explains the competitive explanations of racial unemployment as well as the objections to racial explanations and solutions. Unemployment has a variety of descriptions and causations — structural, frictional, seasonal, and cyclical. A consideration of the literature on unemployment could have avoided its racial classification. With this racial classification come racial solutions that can be neither consistent nor effective.

The problems of the poor and ghetto underclass have been researched ad nauseam. It is not that these social categories are over-researched relative to the attention paid to unreasonableness and moral degeneration in the suburbs and corporations. The writings of Barry Commoner, Ralph Nader, and others give ample testimony to the comparatively astronomical level of "corporate crimes," as well as chronic patterns of (global) ecological and human destruction.[53] Insofar as the level of human destruction in "the internal third world" is related to the political and entrepreneurial leadership in U.S. society, "the underclass" does not reside in the inner city. Researchers could turn their critical attention to the doctrinal allegiances of the suburban underclass. Nor must its values be the ultimate object of analysis. Corporate and legislative decisionmakers are caught up in the web of educational inputs that provide the theories and premises underlying their decisions. If the monumental paradoxes in American society are taken as an index of the reasoning capacities of its leaders, qualitative educational deprivation is not a fixture only of the so-called inner city. The educationally induced incapacity to reason logically permeates corporate boardrooms, legislatures, and alleys.[54]

Formal and informal educational inputs that foster a preoccupation with making money are a second critical but rarely researched factor. If money defines happiness, an end-state of consumption, then making money is pursued by any means necessary. Corporate and political leaders, unemployment and unemployability are but the price others must pay for economic growth and financial security. If so, then, despair grows in the so-called inner city, and it creates underworld explosions whose after-shocks inexorably move into the suburbs. Pity, protests, punishment, and prisons, or sporadic welfare and urban renewal programs are not meant to eradicate conditions of human wastage. Certain fundamental premises about education, economy, and social change will have to be revamped, if rational economic and social policies are to be considered. If the dissolution of the Soviet Union has proven anything, it is that a given social organization will not survive policies based on contradictions.

Consider some of the contrary conclusions in the literature on ethnicity. Culture is too complex a phenomenon for ethnic groups to be defined as culture units. Ethnic groups are internally, culturally, and socioeconomically differentiated. They possess crisscrossing values, beliefs, and situational identities; they compete among themselves over status and material resources, and are at varying levels of generational assimilation and acculturation. Finally, they are not politically cohesive. Thus, political scientist Cynthia Enloe argues that Roman catholics do not constitute an ethnic group and notes that American Indian tribes have disagreed over criteria of membership.[55] Sociologist Harry H. L. Kitano writes that the classification Asian Americans is an "incredible stereotype."[56] As with racial classification, ethnic classification fails to avoid problems of ambiguity and arbitrariness.

The allocation of persons to groups results in individual successes and failures being presented as group phenomena. A person defined as black, Italian, Native American, or Asian "makes it" and is held up as a racial or ethnic symbol. His or her success, however, could have been unrelated to racial genes or group culture. Racial and ethnic classifications simply force group evaluations of all social phenomena. On the other hand, America's legal and moral framework derives from the emphasis on individual-natural rights that formed the philosophical basis of the Enlightenment and the American Revolution. The Revolution, however, was not supplemented by educational policies designed to generate respect for reason and individual rights. Certain groups — for example, women, Indians, and Negroes — were to be kept in their natural places. Educational inputs were designed to serve that purpose. The end result is that neither whites nor nonwhites are educated in a humanistic sense.

Gunnar Myrdal's *American Dilemma* discovers a deeply rooted value conflict in American society.[57] The society is committed to both equal opportunity for *individuals* and *collective* racial judgments. This duality may be rephrased as a commitment to both individualism *and* group classification. However, it represents not a moral conflict but a flawed reasoning that is also expressed in a claim to an exclusive racial or ethnic identity. As psychiatrist George Devereux writes: "in order to have an ethnic identity, one must first be human. Humanness implies a capacity to be unique, for individuation is more characteristic of man than of the amoeba."[58] Identity is "the absolute uniqueness of an individual"; it reflects the human capacity for choosing: "I am unique. No other person is like me. I am not unique; I am a WASP, like other WASPs. I am unique in that I can choose to be a WASP or a non-WASP because I am human." Whatever choice is made, it is due to the primacy of humanness. To claim a racial or ethnic identity as opposed or prior to a human identity is self-contradictory. This claim is itself predicated on being human. An insistence on being white, black, Hispanic, or Jewish *and* human is tautological.

Given education's neglect of philosophy and critical thinking, the contradictions in racial and ethnic studies escape recognition and critical scrutiny. Some scholars advocate market, that is, individualist-meritocratic, solutions to racial and ethnic (group!) problems. Others propose multiculturalism, which will lead to an intensification of racial and ethnic consciousness. All such solutions fail. The image of racial and ethnic inequalities is generated by racial and ethnic consciousness and remedies in the first place. Public policies that address racial and ethnic issues are bound to conserve racial and ethnic problems. Non-recognition of this contradiction suggests that what is lacking is respect for logical and consequential reasoning. In this sense, America's dilemma is not moral but educational. It cannot be resolved until public policies concentrate on what the founding fathers ignored — the quality of education necessary to foster logical reasoning about racial and ethnic classifications.

NOTES

1. Edward Murguia, *Assimilation, Colonialism, and the Mexican American People* (New York: University Press of America, 1989), p. 49.
2. Edward Tylor, *Primitive Culture: Research into the Development of Mythology, Philosophy, Religion, Language, Art,and Custom* (New York: Holt, 1889). See also Bernard Bernardi (ed.), *The Concept and Dynamics of Culture* (The Hague: Mouton Publishers, 1977).
3. Alfred Kroeber and Clyde Kluckhohn, *Culture, A Critical Review of Concepts and Definitions* (Cambridge, MA: Harvard University Peabody Museum of American Archaeology and Ethnology Papers, 1952), p. 86.
4. See George Stocking, "Introduction: The Basic Assumptions of Boasian Anthropology," in George W. Stocking, Jr. (ed.), *The Shaping of American Anthropology, 1883-1911: A Franz Boas Reader* (New York: Basic Books, 1974), pp. 1-20.
5. Reid Luhman and Stuart Gilman, *Race and Ethnic Relations: The Social and Political Experiences of Minority Groups* (Belmont, CA: Wadsworth,

1980), p. 6. A random transition from racial to ethnic relations is illustrated in the writings of: Thomas Sowell, *Race and Economics* (New York: David McKay, 1975), and *Ethnic America: A History* (New York: Basic Books, 1980); John Rex, *Race Relations in Sociological Theory*, 2nd ed. (London: Weidenfeld and Nicholson, 1983), and *Race and Ethnicity* (Milton Keynes: Open University Press, 1986); Michael Banton, *Race Relations* (London: Tavistock, 1967), and *Racial and Ethnic Competition*; Pierre L. van den Berghe, *Race and Racism: A Comparative Perspective* (New York: John Wiley, 1967), and *Race and Ethnicity* (New York: Basic Books, 1970).

6. Henry L. Gates, "Critical Remarks," in David Goldberg (ed.), *Anatomy of Racism* (Minneapolis, MN: University of Minnesota Press, 1990), p. 326.

7. See Robert E. Kuttner (ed.), *Race and Modern Science* (New York: Social Science Press, 1967); Vernon Reynolds, "Biology and Race Relations," *Ethnic and Racial Studies* 9, no. 3 (1986), pp. 373-381.

8. Franz Boas, *Race, Language and Culture* (New York: Macmillan, 1940), p. 259. See also George W. Stocking, Jr. (ed.), *The Shaping of American Anthropology, 1883-1911: A Franz Boas Reader* (New York: Basic Books, 1974), pp. 219-257, 310-330; and *Malinowski, Rivers, Benedict and Others: Essays on Culture and Personality* (Madison, WI: University of Wisconsin Press, 1986); Melville J. Herskovits, *Franz Boas: The Science of Man in the Making* (New York: Charles Scribner's Sons, 1953); Clifford Geertz, *The Interpretation of Cultures* (New York: Basic Books, 1973).

9. As George Stocking writes: "culture and personality became in a sense the functional equivalent of race, explaining the same sort of (presumed) psychological uniformities in very terms, as culture took over the sphere of determinism that had been governed by 'race.'" "Introduction: The Basic Assumptions of Boasian Anthropology," in George W. Stocking, Jr. (ed.), *The Shaping*, p. 5. See also Franz Boas, *The Mind of Primitive Man* (New York: Macmillan, 1938), and *Race, Language and Culture*, pp. 243-304.

10. Alfred L. Kroeber, *The Nature of Culture* (Chicago: University of Chicago Press, 1952), p. 5.

11. Franz Boas, *Race, Language and Culture* (New York: Macmillan, 1940), p. 259.

12. Walter Jackson, "Melville Herskovits and the Search for Afro-American Culture," in Stocking, Jr. (ed.), *Malinowski, Rivers, Benedict and Others*, p. 225.

13. See Alfred Kroeber, *Nature*.

14. See Andrew Greeley, *Why Can't They Be Like Us? Facts and Fallacies About Ethnic Differences and Group Conflicts in America* (New York:

Institute of Human Relations Press, 1969); Richard J. Meister (ed.), *Race and Ethnicity in Modern America* (Lexington, MA: D. C. Heath 1974); Leonard Dinnerstein and David M. Reimers, *Ethnic Americans: A History of Immigration and Assimilation* (New York: Dodd and Mead, 1975); William J. Wilson, *The Declining Significance of Race: Blacks and Changing American Institutions* (Chicago: University of Chicago Press, 1978); Thomas Sowell (ed.), *Essays and Data on American Ethnic Groups* (Washington, DC: Urban Institute, 1978); Stanley Lieberson, *A Piece of the Pie: Blacks and White Immigrants Since 1880* (London: University of California Press, 1980).

15.   Irving Levine writes: "Ethnicity, in short, means the culture of people and is thus critical for values, attitudes, perceptions, needs, mode of expression, behavior, and identity." "Statement," in U.S. Commission on Civil Rights, *Civil Rights Issues of Euro-Ethnic Americans in the United States: Opportunities and Challenges* (Washington, DC: U.S. Government Printing Office, 1979), p. 6. For a synthesis of various theories of ethnicity, see Ronald A. Reminick, *Theory of Ethnicity: An Anthropologist's Perspective* (Lanham, MD: University Press of America, 1983).

16.   Gary Nash, *Red, White, and Black: The Peoples of Early America* (Englewood Cliffs, NJ: Prentice-Hall, 1979), pp. 2-3.

17.   Stephen Steinberg, *The Ethnic Myth: Race, Ethnicity and Class in America* (New York: Atheneum, 1981), p. 3.

18.   For a restatement and comparisons of cultural pluralist advocacies, see Fred Matthews, "Cultural Pluralism in Context: External History, Philosophic Premises and Theories of Ethnicity in Modern America," *Journal of Ethnic Studies* 12, no. 2 (Summer 1984), pp. 63-79. See also Arthur M. Schlesinger, Jr., *The Disuniting of America: Reflections on a Multicultural Society* (Knoxsville, TN: Whittle, 1991).

19.   See Nathan Glazer and Daniel P. Moynihan (eds.), *Beyond the Melting Pot: The Negroes, Puerto Ricans, Jews, Italians, and Irish of New York City* (Cambridge, MA: MIT Press, 1963); Greeley, *Why Can't They Be Like Us?* chapter 5; Ronald Pawalko, "Racism and the New Immigration: A Reinterpretation of the Assimilation of White Ethnics in American Society," *Sociology and Social Research* 65, no. 1 (October 1980), pp. 56-77; U.S. Commission on Civil Rights, *Civil Rights Issues of Euro-Ethnic Americans in the United States: Opportunities and Challenges* (Washington, DC: U.S. Government Printing Office, 1979).

20. Murray Friedman, "Is White Racism the Problem?" in Peter Rose (ed.), *Nation of Nations: The Ethnic Experience and the Racial Crisis* (New York: Random House, 1972), p. 280.

21. Michael Novak, *The Rise of the Unmeltable Ethnics: Politics and Culture in the Seventies* (New York: Macmillan, 1972), p. 30.

22. See Nathan Glazer, *Affirmative Discrimination: Ethnic Inequality and Public Policy* (New York: Basic Books, 1975); A. H. Goldman, "Limits to the Justification of Reverse Discrimination," *Social Theory and Practice* 3, no. 3 (Spring 1975), pp. 289-306; Barry Cross (ed.), *Reverse Discrimination* (New York: Prometheus, 1977).

23. Andrew Greeley, "The Ethnic Miracle," in Yetman (ed.), *Majority*, p. 269.

24. Lieberson, *A Piece of the Pie*, p. 25.

25. Nathan Glazer, "Blacks and Ethnic Groups: The Difference, and the Political Difference It Makes," in Nathan Huggins, Martin Kilson, and Daniel Fox (eds.), *Key Issues in the Afro-American Experience*, vol. 2. (New York: Harcourt Brace Jovanovich, 1971), p. 209.

26. See Malcolm X, *Malcolm X on Afro-American History* (New York: Pathfinder Press, 1967); Stokely Carmichael and Charles V. Hamilton, *Black Power* (New York: Vintage Books, 1967); James A. Kushner, *Apartheid in America* (New York: Associated Faculty Press, 1980); Haki R. Madhubuti, *Enemies: The Clash of Races* (Chicago: Third World Press, 1978); Frances Welsing, "The Cress Theory of Color-Confrontation," *The Black Scholar* 5, no. 8 (May 1974), pp. 32-40.

27. Frederik Barth, "Introduction," in Frederik Barth (ed.), *Ethnic Groups and Boundaries: The Social Organization of Culture Differences* (Boston: Little, Brown, 1969), p. 14.

28. See Abner Cohen, "'Introduction': The Lesson of Ethnicity," in Abner Cohen (ed.), *Urban Ethnicity* (London: Tavistock, 1974), pp. ix-xxiv. See also Ronald Remnick, *Theory of Ethnicity: An Anthropologist's Perspective* (Lanham, MD: University Press of America, 1983).

29. See William J. Wilson, *The Declining Significance of Race: Blacks and Changing American Institutions* (Chicago: University of Chicago Press, 1978); William J. Wilson, "Race-Oriented Programs and the Black Underclass," in Clement Cottingham (ed.), *Race, Poverty and the Urban Underclass* (Lexington, MA: D. C. Heath, 1982), pp. 113-132; Glenn Loury, "Internally Directed Action for Black Community Development: The Next Frontier for the 'Movement'," *Review of Black Political Economy* 13, no. 1-2 (Summer-Fall 1984), pp. 31-46; Walter Williams, *The State against Blacks* (New York: McGraw-Hill, 1982); and *America: A Minority View-*

point (Stanford, CA: Hoover Institution Press, 1982); Thomas Sowell, "The Use of Government for Racial Equality," *National Review* 33 (September 4, 1978), pp. 1000-1016; Shelby Steele, *The Content of Our Character: A New Vision of Race in America* (New York: St. Martin's Press, 1990).

30. Glenn Loury, "Economics, Politics, and Blacks," *The Review of Black Political Economy* 12, no. 3 (Spring 1983), p. 49.

31. Lieberson, *A Piece of the Pie*, p. 365.

32. Daniel P. Moynihan, "The Negro Family: The Case for National Action," in Lee Rainwater and William Yancey (eds.), *The Moynihan Report and the Politics of Controversy* (Cambridge, MA: MIT Press, 1967), p. 51.

33. Sowell, *The Economics and Politics of Race*, p. 282. See also Thomas Sowell, "Culture — Not Discrimination — Decides Who Gets Ahead," *U.S. News and World Report* (October 12, 1981), pp. 74-75.

34. William J. Wilson, "The Urban Underclass," in Leslie W. Dunbar (ed.), *Minority Report* (New York: Pantheon Books, 1984), pp. 109-110. See also William J. Wilson, "Studying Inner-City Dislocations," *American Sociological Review* 56, no. 1, (February 1991), pp. 1-14.

35. William J. Wilson, *The Truly Disadvantaged: The Inner City, the Underclass, and Public Policy* (Chicago: University of Chicago Press, 1986), p. 12.

36. Ibid., p. 61.

37. John Rex, "The Role of Class Analysis," in John Rex and David Mason (eds.), *Theories of Race and Ethnic Relations* (London: Cambridge University Press, 1986), p. 75.

38. Herbert Gans, "Fighting the Biases Embeded in Social Concepts of the Poor," *The Chronicle of Higher Education* 38, no. 18 (January 8, 1992), p. A56.

39. See Sterling Stuckey, *Slave Culture: Nationalist Theory and the Foundations of Black America* (New York: Oxford University Press, 1987); Allen, *Black Awakening*; Marable, *How Capitalism*. Joe R. Feagin, *Social Problems*, 2nd ed. (Englewood Cliffs, NJ: Prentice-Hall, 1986), chapter 4; Robert Staples (ed.), *The Black Family: Essays and Studies*, 3rd ed. (Belmont, CA: Wadsworth, 1986), chapter 1; Barrera, *Race and Class,* chapter 7.

40. Sowell, "Three Black Histories," in Sowell (ed.), *Essays*, p. 49.

41. See "The Black Conservatives," *Newsweek* (March 9, 1981), pp. 29-33. See also Loury, "Internally Directed Action."

42. Mary Frances Berry and John W. Blassingame, *Long Memory: The Black Experience in America* (New York: Oxford University Press, 1982), pp. 261-262.

43. James S. Coleman et al., *Equality of Educational Opportunity* (Washington DC: U.S. Department of Health, Education and Welfare, 1966).

44. See U.S. National Commission on Excellence in Education, *A Nation at Risk* (Washington, DC: U.S. Government Printing Office, 1983); Jonathan Kozol, *Savage Inequalities: Children in America's Schools* (New York: Crown, 1991).

45. Robert L. Green, *The Urban Challenge: Poverty and Race* (Chicago: Follett, 1977), p. 49.

46. In Williams' words: "The thesis of this book is that black handicaps resulting from centuries of slavery, followed by years of gross denial of constitutional rights, have been reinforced by government laws. The government laws that have proven most devastating for many blacks, are those that govern economic activity." *The State against Blacks*, p. 125. These remarks hardly suggest "conservatism."

47. See Steinberg, *Ethnic Myth;* Sowell, *Ethnic America.*

48. Jaslin U. Salmon, *Black Executives in White Businesses* (Washington DC, University Press of America, 1979), chapter 7.

49. Charles V. Willie, *Race, Ethnicity and Socioeconomic Status* (New York: General Hall, 1983), p. 4. For other criticisms of Wilson's analysis, see Melvin Oliver, "The Enduring Significance of Race," *Journal of Ethnic Studies* 4 (1980), pp. 79-91; Alphonso Pinkney, *The Myth of Black Progress* (Cambridge: Cambridge University Press, 1984); Bart Landry, *The New Black Middle Class* (Berkeley, CA: University of California Press, 1987); Charles V. Willie, *The Continuing Significance of Race: A New Look at Black Families* (New York: General Hall, 1981).

50. See Arthur Jensen, *Straight Talk about Mental Tests* (New York: Free Press, 1981).

51. See van den Berghe, *Race and Racism*, pp. 4-5.

52. See Charles Murray, *Losing Ground: American Social Policy 1950-1980* (New York: Basic Books, 1984), pp. 270-272. See also William O'Hare, Taynia Mann, Katryn Porter, and Robert Greenstein, *Real Life Poverty in America: Where the American Public Would Set the Poverty Line* (Washington, DC: Center on Budget and Policy Priorities, 1990).

53. See Ralph Nader, Richard Brownstein, and John Richard, *Who's Poisoning America: Corporate Pollution and Their Victims in the Chemical Age* (San Francisco: Sierra Club Books, 1981); Barry Commoner, *The Politics of*

Energy: The Poverty of Power (New York: Knopf, 1979); Alan R. Block and Frank R. Scarpitti, *Poisoning for Profit: The Mafia and Toxic Waste in America* (New York: Wiliam Morrow, 1985); Richard Quinney, *Class, Status and Crime* (New York: Longman, 1980).

54. See Paul Fussell, *BAD: Or the Dumbing of America* (New York: Summit Books, 1991); Allan Bloom, *The Closing of the American Mind* (New York: Simon and Schuster, 1986); Richard Paul, *Critical Thinking: What Every Person Needs to Survive in a Rapidly Changing World* (Rohnert Park, CA: Center for Critical Thinking and Moral Critique, 1990).

55. Cynthia Enloe, *Ethnic Conflict and Political Development* (Boston: Little, Brown, 1973), pp. 17-23.

56. Harry H. L. Kitano, "Asian Americans: The Chinese, Japanese, Koreans, Philipinos and Southeast Asians," in Milton Gordon (ed.), *America as a Multicultural Society* (Philadelphia: The American Academy of Political and Social Sciences, 1981), pp. 125-138.

57. Gunnar Myrdal, *An American Dilemma: The Negro Problem in Modern Democracy*, vol. 1 (New York: Harper and Row, 1944), p. xlvi.

58. George Devereux, "Ethnic Identity: Its Logical Foundations and Dysfunctions," in George de Vos and Lola Romanucci-Ross (eds.), *Ethnic Identity: Cultural Continuities and Change* (Palo Alto, CA: Mayfield, 1975), p. 43.

4

Racialization through Race-Class Analyses

Over the past decade there has been a proliferation of "race-class analyses," or class analyses of racial minority experiences.[1] In this literature, "race" is used to refer to persons, who are also ascribed a "class" position, and vice versa. This chapter presents a detailed examination of these writings; it seeks to demonstrate that race-class analyses contain a variety of logical flaws that annul any claim to being scholarship.

First, racial and class theories are separate and distinct theories of society that, however, share a realist proof structure and a "humanist" problematic that seeks to unravel the essential nature of human beings.[2] It is these commonalities that allow but also vitiate combinations of race and class. Racial and class theories embody claims on "the real world," as their object of analysis and the basis of the accuracy of their descriptions (see "proof structure," row 5 of Figure 1.1). A significant pattern of intellectual exchanges emerges between advocates of racial and class analyses: Class relations are "real." No, race relations are "real." Race is an ideological instance, and class the reality. No, class is a Marxist superimposition on racial realities. This stalemate is well expressed by Raymond Franklin and Solomon Resnik: "In the end we have come full circle. While race and class analyses are in theory diametrically opposed, and while the proponents of each are in bitter disagreement, the black reality requires that they be combined."[3] But why is the reality "black" and not "class"? Does not the presumption that the reality is racial preempt the viability and relevance of class?

The "bitter disagreements" are at least half a century old. They flow from the fact that race-class analysts are caught up in the contradiction of separating race and class in order to combine them. The field is, therefore, characterized by analytical stalemates and a stultifying repetetion. Some race-class analysts conceive race, or racial experiences, as a reality to which class, a theory, is to be applied. Others reverse the relationship, while still others entirely rule out considerations of race in a class analysis. Each, however, claims to be presenting the picture of the real social world. The insoluble nature of these problems rules out the possibility of coherence and conclusiveness in race-class combinations.

Second, the race-class literature continues a tradition of ascribing some analytic value to race, on grounds that "actors," who are being saturated with racial descriptions, impute meaning to race. Within this self-serving practice, race-class analyses are part of the racialization of social relations.

Third, the deconstructive implications of various definitions of class are not rigorously examined. Class is subjected to numerous "ideological" and "fractional" qualifications in order to accommodate race. Thus, class, in the classical Marxian formulation, is implicitly deconstructed. Class analyses of racial experiences thereby become a race-saving device.

Fourth, race-class analyses do not address relevant questions of analytical irreducibility and congruency between classification and explanation. Such consideration is required in order to discern whether race and class can be combined. It may be argued that racial and class classifications are part of two irreducible theories of society. Their criteria of classification logically entail specific types of explanations. Explanations such as racism and genetic attributes are specific to a racial theory of social relations, just as a class explanation is entailed in political economic descriptions of society.

Finally, materialist or political economic analyses of race relations are necessarily rife with inconclusive disputes, because racial classification necessitates reference to racial motives in the explanation of behavior. Materialist analyses, however, develop racial descriptions then prioritize political economic variables. The racial theory is used to define events as "racial experiences," to which class is applied. These analyses, then, are attempts at class explanations of racial experiences. Such attempts, however, are criticized as economic reductionist and economic determinism. On the other hand, any insistence on the racial nature of experiences is met with the charge of race essentialism and subservience to ideology — that is, of conceptualizing race as if it is something immanent and endemic to society, rather than a feature of a specific, capitalist social formation.

The contradictions within race-class analyses contain a noteworthy philosophical element. The basis of attempted combinations of race and class is a common conception of knowledge (epistemology) claiming that theories are approximations of "the real world," which is something beyond theories and concepts. This conception of knowledge confounds the combination of race and class. Any "real" social phenomenon can be characterized as class or racial by different observers of the economic or the anatomical attributes of the persons involved. It is significant that throughout the race relations literature, the numerous references to the real, social reality, and the real world are not accompanied by any definitions. It is tempting to suggest that social scientists should get their philosophical act together, abandon the game of hide and seek with "the real world," and conceive of races and classes as products of classifications that form part of racial and class theories of society.

PROBLEMS IN RACE-CLASS COMBINATIONS

This issue of the enduring or declining significance of race resurfaced with greater force after the publication of William J. Wilson's *Declining Significance of Race* in 1978. However, the call for an inclusion of "class" in studies of "race relations" was voiced as early as the 1930s by sociologists such as W. Lloyd Warner, John Dollard, and Robert Park.[4] In 1948 it was strongly advocated by Oliver C. Cox in *Caste, Class and Race*, which utilized Marxist class criteria and offered trenchant criticisms of "the caste school of race relations."[5] Early race-class studies addressed, in particular, the issue of whether blacks and whites belonged to separate status systems. Their comparisons with caste and class reflect the influence of Max Weber's writings on social stratification.[6]

In Weber's analysis of class and status, an individual's place in the stratification system is dependent on marketable skills or type of occupation, ownership of goods, quality and quantity of consumption, power or authority, and social honor. In the early integration of race, class, and caste, some sociologists argued that disparities in consumption patterns, the extent of racial segregation, inequality, and deprecation of "Negroes" were so exhaustive that stratification in American society, especially in the South, could be said to resemble India's caste system. Equal-status social intercourse between "whites" and "Negroes" was minimal. The latter were regarded as degraded and dishonored. These elements, together with the persistence of white supremacist beliefs, suggested that "Negroes" were a lower caste, or a lower status group, but definitely in a separate class system.

Sociologist Arthur Marwick's description captures the general thesis.

> The picture which emerges is not of a social structure in which all the upper floors are occupied by whites with the basement being crammed with blacks, but rather of two houses standing side by side: a tall one with a shallow basement, and a much lower one with a deep basement, the whites being in the former, and blacks in the latter.[7]

Warner and Dollard had observed and interpreted this situation as a pattern reminiscent of caste distinctions. It was this interpretation that Oliver Cox sought to replace with a class analysis.

Because criteria of class demarcation vary within Marx and Weber's analyses, the occupants of Marwick's two houses would be elsewhere located in a Marxian scheme. Members of the so-called black middle class, or "black bourgeoisie," would be assigned to the working class, because, for Marx, wage earning defined membership in the working class. When it is said that over 70 percent of the U.S. population generally claim to be "middle class," it should be added that this "middle class" is a Weberian construct. Over 90 percent of this population would be located in a proletarian basement if Marxian criteria of class demarcation were to be employed. Class location depends on criteria of classification.

A sharper clarification of these criteria could lead to a resolution of some of the difficulties in establishing the nature of the relationship between race and class. Indeed, what various types of race-class analyses share is a deep dependency on the theoretical legacies of Marx and Weber. These, however, are contrasting legacies; they generate different images of stratification.

The merging of race and class presents special difficulties, for their differentiation must first be established definitively. However, what if race relations are class relations in disguise, in which racial utterances represent false consciousness, an effect of policies of racial division to ensure class domination? Even if race and class are inter- active, for the purpose of explanation, some primacy must be demon- strated. Why would class emerge out of racial conditions; or is it the reverse? Moreover, which conception of class is applicable to race relations, the Marxian, Marxist, Marxist-Leninist, or the Weberian? Is race the noneconomic and class the economic? As sociologist James Geschwender writes:

> The most difficult challenge facing any school of thought on race relations in America which introduces the variable of class in relation to race is: What is to be done with the noneconomic variable of race within the framework of an economic analysis conceding the presence of racism transcending class lines?[8]

Other questions that should also be raised are: Can race relations be otherwise explained, given that race is itself presented as an explana- tion? Can they be explained by class, without being implicitly recon- ceptualized as class relations? How do race relations and class relations differ, if race relations are both subjective, ideological social processes and political economic relations of exploitation? Is class to be defined as an economic category, a political economic, or a cultural entity? Should race relations themselves be subjectively or materialistically conceived? If they are economically conceived, is there space left for class? Are class and economics identical concepts? What are the criteria of an adequate explanation of either race or class problems?

These questions give testimony to underlying issues of theoretical complementarity, reducibility, and commensurability between racial and class theories of society. In his landmark work, *The Structure of Scientific Revolutions*, historian of the philosophy of sciences Thomas Kuhn writes: "To the extent . . . that two scientific schools disagree about what is a problem and what a solution, they will inevitably talk through each other when debating the relative merits of their respective paradigms."[9] Scholars dealing with race relations have rigorously avoided this particular philosophical issue. This avoidance could be at the root of the controversies over race and class as well as attempts at combinations. Arguably, the concept of class is part of an autonomous theory of history. "The history of all hitherto existing societies is a history of class struggles" — so wrote Karl Marx in *The Communist Manifesto*. Compare this with Arthur de Gobineau's "I was gradually penetrated by the conviction that the racial question overshadows all other problems of history." Ostensibly, then, racial and class theories of history and society are competitive and even mutually exclusive. They contain different structural components such as classificatory criteria, conceptions of social causation and stratification, and different prescriptions for social transformation. In Althusserian terms, race and class are variations within a humanist problematic.[10]

In the class theory, social agents are identified within political economic conditions and market situations, as in the Weberian variant of class analysis. The fundamental relations of differentiation are also political economic. Hence, policies and behavior are said to be shaped by considerations of economic interests that are determined by market forces or relationships to the means of production. By contrast, as sociologist Harold Wolpe writes of the racial theory:

> The central concern for race-based theories, of whatever variety, is the existence of structures of racial inequality, that is, of racial stratification which is generated by racially motivated processes. Indeed, the social structure is conceived of as an hierarchical racial order constituted by competing and unequal racially defined groups which are assumed to be internally homogeneous.[11]

These stipulations of racial and class theories suggest that any attempt to combine them is bound to be a failure.

Race-class analysts circumvent the problems posed by the mutually exclusive nature of racial and class theories by conceiving racial structures as *the* reality, and class a concept that is to be applied. What race-class analyses then become is a discovery of class elements in racially motivated policies and decisions. By implication, class is a subordinate research category. However, the procedure can be reversed. Let class relations be "the reality," and race a concept that guides the search for racial factors. Radically divergent explanations are bound to emerge, and the issue of whether the society is structured by race or class remains unresolved. This indeterminacy is compounded by considerations of different definitions of class in Weberian, Marxian, and Marxist writings and the general question of the relevance of Marxism to racial experiences.

Insofar as racial and class theories contain mutually exclusive analytic components, they are not combinable. The classificatory criteria that produce black people and white racism belong as exclusively to the racial theory as the bourgeoisie is part of the class theory. The idea of a black bourgeoisie, then, is incoherent. The skin color, hair type, and facial form of the bourgeoisie cannot be of analytic significance. Black cannot qualify bourgeoisie, just as "yellow" cannot describe logarithms (as Marx has stated). Racial and class theories are separate and distinct. If references to class are necessary to studies of race relations, it is but a demonstration of an analytic incompleteness in the theory that is based on a racial classification of "actors."

In general, studies of social relations manifest constant shifts in the utilization and combination of racial, ethnic, and class categories. However, such combinations present difficulties for an evaluation of explanations. If a flaw is demonstrated in the class explanation of race relations, a cultural or ideological factor can be tacked on. Would this still be a class analysis? If race is said to be insignificant, more data on black poverty is presented to demonstrate its "enduring" or "inclining" significance. The overall effects are an endless development of explanations, disputes over the status of racism, and increasing mounds of empirical data. Given this persistent stalemate, political denunciations play a large role in race relations studies. For example, sociologist Alphonso Pinkney writes:

> Black social scientists, as well as white, appear to be supporting the growing conservative movement in the United States. That white social scientists should engage in these activities is not surprising. However, black sociologists who support the conservative movement are not unlike government officials in (formerly) South Vietnam who supported American aggression against their own people.[12]

These remarks testify to a major difficulty in discussions of so-called racial experiences. Scholars themselves are racially classified and allotted certain roles, and commentators on "the black experience" should themselves be black, as it is assumed that white scholars cannot know the meaning of being black. Black scholars, however, are further required to take a racial liberationist position. Otherwise, they are but collaborationists, "misguided brothers," and Uncle Toms. Thus, users of the racial theory are hoisted on their own philosophical petard. If race is socially significant and theorists themselves may be racially classified, race may be regarded as an influential variable on all studies of racial experiences. These studies, then, are intrinsically racially partisan and politically biased, especially as race is also considered an "ideology."

The treason allegedly committed by certain black social scientists was to suggest that class, rather than race, was the decisive factor in shaping the black experience in modern America. Pinkney's rejection of the reasons for the explanatory shift from race to class is justifiable. Class cannot explain racially-described relations, without giving rise to the implication that the term race relations was a misnomer in the first place. A description, or classification of a population necessarily influences the nature of the explanation of its relationships. Consistency, then, must be maintained between classification and explanation. A racial description of persons necessitates references to racial motivations in explaining their behavior. Otherwise, the description is of no significance and could be disregarded. Social scientists should be reminded of the explanatory implications of classificatory criteria.

Pinkney's remarks, however, indicted the politics of "black sociologists."

If the object of study is black and white people, explanations must be racial. If persons are given a dual classification, as in poor Puerto Ricans, middle-class Asian Americans, and white capitalists, explanations of their actions must be similarly many-layered. This, in turn, requires their individual weighting. A *white* employer may be racist, but be also interested in profit maximization. A racism-explanation of this employer's policies can, therefore, be repudiated through an emphasis on economic motives. A claim that motives are, or may be, both racial and economic must be supported empirically. The employer has to be asked to specify his or her motives, and this process involves issues of deception, "ideological" self-deception, and biases in questionnaires. What is clear is that the term white employer derives from a combining of racial and class categories. The result is inconclusive. A racial, or an economic, explanation of this employer's decisions could be deemed "reductionist." But "reductionism" is an esoteric term of negative characterization, a mere expression of disagreement. The analysis to which it is applied could still be logically sound.

Problems of *immigrants* must be discussed as effects of immigration policies. On the other hand, immigration policies may be part of foreign and economic policies and expressive of racial considerations. When such connections are demonstrated, the classification of the problems must also undergo a corresponding transformation. If this relationship of consistency is not observed, social scientific theories will be caught up in a circle of plausible but competitive political, economic, and sociological explanations of the "same" problem.

In order to avoid this state of perpetual challenge and counterchallenge and the personalization and politicization of scholarly exchanges, attention should be directed at the logical structure of arguments, definitions of analytic components, and the boundaries among racial and class theories. This would prevent controversies over the political status of authors' works and the politics of the authors themselves. In terms of the logical structure of arguments, it is of no significance whether Karl Marx, Max Weber, Oliver Cox, and William J. Wilson are black-skinned or white-skinned, or whether they are class or racial theorists. Indeed, their writings do not represent an internally consistent, unilinear system of arguments. Therefore, what should be investigated are the implications of the specific analytical components of various theories. The evaluative focus should be on criteria of classification, causation, proof structure, and solutions, not the racial, ethnic, or class attributes of theorists.

Lack of attention to these philosophical issues introduces arbitrariness, circularity, and inconclusiveness into the study of social relations. Sociologists Raymond Franklin and Solomon Resnik's remarks express this condition.

> Almost every analyst dealing with the black condition uses the class concept in some way. As the emphasis on race increases, however, the emphasis on class frequently decreases, and vice versa. Where the emphasis on race predominates, as among the race analysts, the emphasis on class as a primary determinant of the problems of blacks diminishes. When race advocates use the concept of class (usually defined in terms of income level), it is seen primarily as a result of racism. As we move away from racial analysis towards ethnic analysis, the importance of race recedes and class becomes more important. The ethnic analysts often assert that black problems stem in large part from the fact that so many blacks are lower class, and at times this emphasis becomes so dominant that ethnicity is virtually disregarded. As we move towards the end of the spectrum, class predominates at the expense of both race and ethnicity.[13]

Racial, ethnic, and class theories all contain references to "reality" or empirical data as their proof of the "truth" of arguments. It would appear that because the theories deal with the same social reality, their combination presents no analytical difficulties. After all, as social reality is multilayered, race, ethnicity, and class may be said to intersect in the real world. This reference to social reality, however, presents a further difficulty: How can disputes over explanations of race relations be settled if any disputant can claim a purchase on reality, or randomly point to nonracial factors to defend a racial explanation? Verification of claims on reality is necessarily caught up in endless rounds of conflicting observations.

Not surprisingly, race-class combinations have provoked the same accusations of economism, one-sided determinism, and reductionism as the use of an undiluted racial or class analysis. Decade after decade, controversies are repeated over the comparative class situation of races as well as the viability, significance, and interchangeability of racial, ethnic, and class analyses. The termination of these controversies necessitates a recognition that racial, ethnic, and class theories comprise alternative analytic components. Their combinations are bound to sin on the side of incoherence and provoke unending disputes.

Certain arguments from the writings of four eminent scholars of racial and ethnic relations — Leo Kuper, Oliver Cox, Pierre L. van den Berghe, and Percy Cohen — demonstrate why there must be a perpetually revolving circle of ambiguity and contradictions within race-class analyses. Kuper suggests that it is difficult to demarcate racial from class stratification:

> Clearly racial differences are of a more enduring nature than class differences, and there are very extensive social correlates of racial differences in many racially structured societies. In some critical respects relevant to conceptions, class structures and racial structures constitute different systems of stratification, however much they may overlap.[14]

However, these propositions are incomplete as an argument. To be more than mere assertions, definitions of race and class should be outlined, especially as the second sentence states "relevant to conceptions." Kuper's assertions reproduce the play on race and class that fertilizes race-class analyses. In one breath, as it were, racial differences are more enduring than class differences, correlative with class, different from class, and overlapping with class. But Kuper offers a key phrase — "relevant to conceptions" — because the discovery of the balance between racial and class differences depends on a specification of the criteria of demarcation between race and class.

If a class society is conceived as racially structured, or vice versa, the means of discovering this structuring must be made clear. These means cannot be actors' verbal responses to questions on their racial identity. Racial beliefs and the racial self-identification of respondents are symbolic, questionnaire-design dependent, and internally inconsistent.[15] Such expressions cannot constitute proof of racial stratification. The term racial stratification is also a tautology, if members of a racial group are identified through their socioeconomic attributes and political relations. If black workers are a racialized class fraction, the fraction is of race, not class. In effect, race-class combinations contravene elementary logical rules. Only studies not sensitive to such rules could further their development.

While Kuper posits similarities and distinctions between racial and class differences, Oliver Cox advances an identity of race and class relations. He writes: "Here, then, are race relations; they are definitely not caste relations. They are labor-capital-profits relationships; therefore, race relations are proletarian bourgeois relations and hence political-class relations."[16] Race relations are a subspecies of class relations.

On the other hand, Pierre L. van den Berghe writes:

> I was also in good company in emphasizing the irreducibility of ethnic and/or racial membership to class affiliation, and vice versa. Class, ethnicity and race, I asserted are fundamentally different principles of social affiliation, although each of them must be looked at in both subjective and objective terms.[17]

In sum, race relations are distinct from class relations, expressions of class relations, overlapping with class relations, and identical to class relations. But what are class relations? Sociologist Percy Cohen denies that they are clearly distinct from race relations.

> After all, the upper and middle classes of any nationally homogeneous society exploit their own internal proletariat as mercilessly as is necessary and for as long as is necessary, while justifying this in terms of various doctrines (including that of eugenics, a parallel to 'scientific' racism) . . . and stereotype their social inferiors as lazy, immoral and unsuited to participate in the political community.[18]

Ruling classes behave just like ruling races, and class domination is not without racial undertones. Moreover, as Kuper suggested, racial and class stratification overlap and Cox noted that race relations are disguised class relations. Class situations are racial situations, and vice versa. How then is it possible to combine race and class? Surely the study of social relations ought to be rescued from this level of collective incoherence.

Attempts to merge and separate biological descriptions and social relations necessarily produce contradictions. The process represents a "play" in terms of its implications of denial and endorsement. Unlike class or economic relations, race relations are biologically defined. Yet this biological definition may be said to be a manifestation of class struggles. Herbert Seligmann writes:

> The doctrine of race was . . . born of group struggles having their basis in fields far removed from biological or ethnic considerations. The struggles were those of the bourgeoisie against the privileges of the nobility, which privileges were dated back to the Germanic conquests of Europe. Clearest expressions of the class basis for racialism was given by Count de Boulainvilliers, who asserted that the French people was composed of two races, of which one, the nobility, was descended from the Germanic conquerors, the remaining bulk of the population from the conquered Celts and Romans.[19]

If racial characterizations derive from class developments, a racial analysis of class relations or a class analysis of race relations would be specious. Logically, then, a race-class explanation of "a black experience" would be compounding of ambiguity, a continuation of a game without rules, for his experience is already one of class. But then, why is it "black"?

THE NEED FOR CONGRUENCY BETWEEN DESCRIPTIONS AND EXPLANATIONS

Race-class analyses do not successfully marry the analytical categories of racial and class theories. But what constitutes a successful merging of theoretical frameworks? This question does not appear in the literature on racial and class experiences. Its consideration is a requirement, however, for it would force a clarification of the specific structures of racial and class theories. Given also the relative dearth of delineations of class in race-class studies, Marxian and Weberian class analyses are not fully differentiated. Possessors of certain marketable aptitudes are categorized as middle, or upper class, while in Marxian terms they are characterized as working class. Terms such as eth-class, caste-class, race-class, and social race are an implicit recognition of the analytical difficulties involved in categorizing human beings who, by definition, possess innumerable attributes, including the faculty for self-classification.

A principle of congruency between classification and explanation should be observed in social studies. This principle suggests that, if social relations are classified as racial, their explanation should be restricted to racial variables. The description of the object of study, or the entity that is to be explained, necessarily affects the type of explanation. To observe "raindrops" is to utilize specific classificatory criteria distinguishing rainfall from other liquids as well as notions of cloud formation, atmospheric pressure, and cloud-bursts interpenetrating with dust particles. This observation, then, is undergirded by a theory; it implies the nature of the explanation of the observed object. Observation of a *black* experience implies a notion of racial causation. If class is to explain race, descriptions of racial experiences must be free of class elements. Otherwise, they could be designated class experiences.

The principle of congruency implies the existence of boundaries between social theories so that a racial explanation of class experiences would result in a sterilization of class. Similarly, if racial experiences are to be explained by class, then their racial nature is dissolved and was, indeed, a misnomer. These strictures take on added significance in light of criticisms of race as a type of classification.

Social scientists may be flogging a dead horse of race relations. Sociologist Michael Banton writes:

> Most sociologists would now agree that there is no distinctive class of
> social relations to be identified as racial relations. The assumption that
> there was such a class was a product of racial consciousness that
> developed among white people in the United States and North Western
> Europe in the latter part of the nineteenth century.[20]

Some objection may be raised regarding the tautological status of the phrase "racial consciousness that developed among white people" as well as the contradiction implicit in denying the existence of race relations and identifying "white people." The classifications black experience and white people themselves form part of the study of racial relations. The introduction of class is an embryonic reformulation of relations.

If a black experience can be reconceptualized as a race-class experience, it can also be reconstructed as a class experience or a human experience lived by persons who are classified as blacks. How can an experience undergo so many divergent qualifications? In order to resolve this issue, social studies will have to be more sensitive to philosophical issues in social sciences. Thus, the significance of sociologist C. Stephen Fenton's caution cannot be overemphasized:

> The reader should keep in mind a distinction between race as explanans and race as explanandum. When "race" is taken to be the key to understanding history, civilization, or differences in specific traits, we have "race" used as something which can explain; when we seek to explain (for example) race prejudice, "race" (or associated sentiments and behavior) is being explained, implicitly, by reference to "something else." But the distinction is much complicated by the shifting senses in which "race" is (or is not) taken to be real.[21]

Some of the implications of the premise that "races" are "real" will be analyzed subsequently. Suffice it to mention here that this premise functions to avoid having to define "races."

If racial experiences are to be explained, the description racial must be investigated and logically justified. If racial experiences are to be explained with reference to class, they must first be shown to be racially structured. On the other hand, the development of a class explanation seeks to displace the racial description, or at least demonstrate its subordinate status, as in the idea of the black working class, not working-class blacks. In effect, the description is racial, but the racial structure must be demonstrated to be of class. Such a demonstration must be by fiat. What was racial dogmatically becomes class. The reference to racial descriptions as "symbols," or false (class) consciousness, does not escape the dogmatism. A black experience cannot be described as an expression of class relations, without compromising the racial characterization of the experience. On the other hand, if racial experiences are class-structured, what justifies the racial description in the first place? One of the cardinal weakness in race-class analyses, then, is inattention to the logical implications of descriptions or classifications.

MARXIAN CLASS CONCEPTIONS AND RACIAL EXPERIENCES

Variations within definitions of class are embedded in the sociological tradition. Marxian and Weberian contributions provide the foundations of these variations. However, there is no systematic theory of class in either Marx's or Weber's writings.[22] Their writings contain numerous incompletely formulated arguments on the subjective-objective dimensions of class. In both sets of writings, class straddles a range of objective conditions and subjective attributes. Relationship to the means of production and ownership of property are also central to both conceptions. However, in Marx's analysis, it is ownership of specific means of production — investment goods — that polarizes the population into classes. In Marx's writings, then, the term class refers to persons bearing relationships and thus also qualifies social processes, including consciousness, interests, and action. In some of his formulations class position, class interests, class consciousness, and class action are unilinear developmental processes. The proletariat evolves historically into a revolutionary force that transforms capitalist society.

An objective definition of class is predicated on ownership and nonownership of the means of production. This criterion, however, generates a distinction between capitalists and laborers, not ruling and revolutionary classes. Owners and nonowners of the means of production constitute a statistical aggregate. Classes refer to socially significant and politically organized groups. Marx's fragmentary references to class consciousness suggest a recognition of this distinction. Indeed, his reflections on class consciousness are not only fragmentary, they also place class within a subjective-objective dichotomy that continues to plague "Marxist" theories of social change. Some theorists would claim that, in Marx's writings, class is not economistic, objective, monolithic, or subjective. Rather, it is dialectically and contingently conceived, recognizing the concretely fractionalized nature of class formation. Others would regard such a reading of Marx as an opportunistic revisionism that reduces class to Weberian interest and occupational groups and class struggles to a voluntarist workerism.[23] A return to Marx's formulations does not resolve these intra-Marxist disputes.

The unfinished delineation of class in volume 3 of *Capital* mentions "three great classes," wage laborers, capitalists, and landowners. Each owns a different kind of means of production and enjoys a different source of income.[24] Classes, then, are objectively constituted. However, in *The German Ideology*, Marx writes: "The separate individuals form a class only insofar as they have to carry on a common battle against another class; otherwise they are on hostile terms with each other as competitors."[25] Classes are politically interdefined. If there is no bourgeoisie, the proletariat is also nonexistent. But between the bourgeoisie and the working class there are middle classes, or a petite bourgeoisie, just as there is a lumpen-proletariat within the working class.

In *The Poverty of Philosophy*, Marx announces a distinction between a class for itself and a class opposed to capital.

> The domination of capital has created for this mass of people a common situation with common interests. Thus this mass is already a class, as opposed to capital, but not yet for itself. In the struggle, of which we have only noted some phases, this mass unites, it is constituted as a class for itself.[26]

This implies that there is no identity or interchangeability between capitalists and bourgeoisie and between laborers and proletariat. Wage laborers are not, by definition, a revolutionary agent of social transformation; they *become* a proletariat during intellectual and political struggles.[27]

In *The Eighteenth Brumaire of Louis Bonaparte,* Marx proposes that a collective identity, common interests, and organizational cohesion are central to the formation of a class.[28] Hence, capitalists and wage laborers are not necessarily classes; they are classes in themselves, until their respective class interests structure their behavior. Then they become classes for themselves — cohesive, collectively goal-oriented, and organized. It follows that intellectual and political interventions are necessary for the transformation of social categories into self-conscious actors. Workers are not naturally an actively engaged class; they are made into such a force through exposure to class explanations of their life circumstances. Ideas become a "material force" when grasped by the masses. Class consciousness and organization are not to be left to inexorable historical forces. *Capital* must become "the Bible of the working class" if revolutionary consciousness and organization are to develop. Its propositions represent an attempt to create that class, in the form of revolutionary political practices. Class formulations are necessary for class formation. Must these formulations be logically rigorous, or can they simply be said to be reflecting real-world contradictions? In other words, should class be discarded, if it is demonstrated that the basic criterion of classification — a given relationship to the means of production — is anomalous? Or should it be said that anomalies reflect contradictory or "ambiguous" locations in "real" social conditions? The "real" emerges here as an escape hatch for a logically inadequate social theory. If the theory does not fit, alter the "real world," theoretically.

The capitalist-laborer distinction, which is central to the construction of class, is organized around ownership of means of production. Capitalists own the means of production, while laborers own nothing but their power to labor. Marx argues that the birth of capitalist production is predicated on the existence of owners of labor — "free laborers." However, as labor power is also a means of production, all individuals own some means of production. What identifies the capitalist is ownership of goods that, when invested, become capital — merchant's capital, industrial capital, or finance capital. The capitalist's income derives from these investments. The distinction between capitalists and workers, then, attempts to set limits on what laborers can do. For example, wage laborers cannot obtain their income from investments and profit. Otherwise, they would have a foot in both class camps. What, then, is their class status?

The identification of "capitalists" also produces ambiguities, if no limit is set on what they can do. For example, the demonstration that the capitalist is a nonproducer is stymied by the recognition that some shareholders-investors do labor in the enterprise. Therefore, they are both capitalists and laborers who produce surplus value, unless there is some peculiarity about their labor. Hence, a distinction must be constructed between productive and unproductive labor in order to maintain the contrast between capitalist and laborer.[29] Certain types of labor are deemed "unproductive," that is, not directly contributing to the production of surplus value. However, the definition of surplus value contains no such distinction. The capriciousness of the productive-unproductive distinction is illustrated in discussions of the nature of domestic labor. Radical and socialist feminist writings suggest that housework is a form of unpaid labor, that constitutes the second pillar of the dual exploitation of female labor.[30] Housewives are a domestic proletariat engaged in the production of surplus value. But this implies that they are "exploited" by their husbands, who are themselves exploited by capitalists, whose labor has the same unproductive status ascribed to housewives.

A second, critical weakness in the definition of class in terms of relationship to the means of production pertains to the role of savings and investment. Labor power is also means of production. Its sale can be considered an investment of "human capital."[31] All individuals, then, own and control some form of capital. Thus, nonownership/noncontrol of means of production cannot be a criterion of class demarcation. However, if it is the ownership of "stored-up labor" that separates capitalists from workers, then it must be demonstrated that no wage laborer can ever acquire investment goods. Yet Marx's analysis of capitalism does not demonstrate that workers' earnings cannot be saved, invested, and thereby become part of capital accumulation. Workers, senior citizens, and trade unions that invest their pension funds would be both capitalists and members of the working class. Wage laborers can derive substantial interest and income from savings and investments. The distinction between capitalists and workers or the "objective" conception of class does not unambiguously separate classes. How can a project of social revolution be built on such an unstable theoretical foundation?

It is not necessary to be a Marxist, non-Marxist, or anti-Marxist to conclude that Marxian criteria of class membership and conceptions of class action are anomalous and incoherent.[32] Even if class is identified according to source of income, it does not follow that the interests or behavior of members of that class must, or will be, class-determined. A common source of income does not imply similar perceptions of interests. Nor is the legitimacy of the class concept assured by its Marxian or Marxist paternity. Indeed, elements in the derivative Marxist literature on class are critical of traditional formulations and present tentative, inconclusive, and even conflicting alternatives. Internal controversies revolve around whether classes are economic or political, monolithic or fractionalized, subjective or objective, naturally or potentially revolutionary, "things" or a relation.[33] It may even be claimed that certain "Marxist" critics of "traditional Marxism" have declared a virtual obituary on class.[34]

The idea of a historical rise and fall of classes harbors the same historicism as biblical and Hegelian prophecies. Indeed, Marxist class analyses contain mere fiats on class contradictions, class struggle, and history. In order to recognize that social relations are disguised forms of class struggle, it is necessary to endorse the idea of class contradictions being the dynamic of human history. Historical class analysis, then, is irrefutable; it presupposes what is to be proven. Class is as omnipresent as the Holy Spirit, and, therefore, no social phenomenon can be said to be free of class connotations. The notion that class struggle is the dynamic of history is both teleological and theological. Its advocates must respond to criticisms with accusations of non-Marxism, class biases, anti-Marxism, and of ignoring history, that is, the Marxian analysis of "the past." This refutation of class in traditional Marxism is not addressed in race-class analyses.

Class analyses of race relations require a reformulation of the objective, bipolar definition of class developed in so-called classical Marxism. Class cannot be defined solely in terms of relationship to the means of production. This is perhaps the most influential revision of *one* of Marx's specifications of class. In *Race, Class and the Apartheid State*, sociologist Harold Wolpe raises objections to any economic-reductionist conception of class that ignores the omnipresence of class fractions and divisions along political, ideological, and cultural lines.[35] By implication, structures of racial inequality and conflicts could be specified as (disguised) class phenomena. "Racial groups" could be regarded as fractions of class relations by virtue of the noneconomic or cultural and ideological constituents of social processes. "Race relations" may be called ideologically distorted "class relations." But could not "class relations" be deemed ideologically or culturally distorted "race relations"? Subjective or ideological conditions can be invoked to reduce any alleged primacy of class over race to the status of a mere assertion that can be reversed. As sociologist Paul Gilroy writes: "The cultural politics of race can be more accurately described as the cultural politics of racism's overcoming. It challenges theories that assert the primacy of structural contradictions, economic classes, and crises in determining political consciousness and collective action."[36] Class is subordinate to race. But in this realm of assertions and counterassertions, race is subordinate to class.

References to *culturally* based class fractions involve a subjective level of analysis that has to be sustained with empirical research in which income and wealth are measured to prove class positions. In such research, black workers would be asked about their racial and class experiences. They can come out of this research as anything the researcher chooses, as blacks, working class blacks, black members of the working class, the poor, or an underclass. Racial interests may be disguised class interests, and vice versa. Either way, race remains intact, as a reality.

In order to accommodate race in a Marxist class analysis, the definition of class must include noneconomic entities and subjective preferences, such as interests. Class, then, must refer to not just means of production, but also social relations of production — that is, political and technical relations of production. These refinements constitute the basis of a revision of the objective definition of class, which was central to "classical Marxism," and a focus on "class fractions" or divisions. This notion is developed principally in the writings of sociologists Nicos Poulantzas and Erik O. Wright.[37] Class is redefined to include economic, occupational, political, and ideological dimensions that are considered to be intrinsic to class relations. Thus, despite definitional references to superstructural elements such as culture, politics, and ideology, class fractions are said to be still "objective." Class boundaries are allegedly structured around not just buying and selling of labor power but also around job types, degree of worker autonomy, functional significance for capital accumulation, and the degree of control over labor processes. Thus, there are numerous fractions within the two major class groupings, some of whose members straddle more than one class position. Such persons occupy contradictory locations within class relations in the sense of sharing "interests" with persons in other locations.

The fractional conceptions of class developed in the writings of Wright and Poulantzas must be characterized by arbitrariness, tautology, and equivocation. First, the concept of interest is not clarified, and clarified it should be, because, as sociologist Steven Lukes points out, interests can be "subjective," "objective," and "real."[38] An adequate exposition of the concept of class fractions must specify which types of interests are shared by managers, secretaries, and mechanics. The objective nature of class fractions cannot be simply asserted if the shared interests are subjective. Thus, advocates of a revision of the objective definition of class are in dispute regarding who should be excluded from which class.

Second, in Wright's analysis, the term class does double duty, and indeed, the objective bipolar definition is retained. Two major classes are identified — capitalist and workers. But then some persons — managers, the petty bourgeoisie, and unproductive workers — are said to float between these classes. In other words, the focus on the different workplace relations and conditions experienced by groups of workers presupposes usage of an objective definition of class to identify these workers. However, the discovered groups or fractions, such as managers and supervisors, cannot also be *class* fractions without advancing a new set of criteria of class demarcation.

Third, authority relationships in labor processes and ideological elements cannot be a defining feature of class demarcation if they are themselves reflections of "class struggle." Note the tautological status of Wright's formulation: "If a class concept is to explain anything it must provide the basis for explaining class struggles, the formation of people into classes and organized social forces."[39] But how did the struggles become "class struggles?" The class concept cannot "explain" its own qualification of struggles, which is the basis of defining the concept itself. As regards ideologically based fractions, which and how many "ideologies" operate in capitalist society? John Rex, for example, detects an independent *racist* ideology: "Once racist ideology emerges as a means of justifying opposition, conflict or exploitation, it can take on a life of its own and begin to operate as an additional factor, determining the nature of group boundaries, and promoting group conflict both within and independently of classes."[40] Naturally enough, Rex's writings sought to spawn a virtual subfield of race relations studies in British society.

Fractions should be named after the ideologies that form them. If the ideology is racist, then the social structure is being conceived as racial, not class, and the fractions are racial. By contrast, a capitalist ideology presupposes a capitalist mode of production in which workers, not black and white workers, sell their labor power. However, enough has been written on ideology to support the anthropologist Clifford Geertz's claim that "ideology has become thoroughly ideologized."[41] Given the variations within the concept of ideology, innumerable ideologically based class fractions can be discovered within any given class.

These criticisms constitute a dissolution of the idea of class fractions, unless class is an immanent entity, a reality that as such remains irrefutable irrespective of contrary evidence. Such a conception of class reflects the dogmatic content of racial and class theories. "Social races" (the alternative conception proposed once objective races were discredited) were also characterized as a reality, and defined with reference to political and ideological factors. The idea of class fractions remains arbitrary and incoherent, whether based on culture, occupations, labor processes, or ideology. Its retention in race-class studies serves the purpose of claiming that black workers are a racialized fraction of the working class. This assertion presupposes that the working class is white, just as Marx assumed that it is male.

Class, as a classificatory scheme, has been unwittingly dissolved through the exposé of the ambiguities, arbitrariness, and analytical regress involved in its specification. In order to identify classes, a whole battery of other concepts must be specified, such as means of production, the capitalist mode of production, ideology, exploitation, class struggle, and surplus value. But the specification of surplus value, for example, depends on a prior identification of exploitative relationships between classes.

Sociologist Alain Touraine suggests a way out of the impasse surrounding class, arguing that there is no class analysis in Marx's writings. The originality of Marx's social theory lies in its movement away from persons as classes into class relations. Touraine writes: "Sociological concepts are able to deal only with social relations. The fundamental contribution of Marx in this domain was to replace an explanation in terms of classes with an analysis in terms of class relations and their determining role in social organization."[42] Marx himself writes that the discovery of classes belongs to "bourgeois historians":

> And now as to myself, no credit is due to me for discovering the existence of classes in modern society or the struggle between them. Long before me bourgeois historians had described the historical development of this class struggle and bourgeois economists the economic anatomy of the classes. What I did that was new was to prove: 1) that the existence of classes is only bound up with particular historical phases in the development of production, 2) that the class struggle necessarily leads to the dictatorship of the proletariat, 3) that this dictatorship itself only constitutes the transition to the abolition of all classes and to a classless society.[43]

Marx does not claim to have discovered classes; he identifies their transitory presence and stresses the significance of their struggles for historical-social change. His endorsement of the discovery of classes is also a means to an end of generating a revolutionary consciousness and political struggles that would lead to the transformation of capitalism.

Class consciousness is to be developed by theoretical practice, but even revolutionary class consciousness is a form of false consciousness derived from the alienation intrinsic to capitalist commodity production. It will be transcended in the aftermath of the socialist revolution. The development of revolutionary class consciousness is a function of the dissemination of class analyses. Thus, the unity between theory and practice is assured. For Marx, theorizing is a specific political practice aimed at the overthrow of capitalist society. What, however, is the purpose of race-class theorizing? What is the value of the race-class consciousness being fertilized by race-class analyses? Is a racial war in the offing, or is the forging of race-class consciousness an attempt at so-called black-white working class unity? How can such unity be achieved, given attempts to prove the dehumanizing specificity of a black experience and the racist nature of privileged whites? Will the resultant militant racial consciousness not displace class consciousness or disfigure the development of a revolutionary class consciousness? On these questions, there is a silence.

Some post-Marxian and Marxist-Leninist verdicts on class and revolution may be recalled in order to illustrate further the incoherence of race-class analyses and support a claim that class analyses of racial conditions derive from expectations that were not fulfilled by the proletariat. In *What Is to Be Done* Vladimir Lenin claims that the working class is not an intrinsically revolutionary force.[44] It needs revolutionary theory and organization to become a force for socialist transformation. Class solidarity is a function of the development and dissemination of class analyses of the capitalist social formation. Revolutionary class consciousness materializes out of intellectual, political, and organizational practices of revolutionaries, namely, communists. In Lenin's emphasis on the "vanguard" role of activists, however, the party easily becomes a dictatorship over the proletariat as evinced in the emergence of Stalinism. The idea of social change based on a concept of historical class struggle and ultimate proletarian rule was shaken by developments in Stalin's Eastern Europe.

The nonemergence of a revolutionary class consciousness in the West also contributed to the development of theses of working class "economism" and "bourgeoisification" and of "one-dimensional man."[45] Notions of working class ideological capitulation and working class racism were advanced as explanations of the historical failure of proletarian solidarity. White workers in the West have sold out to their exploiters; they even colloborate in the superexploitation of "third world" workers. It is in the context of these doubts about the viability of social transformation through class struggle that some analysts turn a hopeful gaze on so-called nonwhite workers. This superexploited section of the working class would be the agent of revolutionary social change in advanced capitalist society.

The superexploitation thesis asserts that blacks are exploited as a race and as workers. The superexploitation of black labor is said to be evinced in lower wages, denial of benefits, an occupational "glass ceiling," and early redundancy. However, the qualification of the term exploitation does not derive from Marx's *Capital*. Indeed, the concept racial superexploitation is an analytical miscarriage, insofar as Marx's conception of exploitation is being advanced.[46] The conditions that are said to represent superexploitation are not restricted to so-called black workers; they reflect *capitalist* exploitation within a state of relatively weak labor organization. Because some white workers must also be unorganized and vulnerable, "superexploitation" accompanies capitalist labor processes, and cannot be caused by racial considerations.

In Marx's *Capital*, exploitation is an indivisible process; it is rooted in the ratio between the value of the goods produced by the whole working class and the value of its reproductive consumption; it therefore pertains to classes, not racial or ethnic groups. Indeed, Marx conceives capital as a fetishized social relation that exercises true overlordship in economic relations.

> The individual producer deals with his fellow men only through the market where prices and amounts sold are the substantive realities, human beings being merely their instruments. These quantities vary continually independently of the will, foresight and action of the producers instead of being ruled by them, a state of society in which the process of production has mastery over man instead of being controlled by him.[47]

All producers are victims of capitalist commodity production. Their anatomical differences may be considered significant by biological-classificatory sciences; these differences, however, are unrelated to capitalist exploitation.

The analysis in Marx's *Capital* contains an implicit suggestion of *what is not to be done* in attempting to eradicate the exploitation of the working class. To capitalize on race consciousness as a means of fomenting revolutionary class consciousness is self-defeating. The use of class to analyze or explain race relations results in a schizoid race-class consciousness. The dissemination of racial analyses develops race consciousness, just as class consciousness is a function of the propagation of a class theory of social relations. If race is an ideological construct used by the ruling class to perpetuate the status quo, it cannot foster a revolutionary working class consciousness.

The dissolution of class into ideologically and occupationally based "class fractions" allows race-class combinations. These combinations play on the subjective-objective constituents of race and class and are bound to proliferate uncontrollably. Figure 4.1 identifies twenty definitional referents of race and class. Each referent is susceptible to further decompositions and subspecifications. Combinational possibilities are, therefore, infinite. For example, racism necessarily has multiple meanings as it is a mental state of whites, or practices allegedly flowing from their prejudiced minds. Once whites and blacks are identified, there can be no control over ascriptions of a racist motive or the discovery of racial intentions and interests.

The figure illustrates many possible types of race-class combinations. Indeed, given the multiplicity of definitions of race and class, the combinational possibilities are virtually innumerable. These various definitions of race, class, and their connections could produce hundreds of racial and class situations with countless determinations. They may be further counterposed, intersected, and interchanged, ad infinitum.

Figure 4.1 clarifies the conceptual roots of some of the disputes over race and class. In *The Declining Significance of Race*, William J. Wilson proposes that race is periodically dominant in the American polity and economy up to the end of the nineteenth century.[48] This

Figure 4.1
CONCEPTIONS OF RACE, CLASS, AND THEIR CONNECTIONS

	Race		Class		Connections	
R1	racism	C1	capitalist interests	Con 1	reciprocal determination between R and C
R2	racial discrimination	C2	the bourgeoisie	Con 2	R is subspecies of C
R3	racial prejudice	C3	corporations	Con 3	R is functionally necessary to C
R4	racial policies	C4	the state	Con 4	R is an anachronistic survival of C
R5	racial statements	C5	status groups	Con 5	R is a necessary byproduct of C
R6	racial inequality	C6	income levels	Con 6	R is caused by C
R7	racial conflicts	C7	production relations	Con 7	R is periodically subordinate to C
R8	racial ideology	C8	life-styles	Con 8	R is structurally subordinate to C
R9	racial domination	C9	property owners	Con 9	R is periodically dominant over C
R10	racial classification	C10	occupations	Con10	R is structurally dominant over C

represents Con 9. A second proposition is that race is structurally subordinate to class in twentieth century industrial capitalism, Con 8. The thesis of structural subordination is based on premises on the roles of rationality and market forces in economic life.

1. The operation of modern capitalist enterprises and the racial allocation of rewards are incompatible because such allocation contravenes a fundamental capitalist principle of rationality.
2. The exigencies of markets must ultimately overwhelm racial considerations.

In repudiating these propositions, critics merely invoke Con 10, race (racism) is structurally dominant over class (labor policies) in modern industrial capitalism, and Con 2, racial discrimination can be a rational a means of increasing the rate of profit.

Disputes necessarily erupt over the relationship between racial and class processes. However, they cannot be resolved logically, for the disputants claim to be observing social reality. Within a definition of race based on skin color, facial form, and hair type, one may, by simple correlation, observe racial socioeconomic stratification. However, this "racial reality" may be conceived as class stratification, or as an ideologically disguised form of class stratification. Thus, many perceptions of social reality emerge. Hundreds of graduate theses and scholarly papers could be developed from the intersection of race and class. Indeed, an infinite number of revelations about race and class must be expected precisely because race and class are mutually (in)eligible suitors.

MATERIALIST ANALYSES OF A BLACK EXPERIENCE

Given the multiple variations in the Marxian conception of class, to claim an explanation as class or "Marxist" would be to invite further controversy. Not all references to class or economic and class factors deserve or suggest a Marxist approach. However, two propositions, which express clear links with Marx's historical materialism remain influential in race-class analyses:

1. Being determines consciousness.
2. In the investigation of social processes, attention must first be paid to the economic interests underlying action and policies.

These propositions form the core of materialist analyses of race relations. One such analysis is exemplified in Cox's *Caste, Class and Race*, which locates racism in capitalist and imperialist exploitation of "black labor." *Caste, Class and Race* is generally taken to be a Marxist analysis, although Cox himself disclaims this status.[49] Racism, as a belief, is conceived as a rationalization, or an ideological spin-off from past conditions of exploitation. As policies and action, it is an instrument for profit maximization, or a device for the destruction of working-class solidarity. Its instrumental and contingent status implies it should not be the point of departure for the study of race relations.

In a materialist analysis of race relations, racial phenomena are regarded as secondary, and expedient. Racial differentiations are said to be reflections of underlying economic relations. Racist beliefs are not the cause of racial inequality; they are ideological forms specific to capitalist development. In Dennis Forsythe's words: " 'Color' and 'race' are thus significant primarily in their symbolic form, as a means of facilitating the process of capitalist exploitation against a particular group. Race is a powerful symbol, but like all symbolic definitions it is secondary, not a primary reality."[50] Racial antagonisms should be interpreted as forms of struggle over scarce resources, especially employment and higher wages. This type of analysis surfaces in "split labor market theory," which subsumes racial antagonisms under class conflict by conceiving them as integral to capitalist exploitation.[51]

Split labor market theory presents a variant of a materialist analysis; it makes no claim of a Marxist status but adheres to a bipolar conception of class and treats racial antagonisms as a by-product of capitalist relations of production. The socioeconomic conditions facing black workers are said to be a product of intraworking class antagonisms brought about by global capitalist exploitation. All wage laborers are exploited by the capitalist class. Historically different patterns of recruitment, however, generate different levels of remuneration, intense labor competition, and various forms of exclusion by high-priced labor of cheap labor. The global struggle between capital and labor randomly displaces workers from different sectors and regions and fosters labor migration. This migrant labor, however, constitutes a threat to the job security and wage level of indigenous workers. The racial terms expressed during the struggles over access to jobs are culturally or ideologically specific accompaniments of labor competition.

Given the conflict between capital and labor, competition between indigenous and displaced workers is unavoidable. Depending on their volume and level of desperation, displaced workers represent cheaper labor. Hence, they are confronted with protectionist strategies from the established labor force. This protectionism, however, is aimed at preventing employers from utilizing the oversupply of labor. While it harms the immigrant workers, their employment would have led to lower wages and unemployment among the indigenous workers, and a weakening of their organization. Protectionism and trade union discrimination against incoming workers often escalate into violent conflicts in which racial and ethnic categories are voiced. But the core conditions of labor displacement and labor competition must be borne in mind, and they themselves are the result of the exigencies of capitalist accumulation, the evolution of imperialism, and the creation of a third world pregnant with reservoirs of surplus laborers. Split labor market theory, then, implicitly discards the racial classification of political economic processes. However, this does not make it a "Marxist" approach to racial and ethnic relations.

Advocates of a materialist analysis claim differences from orthodox racial explanations, for they seek to ground racial experiences in an economic structure or in political economic relations. Conflicts and antagonisms between black and white workers are regarded as politically and economically conditioned, not a product of racial preconceptions. Indeed, such preconceptions are themselves deemed contingent on economic relations. In *Racism and Migrant Labour*, sociologist Robert Miles argues that relations between nineteenth-century "white" Irish and English workers were racialized, for the Irish were referred to as a distinct race and ascribed a variety of deviant attributes.[52] Miles concludes that racist expressions can emerge even when there are no significant phenotypical differences among workers. Contemporary white working class racism is similar to ethnic and nationalist opposition to the incursions of migrant laborers.

The materialist approach suffers similar philosophical weaknesses as in Marxist analyses. Racism is not recognized as an object or problem peculiar to a racial theory of society. Rather, it is assumed to be part of social reality, of which theorists can offer different interpretations. As a result of this failure to distinguish between problems that are unique to a given theoretical structure, theories and their problems become supplementary and explanations of (racial) problems inferior or superior, according to the level of emphasis on the economic factor. In consequence, materialist explanations mirror their alleged opposites and give rise to an inconclusive prolongation of idealist and materialist exchanges over "race relations."

An "idealist" analysis could claim that political economic relations are shaped by racial beliefs; that the relegation of black workers to the secondary and tertiary labor markets is an expression of deeply rooted ideological legacies of slavery and colonialism; that through intermarriage, successive generations of Irish workers could successfully be integrated into English society; that English beliefs about blacks and the Irish are incomparable; and that any comparison between white ethnic and black experiences thoroughly misunderstands the force of Negrophobia in white culture, politics, and history. These are plausible propositions, given the endorsement of racial classification, and a materialist-idealist stalemate necessarily results.

Second, political economic explanations of black workers' experiences contain no clear definitions of black and white workers or justification why the categories racism and racial antagonisms should be retained. The thesis that relations between races necessarily unfold within political economic processes is compatible with conclusions reached in "the sociology of race relations." This sociology cannot be accused of ignoring economics, or class, for its conflict version is indistinguishable from a materialist analysis of race relations. The latter would be directed at the political economic conditions and relations that give rise to, or become, race problems. A conflict sociological analysis deals with racial problems as they manifest themselves at economic, political, and cultural levels. Both analyses retain the concept of racial problems.

Idealist and materialist analyses of race relations are enjoined within the proposition that race relations are observable, concrete, empirical phenomena. Concepts are being used merely to record and account for racial experiences and conditions. References to the real world, however, cannot settle disputes over the nature of the real world. The so-called real world is being observed by theorists who already hold different perceptions, select different facts, and interpret data differently. No argument, then, can be refuted. Any account of the real world is as good as any other.

Other criticisms may be made of materialist analyses of racial experiences that seek to displace a causal emphasis on racism. First, it is not ascertained that racism is a mere post-hoc factor and not a motivating force. Any demonstration that political economic relations, not racist beliefs, are causally effective has to be inconclusive. It can be argued that a racist belief is not rendered inoperative by the presence of another (economic) belief. Second, it is not clear why the political economic explanation is considered an explanation of *racial* and not of economic relations. Finally, once racial antagonisms are conceded as a reality, they cannot be reduced to ideological and political economic relations, for it is equally plausible to assert, as sociologist Sidney Willhelm does, that economic considerations are subordinate to "genocidal" racist goals.[53] If political economy can be used to explain racism, why cannot racism be used to explain political economy? The answer may be: because being determines consciousness. But any characterization of persons as whites and blacks and discussion of their relations within a political economic framework imply that "being" is "racial."

MARXISM AND RACE RELATIONS

Discussions of the relevance of Marxism to race relations have produced polarized bodies of writings. One claim is that Marxism is intrinsically unable to account for racism and racial conflicts, for it is an economistic doctrine whose point of departure is class interests and modes of production.[54] One of the expressions of its failure is discernible in dogmatic Marxist impositions of class definitions on the black experience and Marxist denials of the actuality of racial phenomena by invoking "false consciousness." As Leo Kuper protests: "Perhaps it is class consciousness which is the expression of false consciousness, obscuring the reality of the racial struggle."[55] Kuper and other critics argue that Marxism also fails at the political level, because it cannot recognize the presence and viability of racial identities and organization within the working class. Sociologically, Marxism is a failure in that it underestimates the pervasiveness of racism. Racism is not a mere rationalization, or reflex, but an autonomous historical catalyst of policies and behavior. An emphasis on economics or class merely distorts the historical picture of racial oppression. Racial differentiations and racial experiences go beyond class relations. Marxist theory, with its built-in class approach, is therefore inapplicable to race relations and racial problems.

Certain raised but unresolved philosophical issues lurk behind discussions over the relevance/irrelevance of Marxism to race relations. First, which class or economic analysis is to be characterized as a Marxist exposition? For example, references to exploitation, class, and ideology in Cox's *Caste, Race and Class* have earned the author a Marxist reputation. But this has been challenged, and the doubts raised about the Marxist status of "economistic" analyses have given rise to claims of many different Marxisms, even within Marx's writings.[56] Which Marxism is to be selected as a test case of the issue of Marxism's applicability to race relations? What are the criteria of an adequate explanation of problems whose racial description is itself questionable? Are race relations so conceptualized as to render any explanation inadequate? Finally, are the classifications used within racial and Marxist theories of social relations commensurate? That is to say, *should* Marxism be asked or used to explain (which conception of) racial experiences?

The claim that Marxist theory is inapplicable to race relations problems is a double-edged indictment. It may be that race relations problems are a flawed classification of social problems. They are often defined ambiguously, as racially prejudiced behavior, racial deprivation, racial tension, racial conflict, and racism. No social theory can adequately explain vaguely formulated conditions, and the concept of race relations lacks stable referents. Many types of "black experiences" have been discovered, and the force of the impact of racism on some experiences is deemed marginal. However, racism itself refers to a variety of entities: a belief system or ideology, discriminatory policies and behavior, theories of genetic inferiority, and socioeconomic inequality. Which of these is Marxism called upon to explain? Indeed, which Marxism is to be called upon?

Sociologist Stuart Hall provides an illuminating analysis of the tensions in Marxist analyses of race relations.[57] According to a certain Marxist tendency, Marxism is a social theory that emphasizes the decisiveness of economic factors in behavior and social change. Race is a mere epiphenomenon, an ideological smokescreen deliberately constructed to obscure and facilitate the exploitation of the working class as a whole. Race consciousness is a form of false consciousness devised to divide the working class or a reflex of capitalist exploitation. Racial antagonisms are "a distorted form of class struggle." Another Marxist tendency proposes, however, that racial problems are not reducible to objective economic positions and falsely conceived interests. Societies may be said to be racially structured insofar as economic interests are sacrificed in order to preserve uneconomic racial positions. Oppression necessarily takes place within both ideological and economic contexts. A Marxism sensitive to plural structures of dominance provides a more sophisticated explanation of distinctive racial formations than the idealist exaggeration of racism or the mechanical materialist reduction of all social processes to economics.

One Marxist tendency derives from a conceptualization of Marxism as an economic analysis in which racism is a merely symbolic phenomenon. Another posits an "overdetermination" or an interaction between base and superstructure in which cultural and ideological elements are relatively autonomous. This tendency underlies the conception of racism as an autonomous ideology that politically mobilizes actors and lives on in the bowels of social systems. Struggles by oppressed black workers are justified and require a separate platform from class struggles.[58] A second implication is that racial divisions and inequalities are not eradicable at a stroke of socialist revolution. Indeed, attempts at their eradication should take primacy over the abolition of class differences, because the dominated races are the real packhorses of capitalist society. These differences within Marxist writings on race relations further invalidate the idea of Marxism as a theoretically homogeneous system. Thus, the classification of certain arguments on race relations as Marxist merely intensifies a controversy over the essence of Marxism.

Stuart Hall's defense of a Gramscian Marxist integration of race and class reformulates Oliver Cox's propositions. Race relations become racial struggles, which are conceptualized as inverted forms of class struggle. Hall writes: "Race is . . . the modality in which class is 'lived,' the medium through which class relations are experienced, the form in which it is appropriated and 'fought through'."[59] This formulation, like the notion of class fractions, implies a definition of class as a self-mutating Hegelian Spirit. Class is not only omnipresent, its chameleon essence makes it interchangeable with race. Indeed, race could be replaced with class without affecting the plausibility, or implausibility, of Hall's remark — "Class is . . . the modality in which race is 'lived,' the medium through which race relations are experienced, the form in which it is appropriated and 'fought through'."

Any form of class struggle in a racially described society can be conceived as a racial struggle, and vice versa. A strike by white workers in protest against equal wages for black workers can be conceived as either or both a racial and a class struggle. Nevertheless, if class cannot be reduced to economics, it cannot be reduced to race either. "Reductionism" can be avoided only when racial and class analyses are recognized as asymmetrical investigations. A social phenomenon can be conceived as a class issue or a race issue, not as a race *and* a class issue, or a race-class issue.

No particular conception of class may be deemed superior because of a closeness to Marx's "meaning." Neither Marxism nor Marx's writings on class represent a coherent analytical system. Indeed, given the derivative status of Marxism, there can be as many Marxisms as there are interpretations of Marx's writings. Thus, the resolution of the contrasting claims on Marxism's relevance to race relations demands, at least, a specification of the particular Marxism in operation and an analysis of the problem of incommensurability. The charge that Marxism is inadequate with respect to racial problems involves the question of whether a theory's adequacy depends on its applicability to problems and data generated by another theory. Any evaluation of Marxism vis-à-vis race relations must demonstrate a logical entailment between racial problems and Marx's analysis of social change. Such a demonstration, however, would confront intractable logical difficulties.

The racial theory identifies blacks and whites. Whatever its internal weaknesses, Marx's analysis of historical transformations and capitalism focuses on *class* relations. The racial attributes of classes are not considered significant. Frank Parkin's comments are relevant:

> Notions such as the mode of production make their claims to explanatory power precisely on the grounds of their indifference to the nature of the human material whose activities they determine. To introduce questions such as the ethnic composition of the workplace is to clutter up the analysis by laying stress upon the quality of social actors, a conception diametrically opposed to the notion of human agents as träger or "embodiments" of systemic forces.[60]

A class analysis categorizes populations according to economic, not anatomical, attributes. In such an analysis, references to anatomical attributes can be only incidental; they can be removed without altering the conclusions in the analysis. By contrast, a racial theory embodies a racial classification of populations and social problems. In order for Marx's analysis to be accused of not being able to explain race relations problems, it must be demonstrated that his analysis can generate racially problematic situations (problems of racial exploitation, racial conflict, and racial oppression).

Even if it is demonstrated that some of Marx's arguments, explicitly or implicitly, lend themselves to the understanding of race relations problems, this would not constitute a Marxist explanation of race relations, or proof of Marxism's relevance to race. Such a Marxism could be repudiated by another Marxism, or the explanation could be deemed not Marxist but materialist, or the race relations problems would have to be redesignated as class problems.

The rivalry between racial and class theories suggests that social theories are differentiated by their classificatory criteria. Whatever the logical flaws in the construction and deployment of classifications such as capitalist and working class, class analyses of social relations cannot advance a notion of racial motivations. The compulsion of the capitalist class to accumulate capital is deduced from postulated laws of economic competition. The working class is protectionist because of a perceived economic threat, not by virtue of racial or national differences. As Marx writes: "The essential condition for the existence and for the sway of the bourgeois class is the formation and augmentation of capital; the condition of capital is wage labor. Wage labor rests exclusively on competition between the labourers."[61] This competition is not racially interpreted, although a national description is used to demonstrate how labor competition obscures the perception of common interests. Marx notes: "Every industrial and commercial center in England now possesses a working class divided into two hostile camps, English proletarians and Irish proletarians. The ordinary English worker hates the Irish worker as a competitor who lowers his standard of life."[62] It is not the "Irishness" of the worker that generates mutually hostile images but labor competition, a feature of wage labor. Marx's analysis does not refer to racial and ethnic antagonisms but to intra-working class competition. It does not accord a "reality" to the racial nature of the slurs hurled at the Irish workers; its object of study is the labor competition that results from "the condition of capital" — wage labor. The alleged failure of Marxist theory to explain race relations derives from an analytical irreducibility between racial and class theories of social change. Marxist political economy need not and cannot explain race relations.

Marx's *Capital* is admittedly pregnant with unresolved issues, such as the relationship between structure and human agency; the genesis of capitalist production; the concepts of tendencies; productive and unproductive labor; and the relationship between value and price. However, what is clear is that the concept of wage labor represents a condition of selling labor power; it implies a labor market that is not amenable to racial qualifications and subdivisions. Concepts such as

the qualitative development of social sciences nor the diminution of racial (class) oppression. Marxism should not explain race relations problems. The idea of Marxism itself needs to be discarded. Class must also be jettisoned, for it is as unfalsifiable as the classification race relations is incoherent.

The common defense against the charge that a class analysis is incapable of explaining race relations or racism is a redefinition of class to accommodate "black workers." The defense against the criticism that race relations are unidentifiable by virtue of the unintelligibility of racial classification is the claim that race is a social reality. Such defenses however, expose philosophical weaknesses in both class and racial theories. If race relations — that is, racial inequality, exclusion, and oppression — are a reality that is reflected or grasped by theories, then it is understandable that "Marxists," materialists, and class analysts pursue their explanation. Once the premise is accepted that racial divisions exist in the real world, theorists are obliged to offer accounts. Silence would be an admission of irrelevance to the real world. So, Marxist, materialist, and class theorists must intervene in the field of race relations.

These interventions have taken three directions. The first adheres to an objective definition of class and maintains that race relations are an ideological phenomenon. What is not made clear is whether "ideology" means misleading ideas, ideas that are part of a capitalist superstructure, or inactive colonial-imperial intellectual legacies. The second direction is subjectivist and accords race a critical ideological significance in class formation and class configurations. Blacks are considered a superexploited class, or a class fraction. The third road is integrationist in that it seeks to merge subjective and objective conceptions of class into an explanatory scheme that locates racial inequality, racial oppression, and racism in the fractionalization of class consciousness, suggesting that black workers are a racialized fraction of the working class. Few scholars attempt to refute the proposition that racial conditions are "real," or to trace it to a specific epistemological condition in social science. As a result, the disputes over Marxism and race relations produce more deprecatory heat than conclusive light.

In these intellectual exchanges, arguments are not refuted but simply dismissed as reductionist, economistic, mechanical materialist, idealist, and essentialist. These are pejorative descriptions whose appreciation requires a substantial appreciation of the history of philosophy and of Marxism.[65] They are not offered for philosophical enlightenment but as forms of denunciation. Hence, these descriptions cut no ice with the opposition, or they are simply reciprocated. And so the intra-Marxist and materialist disputes grow into various class and Marxist "approaches" and schools of thought on racism, racial inequality, and racial oppression. In this sense, the outstanding virtue of "Marxist," political economic, and class analyses of racial experiences and conditions is their demonstration that class and racial classification belong to divergent social theories. Class can explain only relations defined in terms of relations to the means of production, the economic structure, and economic interests — just as biological deficiencies and racism are explanations of racial relations. The attempts to combine the categories of these mutually exclusive theories necessarily result in a proliferation of inconclusive analyses. The results are inconclusive because, in their combination, no definitive explanatory significance can be attributed to either race or class.

The refusal to abandon race relations as an object of study suggests a particular philosophical presence in social studies: the proposition that these relations are "real." This postulate denotes that social sciences emerged from philosophy's concern with the nature of "reality" and from a particular conception of knowledge in which thought and theories are said to reflect the real world. Thus, social scientific theories are constructed to grasp real experiences and are regarded as mirrors of the social world. Idealist-materialist controversies necessarily erupt over the explanation of these experiences, because social reality comprises actors with their subjective attributes as well as material conditions. Are racial experiences to be explained with reference to a material basis, the capitalist mode of production, or to an ideological element, racist beliefs, structure, or culture, or structure and culture? This question raises the more profound philosophical dispute between idealism and materialism. But insofar as social scientists do not analyze the philosophical roots of their disciplines and disputes, their exchanges are bound to remain at the level of dogmatic assertions and mutual denunciation. For example, the race relations approach that focuses on beliefs and culture is deemed "ideological," while an emphasis on the economy as the ultimate locus of racial problems is considered "mechanical materialist." But any suggestion of an autonomous racial ideology invites the charge of idealism, and an integration of ideology and economics runs into the complexities of the base-superstructure distinction in Marx's *Preface to a Contribution to the Critique of Political Economy.*[66] Marxist studies of race relations lead to nothing but perpetual reformulations of Marxism, class, and race relations. The "real world" does not become more knowable.

WEBERIAN RACE-CLASS ANALYSES

A class approach to race relations does not suggest the presence of Marxism, for the class concept is not a monopoly of either Marx or Marxists. Indeed, in studies of stratification, Max Weber's writings on class and status hold a more seminal position than Marx's. Weber identifies classes and class fractions based on ownership of property, productive facilities, services, and marketable skills. This focus on productive attributes allows the construction of a variety of classes and class situations: property classes, commercial classes, social class, class types, class status, and class situations.[67] In Weber's writings, social change is analyzed within a triadic conception of stratification — class, status, and power. Each dimension of stratification is located in related but autonomous economic, status, and political orders. Thus, similarities in economic positions lead to class membership, but not necessarily to class identity and action. Weber thereby repudiates Marx's historical materialist scheme, which presents polarized classes self-consciously acting out their interests throughout history.

One of Weber's basic propositions is that class, status, and political mobilization are segmented and differentiated elements of economic and social organization. The relations of production generate classes, but relations of distribution, or consumption, are also formative of groups that have been left unexplored in Marx's writings on class. As Weber writes: "With some oversimplification one might say that 'classes' are stratified according to their relations to production and acquisition of goods, whereas 'status groups' are stratified according to their relations to the principles of their consumption of goods as represented by special styles of life."[68] Modern industrial society is said to contain complex and interrelated class and status systems. Both systems are populated by disparate groups that reflect ownership of marketable skills and qualitative and quantitative differences in the consumption of specific goods. Class and status, however, are asymmetrically related, because income disparities as well as educational attributes, honorific possessions, and occupations all measure social esteem. Class position, on the other hand, is defined by control over consumer goods and marketable skills. Class is economically determined, while status reflects a positive or negative social estimation of honor. The status system and status groups constitute not a polarization of society but a gradation of positions determined by a variety of symbols to which prestige is attached. Weber was concerned to demonstrate the autonomy of the status system in relation to the economic and political orders. Class and political organization are often contiguous but essentially parallel facets of power. Mere economic power or wealth is no guarantee of social honor or political office. Indeed, the opposite has often been the case.

Weber's second major focus is on differences within the two main social classes defined according to their relations to the means of production. Entrepreneurs represent a positively privileged group, an upper class. The propertyless, or negatively privileged social class is subdivided into a variety of occupational segments on the basis of different levels of marketable skills and the income accruing from the sale of these skills. The result is a tripartite division into upper, middle, and lower classes that may be further subdivided.

Modern sociologists invariably utilize Weberian criteria of classification to generate notions of white-collar (professionals, managers, technical experts, minor entrepreneurs, clerical, service, and sales occupations) and blue-collar workers (skilled and semiskilled workers, factory floor workers), and a lower class (unskilled laborers, entry-level positions). Do these job-type patterns themselves constitute classes, or should income and education also be considered? In *The*

New Black Middle Class, sociologist Bart Landry presents some of the difficulties involved in choosing among skills *and* education, occupation, income, and education to define class and deciding whether skills and education are sources, or consequences, of class position. He writes: "From a Weberian point of view, education is a cause or source of an individual's class position rather than a defining characteristic, and income is one of the many rewards resulting from one's class position. Neither income nor education, therefore, are part of the definition of class."[69] Income may be an index of class position, but it is a function of occupation that is, in turn, generally commensurate with education and skills possessed.

Classified according to income, an innumerable number of class segments can be discovered among the middle class or middle classes. The upper and lower limits of income classes must be definitive but can only be arbitrary. Moreover, income levels are not symmetrical with education or occupation. Some comparatively uneducated persons are in extremely high income brackets in media, entertainment, and sports. The qualifications and incomes of public school teachers vary enormously from state to state. The same may be said of the incomes of managers, secretaries, and taxicab drivers. Income alone cannot define class. However, it is testimony to the difficulties involved in classifying individuals that Landry cannot sustain his rejection of income as a defining feature of class. He writes: "However, the concept of class does not rest so much on the development of an infallible list of occupations for each class as on the existence of overall, gross differences in the real economic rewards received by individuals in different occupational groups."[70] These difficulties plague the identification of the "middle class," which is, therefore not a particularly useful classification; its popularity is in inverse relation to its coherence, and this should be borne in mind in considering notions of the black middle class, the new black middle class, and black middle classes.

In *The Declining Significance of Race*, William J. Wilson uses both Marxian and Weberian criteria of class stratification. According to Wilson's analysis, race and class are complementary in the sense that racial ideologies and the class structure operate serially and create separate contours of racial experiences. Wilson does not reject the "objective" Marxian definition of class. Rather, he suggests that this bipolar model of class (as expressed in split labor market theory) *and* the multilayered Weberian conception of class are periodically applicable to the understanding of the black experience. The bipolar Marxian model fits the early, preindustrial period of crass labor exploitation. On the other hand, the Weberian conception of class is more relevant to contemporary industrial society where race is of "declining significance" and class of increasing pertinence to the understanding of the patterns of urban social differentiation.

The evidence of this declining significance of race is seen in differentiations among urban blacks in spheres of occupation, income, place of residence, education, and life-style. This differentiation testifies to the growing significance of class in modern urban America. Hence, a pure race or class approach cannot capture the changing face and fate of black America. Race and class concepts must, therefore, be combined to illuminate the shifting features of race relations.

Wilson's race-class analysis does not counterpose race and class or subordinate one to the other. Rather, it serially applies Marxian and Weberian conceptions of class and a thesis of an incompatibility between industrialism and a racial division of labor to the black experience. Race is not deemed irrelevant, but of periodically diminishing operational significance. This dynamic integration of economic and ideological developments appears to forestall the accusations of idealism and economism that are generally leveled at the racism and the class explanations, respectively. What it represents, however, is an elaboration of the racial theory of society that includes a play on various meanings of race, racism, and class.

Wilson argues that the force of "race" — by innuendo, racist motives — diminishes in the modern industrial period. This argument is substantiated by an unstated thesis that industrialism is incompatible with racial discrimination. Some blacks will necessarily be incorporated into the developing industrial economy. Capitalism cannot tolerate the waste of human resources caused by racial discrimination. Those blacks who are not being incorporated are victims either of global competition or of deficient welfare, educational, and training policies. In other words, they are an "underclass" that is being ejected by economic forces and by government and corporate policies that are not keeping pace with changes in the world economy. The race of these casualties is not significant, and the remedies should, therefore, not be race-specific. Rather, public policies should focus on those minorities that vegetate on the periphery of the crisis-torn urban economy, as victims of America's deindustrialization.

Wilson claims that, whatever its ideological magnitude, race alone cannot explain the complex vicissitudes of the black experience. A single ideological instance explains social processes only at the risk of vast oversimplification. There is no iron law of race. Racism cannot be immune to the exigencies of the economy and the changing contours of urban political economies. The understanding of certain modern developments, specifically class stratification within the African-American population, and the worsening position of the underclass require a focus on racist discrimination, cultural legacies in the African-American community, and America's post-Vietnam deindustrialization. No single factor explains the whole panorama of black experiences, but if emphasis is to be placed anywhere it should be on the structural dynamics of urban America.

The operation of structural forces in contemporary U.S. society is evident in educational, income, and cultural differences among blacks and the increasing socioeconomic gaps between the black elite and the black underclass. These are class cleavages, and they cannot be ignored. As Wilson defines class: "Class means any group of people who have more or less similar goods, services, or skills to offer for income in a given economic order and who therefore receive similar financial remuneration in the market place."[71] Citing evidence of varying levels of remuneration and life-styles among blacks, Wilson argues that "a preoccupation with race and racial conflict obscures fundamental problems that derive from the intersection of race with class."[72] The demonstration of this intersection is organized around the proposition that the black postbellum experience comprises shifting patterns of racial and class oppression. The total black experience takes shape within three stages of race relations — preindustrial, industrial, and modern industrial. These stages are characterized by a progressive transition from blatant racial oppression, to racial-class oppression and class subordination. However, because the criteria of demarcation between racial and class subordination are not presented, this periodization is obscure. Hence, it may be asked whether it is a case of the black experience being periodized or of different interpretations of events. Both enslavement and postbellum subordination may be interpreted as class exploitation and class oppression. Race, it may be claimed, has always been *insignificant*. Profit and privilege were the fundamental objectives that were to be achieved at any cost. Loudly proclaimed racial defamations were designed to render these goals morally justified, and the racial laws were established to augment them.

In Wilson's analysis, the significance of race declines in the modern industrial period. Some blacks are dramatically improving their market situation. Those who are being held back are victims of the competitive rigors of modern industrialism. This thesis of a periodic transcendence of race by class rests on a distinction between racial and class oppression, a distinction central to the coherence of the propositions that race is of declining significance and that class oppression now supersedes racial exploitation. Wilson's analysis does not investigate the conceptual ramifications of race and class because such an investigation would demonstrate that his propositions derive from consecutive applications of racial and class theories, not from the nature of past and present social conditions. The alleged decline in the significance of race is the result of a change in interpretation of events.

Slavery has been interpreted as blatant racial oppression. Modern capitalism may be said to revolve around economic class exploitation. However, slavery may also be characterized in Marxian and Weberian class terms. As owners of relatively vast amounts of commodities and recipients of a distinct quantity of money not derived from their own labor, the slave owners represented a class. The total "free" population was also differentiated by levels of skills, income, and ownership of land. Although Weber utilizes concepts of free and unfree labor to distinguish between capitalist and slave modes of labor exploitation, there are reasons to conceive of the South's plantations as capitalist enterprises.[73]

Was there not class stratification in preindustrial America? Some historians point to class and status differences among antebellum blacks who were stratified into colored freedmen, urban slaves, house slaves, and field hands, as well as imported, indigenous, male, and female.[74] Patterns of socioeconomic differentiation existed among persons classified as blacks throughout the late nineteenth-century industrialization and both world wars. There have always been "aristocracies of color." Social differentiation among African Americans, then, is not a distinctly modern development. It therefore cannot be used to demonstrate a declining significance of race.

Perhaps the cardinal weakness in *The Declining Significance of Race* is the equivocation surrounding the term racism. It is not defined, but a racist ideology is deemed both inoperative and pervasive in the modern industrial period. If race is taken to mean racism, which racism, it may be asked, has declined? Many kinds of racism permeate the race relations literature — corporate, individual, institutional, cultural, symbolic, intrinsic, extrinsic, white, black, economic, and accommodationist. Wilson's overall thesis would have been strengthened by clarification of key concepts such as industrialism, race, and racism.

The absence of a definition of racism and an ambiguous equation of race and racism prevent the construction of viable evidence of racism's declining significance. In order to substantiate this proposition, it would be necessary to demonstrate not just the emergence of class competition but the ineffectiveness of racist motives, not mere gains from black political agitation but a white change of heart. Wilson admits to the omnipresence of a racist ideology in American society. This ideology, however, he declares impotent by simply asserting the triumph of industrialism and class over race. However, Wilson's analysis does not demonstrate that racism and industrialism are necessarily incompatible. An empirical correlation between industrialization and diminishing racial discrimination is not evidence of a causal connection. Critics will capitalize on this error.

Wilson's analysis repudiates the idea of blacks as an homogeneous social entity, diminishes the explanatory value of racism, and denies the effectiveness of race-specific solutions to racial inequality. Thus, not surprisingly, *The Declining Significance of Race* met a deluge of criticisms. Critics claim that racism *has* been a dominant factor throughout U.S. history, that it did not and cannot simply disappear during the twentieth-century period of industrialism. Racism is said to be "enduring" and "inclining," based on evidence of continued discrimination against blacks in the labor, educational, and housing markets. Black progress is a "myth" and an "illusion." A marginalized black middle class may have emerged over the last decade. The vast majority of blacks, however, remain victims of racist economic and social policies. Racism has not declined in significance; it has not even changed its form. Indeed, it is precisely in the modern period that the civil rights movement had to challenge systematic restrictions and obstacles to black socioeconomic progress and to demand affirmative federal government intervention.

Other critics point out that even if market, occupational, income, and residential differentiations among blacks are cited as proof of a black class structure, it may be argued that, in terms of self-identification, voting patterns, social networks, and situational cohesiveness, blacks act as a racial group.[75] On the other hand, Wilson could claim that their actions may be said to be furthering the interests of a specific class within the black community. For example, all classes of blacks support Jesse Jackson by virtue of his incitement to racial solidarity. But Jackson's promises and programs further the interests of the black working class and lower working class that the Democratic Party has abandoned. Class may be said to be dominant over race.

Wilson's arguments have also been met with political denunciation and statistical repudiation. Charles V. Willie writes: "If race is not an appropriate explanation, why is it that whites of limited education are paid one-third more than blacks who are as qualified as they are? . . . Why is it that only 1 out of every 10 whites is poor compared to around 3 out of every 10 blacks?"[76] Some critics not only challenged Wilson's data on black socioeconomic progress but also redeployed the idea of racism as a dynamic force in both corporate and government policies. These responses are to be expected, because Wilson's analysis does not refute the racial explanation of inequality. It concedes that racism remains an operating ideology; it endorses the racial theory, implicit in the racial data, by focusing on blacks, then doubles back and rejects race-specific explanations, research, and solutions. It separates race from class, then seeks to demonstrate their inseparability.

Regarding the intersection of race and class, the critical question is which is which, at the point of intersection? How are race and class to be defined, once they intersect? They must be specified as mutually exclusive, if one's increasing importance automatically diminishes the other's significance. On the other hand, they cannot be mutually exclusive, because blacks, by definition, belong to a race and, by economic fortunes, a class. This dilemma plagues all class-race analyses. It resides, ultimately, in the equivocation surrounding the terms race and class.

Over a decade ago sociologist James Geschwender wrote:

> All black Americans are simultaneously black and members of a particular class. All white Americans are simultaneously white and members of a particular class. There are proportionately more blacks in the proletariat and more whites in the capitalist class, but each racial group is internally differentiated by class and each class is internally differentiated by race.[77]

To all appearances, certain objective anatomical and economic criteria of differentiation define races and classes, respectively. But as testimony to the looseness of these categories, each race is also internally differentiated by race, and each class by class. Hence, Weberian race-class analyses fare no better than Marxian race-class analyses. Both retain race, dissolve race, emphasize the significance of class, and demonstrate the dissipation of class. In effect, competing emphases on race (white racism, racial competition, white power dynamics, and psychological legacies from slavery) and multiple class explanations permeate studies of the black experience. What has rarely been commented on is that, in these studies, a wide variety of black and class experiences have emerged.

The black experience is a conceptualization of certain events through the prism of the racial theory. Its racial status is taken as a "reality," as if the events of enslavement, segregation, and discrimination could be conceptualized only racially. This racial conceptualization ensures that the persons involved in the events are never given a *human* designation. In this sense, the racial theory continues the tradition in the intellectual sphere, of what both so-called whites and blacks actualize: a contradictory denial of their status as human beings.

Studies of race-class relations manifest constant references to an observed, racial social reality. This is the philosophical claim that allows the continuation of these studies. The assumption about the racial nature of the world takes the place of definitions of terms and the establishment of a relation of logical entailment among propositions. For example, blacks and whites are presented as aggregated socioeconomic categories with specific group experiences. However, it must be noticeable that, as in sociologist Ira Katznelson's attempted definition, the idea of a racial group contains some irrepressible logical flaws:

> A racial group is defined by its relationship to other groups and by its potential as well as actual consciousness. . . . the racial group as a collectivity is a meaningful stratification unit whose members share positions, and therefore objective interests, similar vantage points, and a shared consciousness actual or potential.[78]

In order to identify a racial group, "other groups" must be defined, which entails a definition of yet other groups. A shared consciousness is depicted as both actual and potential. The members of a racial group also share objective interests. These are unfalsifiable claims, which means that the social scientists' judgments on the nature of groups are, by definition, irrefutable. Black people and white people are social scientists' constructs that are used to color experiences.

The idea of a black experience is a specific conceptualization of events, for experience is not separable from human reasoning. Philosopher and educational theorist John Dewey echoes Immanuel Kant's proposition that experience is theoretically constructed. He writes: "in a proper conception of experience, inference, reasoning and conceptual structures are as experiential as is observation, and . . . the fixed separation between the former and the latter has no warrant beyond an episode in the history of culture."[79] The analysis of a black experience as a reality is bound to generate contradictions and controversies, because observational means of proving arguments involve an endless invocation of empirical data and, above all, repetition.

In 1965 Senator Daniel P. Moynihan wrote:

> A middle class group has managed to save itself, but for vast numbers of the unskilled, poorly educated city working class the fabric of conventional social relationships has all but disintegrated. . . . There is considerable evidence that the Negro community is in fact dividing between a stable middle-class group that is steadily growing stronger and more successful, and an increasingly disorganized disadvantaged lower-class group.[80]

Almost identical claims were made in 1957, in sociologist E. Franklin Frazier's *Black Bourgeoisie: The Rise of a New Black Middle Class in the United States*.[81] Two decades later William J. Wilson rediscovered a growing black middle class and almost ten years later an increasing impoverishment of a black underclass. By the late 1980s these writings were supplemented by, among others, Bart Landry's findings on "a new black middle class" that is allegedly ailing and not doing as well as the "white middle class." Surely the intellectual energies invested in these repeated discoveries about race and class could be employed more fruitfully elsewhere. It is therefore tempting to discern a conspiracy to racialize. Yet the temptation must be resisted, for what these race-class echoes and reechoes illustrate is the intellectual waste social scientists incur by neglecting their philosophical roots.

The various perspectives on the so-called black experience do not present any sustained analysis of the criteria used to classify persons, events, and situations. This seriously mars their conclusions because culture, for example, has a multitude of definitions and has been conceived as a product of structures. In *The Underclass*, sociologist Ken Auletta insists that the dichotomy between culture and structure is false and unwarranted.[82] But the concept of underclass has itself been subjected to sharp criticisms by Herbert Gans:

> Underclass is a particularly nasty label, however. Earlier terms such as pauper, vagrant, and tramp were openly pejorative, but underclass is a technical-sounding word that hides its pejorative meaning. Moreover,

once people are labelled as underclass they are often treated accordingly. Teachers decide they cannot learn, the police and the courts think that they must be incorrigible, and welfare agencies feel justified in administering harsh policies. Such treatment sets in motion the self-fulfilling prophecy. If the poor are treated like an underclass, their ability to escape poverty is blocked further. In addition, the term is turning into a racial code word, since by now it is increasingly applied solely to blacks.[83]

Labels or classifications are of enormous policy and behavioral significance, but they have not received the scrutiny commensurate with their popularity in social studies. Professor Gans' comments could be extended to racial descriptions. Such descriptions certainly generate specific expectations and orientations toward the persons so described.

The so-called black experience does not represent the collective experience of persons classified as black people, for it is not the experience that is black. Rather, persons are initially classified as black. This classification is then used to denote and even posed as a determinant of, events and life situations. However, given the existence of alternative classifications, there is no iron-clad obligation to conceive experiences as black or white. Take away the racial classification of persons and their experiences cease to be racial. The proposition that persons are racially classifiable underlies the conceptualization of social processes as racially determined. Other theoretical possibilities are, therefore, open. Events such as slavery, jim crowism and lynchings, internment in concentration camps, refusal of entry to America, and relocation to uninhabitable regions may be read as nonracial experiences. They may be interpreted as examples of human non-consideration of the ineffectiveness of violence. The so-called capitalist class, the slave owners, whites, or whatever, were indisputably members of the human species, albeit influenced by certain incoherent and absurd doctrines on social relations. As Voltaire noted: "People who believe in absurdities tend to commit atrocities." Why, then, do social scientists continue to promote the absurdity of racial classification?

BEYOND RACIAL AND CLASS ANALYSES

The development of the racial theory was inspired by a naturalistic approach to social relations. The classification of persons followed patterns established by natural scientists. It was part of a biological explanation of regional disparities in economic development and civilizations. Biological scientists pursued a natural source of different patterns of culture, achievements, and inequalities among human societies. Thus, the human species was divided into hierarchical biological units in order to explain social divisions. This explanation contains an arbitrary moral judgment on social organization. Some societies and civilizations were described as unequal by virtue of the racial attributes of their members. Subsequent social studies, however, claimed that racial attributes are as likely an explanation of different patterns of consumption and achievement as class or culture. Each of these terms, then, must be rigorously defined, if the explanations are to be mutually exclusive, and if some analytic guidelines are to be established.

Most sociological analyses of race relations admit to the fictitious nature of racial classification, then go on to claim that "social reality" contains intertwining racial, cultural, and class elements and separate, intersect, and combine them at random. But it is not clear whether the combining of race and class explains: (1) racial problems — racial conflict and racial discrimination, (2) a uniform socioeconomic situation of African Americans, (3) the socioeconomic conditions of certain African Americans, or (4) general economic conditions as they affect African Americans.

In the first case, class is inapplicable because the problems are a priori defined as racial. In the second case, the implicit racial causation also nullifies the relevance of class. Secondly, socioeconomic differentiations among African Americans, as in the third case, render racial causation inadmissible. Finally, a demonstration of how general economic conditions particularly affect African Americans constitutes a race-class analysis only if the effects are racially uniform. That is to say, no persons classified as whites must be similarly affected.

The analytical problems in race-class combinations reflect a significant neglect of the discussions among philosophers on the concepts of reality, explanation, and experience. Racial studies are at a standstill.

The same questions are discussed over and over: Are races and classes to be defined subjectively or objectively? Are African Americans a social race, if they are not purposefully organized to realize their interests? Are such interests racial or class, as they represent a challenge to the class structure? Given the variety of black experiences, does not the idea of *a* black experience entail a stereotyping of the persons classified as blacks? These issues cannot be answered adequately without greater attention to the philosophical context of social studies.

Race-class combinations are not a novelty. The founding father of the sociology of race relations, Robert Park, struggled unsuccessfully with different definitions of race relations, did not define the term class, but predicted that class would ultimately transcend race.[84] Critics of a class analysis, however, claim the preeminence of race by pointing to evidence of chronic racial discrimination and structures of racial inequality. These instances are said to prove the durability, if not the ineradicability, of race and racism. However, such evidence can itself be given class and race-class explanations. Clearly, unless social studies become more sensitive to logical rules and conceptual analysis, cycles of race-class analyses will eternally haunt "whites" and "blacks."

Up to the early 1990s the proliferation of race-class analyses continued, despite their ambiguities and contradictions. The logical flaws in classifications by anatomy and economy are tolerated for want of attention to the philosophical elements in racial and class theories of society. The construction of an alternative social theory, then, requires the refutation of certain influential components of the intellectual environment, such as the Hobbesian conception of human nature, both neoclassical and Keynesian recommendations for economic stability and growth, and the distinction between the empirical and the theoretical. These tasks would involve a thorough philosophical reconstruction of social sciences. But philosophy has virtually disappeared from schooling, including the schooling of social scientists. It is, therefore, not surprising that theorists, whose avowed goals are social renewal and ameliorative transformations, doggedly cling to the flawed legacies of race and class.

A substantial number of physical anthropologists and social scientists have deemed the concept of race fallacious, unscientific, ideological, mythical, and political. Categories such as black, brown, and white people belong to the Stone Age of social sciences. Some social scientists, however, continue to ply the population with the idea of belonging to different races and cultures on the grounds that citizens regard themselves as different. Is there no relationship between what social scientists do and how people regard themselves? The study of race relations continues a tradition of concern with differences rather than similarities. The self-serving consequences of this selective propagation of differences are not being considered. But a glance at "nature" might indicate why racial classification and studies of race relations should be terminated.

If "nature" is perceived as different from "us," it is easy to approach "her" as an object for exploitation by us. Hence, an essential "man"–nature separation is implicit in policies that destroy the environment. The notion of essential differentiation is easily transferred to all species and to variations within the human species. Unity and cooperation with other beings cannot be sought after. Modes of economic organization will be founded on observations of differences and the desirability of competition between individuals and groups. We do not seek to give to, but rather trade with, those defined as different. Adam Smith's naturally competitive "traders" and "truckers" are rooted in a similar philosophical anthropology as Marx's conflicting "bourgeoisie" and "proletariat."[85] Racial differentiation is part of a powerful intellectual tradition of divide and compete, even unto self-destruction.

The continuing furor over race can be taken as an indication of a recognition that the idea of human beings belonging to races is self-contradictory. A race refers to a conglomerate of *certain* biological attributes possessed by human beings. Their "belonging" to their biological characteristics would be a case of the tail wagging the dog. What, then, is the status of these "social races"? People in "the real world" do define themselves racially. First, if race is an absurdity, it should be pointed out that people are using an absurd classification. Second, a recognition of certain physical differences does not imply a racial identity. Finally, the idea of a "social race" suggests that racial awareness could be generated by inputs from society's institutions. Hence, the citizen's use of race to define the self may reflect formal and informal educational processes, specifically, the absence of instruction in logic in schools, and the information about races propagated by social scientists, governmental institutions, and media. Their practices create social races that are then cited to continue the practices.

The stalemate among competing explanations of racial experiences and race-class combinations signals the demise of racial and class theories of social relations. Indeed, protests against inhuman treatment and violations of human and civil rights suggest a hidden concern for persons as human beings. A human accent is discernible in the opposition to what is called racism and ethnocentrism, as it is claimed that certain elements of the white ethnic, black, Hispanic, Asian Pacific-American, and Native American experiences are not what should be meted out to human beings. These experiences suggest a terrible dehumanization. By implication, they are experiences of human beings; they are being racialized by the usage of the racial theory. Social scientists generally justify this usage with reference to a reality that is itself a product of the dissemination of the racial theory. Nevertheless, if racial consciousness is the source of discrimination and the scourge of human society, racial classification of persons should be abandoned, for it perpetuates the consciousness of difference that underlies "dehumanization."

The recommendation of an alternative, human classification does not imply that problems of material insecurity and violence would disappear. What would be dissolved is their racial classification. Social problems would be classified as human problems, and reasonable attempts could be made at their resolution. Doing so would take human society into uncharted territory, but unless there is a distinct preference for a known hell over Utopia, a human classification should be propagated. White and black people cannot but eventually initiate processes of separation or mutual elimination. In fundamentalist and separatist readings of "history," these processes have already begun and are most welcome. However, if white people, or black people, are thought of as the enemy, it is suicidal to let them know you think they are your enemy. Nietzsche, despite his reputation as a moral nihilist, gladly endorsed the cornerstone of Buddhism, "It is not by enmity that enmity is ended."[86] A declaration of enmity is necessarily reciprocated. Indeed, it may even be internalized to self-destruction. You love yourself a little less not only when you hate another person, but also when you believe you are hated. America needs to formulate and inculcate a paraphrase of Pogo's words: "I have seen the enemy and it is my blackness/whiteness."

The failure of race-class combinations indicates a paradigm shift or two. Racial and class theories are in the throes of an internal dissolution. Their individual classificatory criteria produce various ambiguities, anomalies, arbitrariness, and self-contradictions; their objects of study require conceptual redefinitions and stipulations of exceptions. They had to be combined, but their combinations become innumerable and implausible. The competition among liberationist perspectives furthers more research and presentation of empirical data repudiating and supporting claims of racial progress. Identical moral claims about the fate and the state of races are repeated century after century. No "oppressed" class, underclass, or race is served by this stalemate. If there are apprehensions about discarding class and racial classifications, philosopher A. N. Whitehead's dictum should be recalled: A science that does not forget its founding fathers is surely lost. The racial and class ghosts of Bernier, Blumenbach, Gobineau, Marx, and Weber need no longer haunt the study of social relations.

NOTES

1. As Robert Blauner writes: "In American society races and classes interpenetrate one another. Race affects class formation and class influences racial dynamics in ways that have not yet been adequately analyzed." Robert Blauner, *Racial Oppression in America* (New York: Harper and Row, 1972), pp. 28-29. See also Robert Park, *Race and Culture* (New York: Free Press, 1950), p. 116; O. C. Cox, *Caste, Class and Race: A Study in Social Dynamics* (New York: Monthly Review Press, 1959), Raymond Franklin and Solomon Resnick, *The Political Economy of Racism* (New York: Holt, Rinehart and Winston, 1973); Dennis Forsythe, "Marxism, Blacks and

Radicalism in Sociology: The Necessary Reconciliation," *The Black Sociologist* 7, no. 1 (1977), pp. 14-22; Edna Bonacich, "The Past, Present and Future of Split Labor Market Theory," in C. B. Marrett and Cheryl Leggon (eds.), *Research in Race and Ethnic Relations*, vol. 1 (Greenwood, CT: Jai Press, 1978), pp. 17-64; Edna Bonacich, "Class Approaches to Ethnicity and Race," in Norman Yetman (ed.), *Majority and Minority: The Dynamics of Race and Ethnicity in American Life* (London: Allyn and Bacon, 1985), pp. 62-78; William J. Wilson, *The Declining Significance of Race: Blacks and Changing American Institutions*, (Chicago: Univeristy of Chicago Press, 1978); James A. Geschwender, *Racial Stratification in America* (Dubuque, IA: William C. Brown, 1980); Mario Barrera, *Race and Class in the Southwest: A History of Racial Inequality* (London: University of Notre Dame Press, 1979); Edward H. Ransford, *Race and Class in American Society: Black, Chicano and Anglo* (New York: Schenkman, 1983); Harold Wolpe, "Class Concepts, Class Struggle and Racism," in John Rex and David Mason (eds.), *Theories of Race and Ethnic Relations* (London: Cambridge University Press, 1986), pp. 110-130; Harold Wolpe, *Race, Class and the Apartheid State* (Paris: UNESCO Press, 1988); John Rex, "The Role of Class Analysis in the Study of Race Relations — A Weberian Perspective," in John Rex and David Mason (eds.), *Theories of Race and Ethnic Relations*, pp. 64-83.

2. See Etienne Balibar, "Paradoxes of Universality," in David Goldberg (ed.), *Anatomy of Racism* (Minneapolis, MN: University of Minnesota Press, 1990), pp. 283-294.

3. Solomon and Resnik, *Political Economy*, p. 183.

4. See W. Lloyd Warner, "American Caste and Class," *American Journal of Sociology* 42, no. 2 (September 1936), pp. 234-237; John Dollard, *Caste and Class in a Southern Town* (New York: Doubleday, 1937). Robert Park, *Race*. For a restatement of the position that American "race relations" are not qualitatively different from "castism," see Gerald D. Berreman, "Race, Caste, and Other Invidious Distinctions," in Yetman (ed.), *Majority and Minority*, pp. 21-39; J. V. Ogbu, *Minority Education and Caste: The American System in Cross-Cultural Perspectives* (New York: Academic Press, 1978).

5. Cox, *Caste, Class and Race*.

6. See Reinhard Bendix and Seymour Lipset (eds.), *Class, Status and Power: Social Stratification in Comparative* Perspective (New York: Free Press, 1966); Hans Gerth and C. Wright Mills (eds.), *From Max Weber: Essays in Sociology* (London: Oxford University Press, 1953).

7. Arthur Marwick, *Class: Image and Reality in Britain, France and the U.S.A. Since 1930* (New York: Oxford University Press, 1980), p. 123.

8. James Geschwender, *Racial Stratification*, p. 105.

9. Thomas Kuhn, *The Structure of Scientific Revolutions* (Chicago: University of Chicago Press, 1970), p. 109.

10. See Louis Althusser, *For Marx* (Middlesex: Penguin Books, 1969); Louis Althusser and Etienne Balibar, *Reading Capital* (London: New Left Books, 1970).

11. Wolpe, *Race, Class*, pp. 13-14.

12. Alphonso Pinkney, *The Myth of Black Progress* (London: Cambridge University Press, 1985), p. 17.

13. Franklin and Resnick, *Political Economy*, p. 158.

14. Leo Kuper, *Race, Class and Power: Ideology and Revolutionary Change in Plural Societies* (New York: Aldine, 1975), p. 61.

15. See A. V. Cicourel, *Cognitive Sociology* (New York: Free Press, 1974); Harold Garfinkel, *Studies in Ethnomethodology* (Englewood Cliffs, NJ: Prentice-Hall, 1967), Mary R. Jackman and Mary S. Senter, "Images of Social Groups: Categorical or Qualified," *Public Opinion Quarterly* 44 (Fall 1980), pp. 341-361.

16. Cox, *Caste Class*, p. 336.

17. Pierre L. van Berghe, "Race and Ethnicity: A Sociobiological Perspective," in Norman Yetman (ed.), *Majority and Minority*, p. 54.

18. Percy Cohen, "Need There Be a Sociology of Race Relations?" *Sociology* 6, no. 1 (1972), p. 100.

19. Herbert J. Seligmann, *Race Against Man* (New York: G. P. Putnam's Sons, 1939), p. 18.

20. Michael Banton, "Epistemological Assumptions in the Study of Racial Differentiation," in Rex and Mason, (eds.), *Theories*, p. 49.

21. C. Stephen Fenton, "Race, Class and Politics in the Work of Durkheim," in UNESCO, *Sociological Theories: Race and Colonialism* (Paris: UNESCO, 1980), p. 175 n.

22. See Anthony Giddens, *Capitalism and Modern Social Theory: An Analysis of the Writings of Marx, Durkheim and Max Weber* (Cambridge: Cambridge University Press, 1971); Frank Parkin, *Max Weber* (London: Tavistock, 1982), chapter 4. For an exposition of some differences between Weber and Marx's conceptions of class, see Zbigniew Jordan (ed.), *Karl Marx: Economy, Class and Social Revolution* (London: Nelson, 1971).

23. See A. Przeworski, "Proletariat into Class: The Process of Class Formation from Karl Kautsky's *The Class Struggle* to Recent Controversies," *Politics*

and Society 7, no. 4 (1977), pp. 343-401; Jean L. Cohen, *Class and Civil Society: The Limits of Marxian Critical Theory* (Amherst, MA: University of Massachusetts Press, 1982).

24. Marx writes: "The owners merely of labour-power, owners of capital, and landowners, whose respective sources of income are wages, profit and ground-rent, in other words, wage-labourers, capitalists and landowners constitute then three big classes of modern society based upon the capitalist mode of production." *Capital*, vol. 3 (London: Lawrence and Wishart, 1974), p. 885.

25. Karl Marx and Frederick Engels, *The German Ideology* (London: Lawrence and Wishart, 1965), p. 69.

26. Karl Marx, *The Poverty of Philosophy* (Chicago: Charles Kerr, 1913), p. 189.

27. See George Lukacs, *History and Class Consciousness: Studies in Marxist Dialectics*, trans. Rodney Livingston (Cambridge, MA: MIT Press, 1972); Quintin Hoare and Geoffrey N. Smith (eds.), *Antonio Gramsci, Selections from Prison Notebooks* (New York: International Publishers, 1971).

28. Marx writes, "In so far as there is merely a local interconnection among these small-holding peasants, and the identity of their interests begets no community, no national bond and no political organization among them, they do not form a class." *The Eighteenth Brumaire of Louis Bonaparte* (New York: International Publishers, 1969), p. 124. See also Anthony Giddens, *Capitalism and Social Theory*.

29. See Ian Gough, "Marx's Theory of Productive and Unproductive Labor," *New Left Review* 16 (November-December 1972), pp. 47-72.

30. See Wally Seecombe, "Housework Under Capitalism," *New Left Review*, 83 (January/February 1974), pp. 3-24; Lise Vogel, *Marxism and the Oppression of Women: Toward a Unitary Theory* (New Brunswick, NJ: Rutgers University Press, 1983), part 4. Janet Collins and Martha Giminez (eds.), *Work Without Wages: Domestic Labor and Self-Employment Within Capitalism* (New York: State University of New York Press, 1990).

31. See Gary Becker, *Human Capital: A Theoretical and Empirical Analysis with Special Reference to Education* (Chicago: University of Chicago Press, 1981).

32. For critical analyses, see Charles F. Sabel, "Ambiguities of Class and the Possibility of Politics," in Andre Liebich (ed.), *The Future of Socialism?* (Montreal: Interuniversity Center for European Studies, 1979), pp. 257-279; Frank Parkin, *Marxism and Class Theory: A Bourgeois Critique*

(London: Tavistock, 1979); Allin Cottrell, *Social Classes in Marxist Theory* (New York: Henley and Melbourne, 1984).

33. See E. P. Thompson, *The Making of the English Working Class* (London: Penguin, 1968); V. I. Lenin, *What Is to Be Done* (Moscow: Progress Publishers, 1923); Stanislaw Ossowski, *Class Structure in the Social Consciousness*, trans. Sheila Patterson (London: Routledge and Kegan Paul, 1979).

34. See Karl Kautsky, *The Class Struggle*, trans. William E. Bohm (New York: Norton, 1971); Louis Althusser and Etienne Balibar, *For Marx*; Anthony Cutler, Barry Hindess, Paul Q. Hirst, and Athar Hussain, *Marx's Capital and Capitalism Today*, vol. 1 (London: Routledge and Kegan Paul, 1977).

35. Wolpe, *Race, Class*.

36. Paul Gilroy, "One Nation Under a Groove, the Cultural Politics of Race and Racism in Britain," in David Goldberg (ed.), *Anatomy*, p. 280.

37. See Nicos Poulantzas, *Classes in Contemporary Capitalism* (London: New Left Books, 1975); Erik O. Wright, "Class Boundaries in Advanced Capitalist Societies," *New Left Review* (July-August 1976), pp. 3-41; Erik O. Wright, "Varieties of Marxist Conceptions of Class Structure," *Politics and Society* 9, no. 3 (1980), pp. 323-370.

38. See Steven Lukes, *Power: A Radical View* (London: Macmillan, 1974).

39. Wright, "Varieties," p. 359.

40. John Rex, *Race Relations in Sociological Theory* (London: Weidenfeld and Nicholson, 1983), p. 198.

41. Clifford Geertz, *The Interpretation of Cultures* (New York: Basic Books, 1973), p. 193. See also George Lichtheim, *The Concept of Ideology and Other Essays* (New York: Random House, 1967); John P. Plamenatz, *Ideology* (New York: Praeger, 1970); Ernesto Laclau, *Politics and Ideology in Marxist Thought* (London: New Left Books, 1977); Paul Ricoeur, *Lectures on Ideology and Utopia* (New York: Columbia University Press, 1986); Martin Seliger, *The Marxist Conception of Ideology* (London: Cambridge University Press, 1977).

42. Alain Touraine, *The Self-Production of Society*, trans. Derek Coltman (Chicago: University of Chicago Press, 1977), p. 176.

43. Marx, *Eighteenth Brumaire of Louis Bonaparte*, p. 139. Italics in original.

44. Lenin, *What is to Be Done?*

45. See Herbert Marcuse, *One-Dimensional Man* (Boston: Beacon Press, 1966), and *Essays on Liberation* (Boston: Beacon Press, 1969); Michael Mann, *Consciousness and Action Among the Western Working Class* (London: Macmillan, 1973).

46. See Arun Bose, *Marxian and Post-Marxian Political Economy* (Middlesex: Penguin, 1975). See also Donald J. Harris, "Capitalist Exploitation and Black Labor: Some Conceptual Issues," *The Review of Black Political Economy* 8, no. 2 (Winter 1978), pp. 133-151.

47. Karl Marx, *Capital*, vol. 1 (London: Lawrence and Wishart, 1972), p. 93.

48. See Wilson, *The Declining Significance of Race*; Bart Landry, *The New Black Middle Class* (Berkeley, CA: University of California Press, 1987).

49. See O. C. Cox, *Caste, Class and Race*, p. xii. Some contradictions in Cox's work are exposed in Robert Miles, "Class, Race and Ethnicity: A Critique of Cox's Theory," *Ethnic and Racial Studies* 3, no. 2 (1980), pp. 169-187. For political economic analyses of immigrant or migrant labor which disavow "race relations," see Stephen Castles and Godula Kosack, *Immigrants and the Class Structure in Western Europe* (London: Oxford University Press, 1973); Robert Miles, *Racism and Migrant Labour* (London: Routledge and Kegan Paul, 1982).

50. Forsythe, "Marxism, Blacks and Radicalism," p. 21.

51. See Bonacich, "The Past, Present and Future."

52. See Robert Miles, *Racism and Migrant Labour*, chapter 6. But see also Victor Perlo, *The Economics of Racism* (New York: International Publishers, 1975).

53. See Sidney Willhelm, *Who Needs the Negro?* (Cambridge, MA: Schenkman, 1970).

54. For similar dismissals of Marxist theory, see Ira Katznelson, *Black Men White Cities: Race, Politics and Migration in the United States, 1900-1930 and Britain, 1948-1968* (London: Oxford University Press, 1973), p. 6; Blauner, *Racial Oppression*, p. 13; Frank Parkin, "Social Stratification," in Tom Bottomore and Robert Nisbet (eds.), *A History of Sociological Analysis* (London: Heinemann, 1979); Sidney Willhelm, "Can Marxism Explain America's Racism?" pp. 98-112.

55. Leo Kuper, *Race, Class and Power*, p. 208. See also Frank Parkin, *Marxism and Class: A Bourgeois Critique* (New York: Praeger, 1979).

56. See Alvin Gouldner, *The Two Marxisms* (New York: Seabury Press, 1980); Shlomo Avineri (ed.), *Varieties of Marxism* (The Hague: Martinus Nijhoff, 1977); Alex Callinicos, *Althusser's Marxism* (London: Pluto Press, 1976); Carl Boggs, *Gramsci's Marxism* (London: Pluto Press, 1976); Wilfrid Desan, *The Marxism of Jean-Paul Sartre* (New York: Doubleday, 1965).

57. See Stuart Hall, "Race, Articulation and Societies Structured in Dominance," in UNESCO, *Sociological Theories*, pp. 305-345.

58. Hall writes: "If ethnic relations are not reducible to economic relations, then the former will not change if and when the latter do. Hence, in a political struggle, the former must be given their due specificity and weight as autonomous factors." Ibid., p. 307.

59. Ibid., p. 341.

60. Parkin, "Social Stratification," in Bottomore and Nisbet (eds.), *A History*, p. 625.

61. Karl Marx and Frederick Engels, *Selected Works*, vol. 1 (Moscow: Progress Publishers, 1969), pp. 45-46.

62. Karl Marx and Frederick Engels, *Selected Writings*, edited by David Mc-Clellan (Oxford: Oxford University Press, 1977), p. 591.

63. See Karl Marx, *A Contribution to the Critique of Political Economy* (New York: International Publishers, 1970).

64. See G. A. Cohen, *Marx's Theory of History* (Oxford: Clarendon Press, 1978).

65. See Leszek Kolakowski, *Main Currents of Marxism: Its Rise Growth and Dissolution*, vols 1-3 (London: Oxford University Press, 1978).

66. See Cohen, *Marx's Theory.*

67. Max Weber, *The Theory of Social and Economic Organization, Economy and Society*, vol. 1, trans. A. M. Henderson and Talcott Parsons (New York: Free Press, 1964), pp. 302-310; Max Weber, "Class, Status and Party," in Hans Gerth and C. Wright Mills (eds.), *From Max Weber*, pp. 150-195. See also Dennis Gilbert and Joseph A. Kahl, *The American Class Structure: A New Synthesis* (Homewood, IN: Dorsey Press, 1982).

68. Max Weber, "Class, Status and Party," in Hans Gerth and C. Wright Mills (eds.), *From Max Weber*, p. 193.

69. Landry, *The New Black Middle Class*, p. 5.

70. Ibid., p. 11.

71. Wilson, *The Declining Significance of Race*, p. xx.

72. Ibid.

73. See Max Weber, *General Economic History* (London: Collier Books, 1961). For a detailed analysis of the issue of relationship between slave labor and capitalism, see Robert Miles, *Capitalism and Unfree Labour: Anomaly or Necessity?* (London: Tavistock, 1987).

74. See Richard Wade, *Slavery in the Cities: The South 1820-1860* (New York: Oxford University Press, 1964); Eugene Genovese, *Roll Jordan Roll: The World the Slaves Made* (New York: Pantheon, 1974); William B. Gatewood, *Aristocracies of Color* (Bloomington, IN: Indiana University Press, 1990).

75. See Marcus Pohlmann, *Black Politics in Conservative America* (New York: Longman, 1990), chapter 3.

76. Charles V. Willie, *The Continuing Significance of Race: A New Look at Black Families* (New York: General Hall, 1981), p. 41. See also Charles V. Willie, "The Inclining Significance of Race," in Charles V. Willie (ed.), *Race, Ethnicity and Socioeconomic Status: A Theoretical Analysis of Their Interconnections* (New York: General Hall, 1983). Melvin Oliver, "The Enduring Significance of Race," *Journal of Ethnic Studies* 4 (1980), pp. 79-91. Thomas D. Boston, *Race, Class and Conservatism* (Winchester, MA: Unwin Hyman, 1988).

77. Geschwender, *Racial Stratification*, p. 264.

78. Ira Katznelson, "Power in the Reformulation of Race Research," in Peter Orleans and William Ellis, Jr. (eds.), *Race, Change and Urban Society*, vol. 5 (New York: Sage Pub., 1971), p. 64.

79. John Dewey, *Logic: The Theory of Inquiry* (New York: Henry Holt, 1926), p. 38. See also Gordon Nagel, *The Structure of Experience: Kant's System of Proof* (Chicago: University of Chicago Press, 1983).

80. Daniel P. Moynihan, "The Negro Family: The Case for National Action," in Lee Rainwater and William Yancey (eds.), *The Moynihan Report and the Politics of Controversy* (Cambridge, MA: MIT Press, 1967), pp. 43-52.

81. E. Franklin Frazier, *Black Bourgeoisie: The Rise of a New Black Middle Class in the United States* (New York: Free Press, 1962).

82. Ken Auletta, *The Underclass* (New York: Random House, 1983).

83. Herbert Gans, "Fighting the Biases Embedded in Social Concepts of the Poor," *The Chronicle of Higher Education* 38, no. 18 (January 8, 1992), p. A56.

84. See Park, *Race and Culture*, pp. 81-84.

85. See Adam Smith, *The Wealth of Nations* (New York: Modern Library, 1937); Patricia H. Werhane, *Adam Smith and His Legacy for Modern Capitalism* (New York: Oxford University Press, 1991).

86. See Friedrich Nietzsche, in *The Portable Nietzsche*, selected and translated by Walter Kaufman (ed.) (New York: Penguin Books, 1968), pp. 587-588.

BIBLIOGRAPHY

Abel, Theodore. "The Operation Called Verstehen." *American Journal of Sociology* 54, no. 3 (November 1948), pp. 211-18.

Acuna, Rodolfo. *Occupied America: The Chicano's Struggle Toward Liberation.* San Francisco: Canfield Press, 1972.

——. *Occupied America: A History of Chicanos,* 2nd ed. New York: Harper and Row, 1981.

Adorno, Theodore (ed.). *The Positivist Dispute in German Sociology.* London: Heinemann, 1976.

Aldrich, Mark. "Progressive Economists and Scientific Racism: Walter Wilcox and Black Americans, 1895-1910." *Phylon* 40, no. 1 (Spring 1979), pp. 1-14.

Allen, Robert. *Black Awakening in Capitalist America: An Analytic History.* New York: Anchor Books, 1969.

Allport, Gordon. *The Nature of Prejudice.* New York: Doubleday, 1958.

Almaguer, Tomas. "Historical Notes on Chicano Oppression: The Dialectics of Racial and Class Domination in North America." *Aztlan: Chicano Journal of the Social Sciences and the Arts* 5, nos. 1 and 2 (Spring and Fall 1974), pp. 27-56.

——. "Race, Class and Chicano Oppression." *Socialist Revolution* 5, no. 3 (July-September 1975), pp. 71-99.

——. "Toward the Study of Chicano Colonialism." *Aztlan: Chicano Journal of the Social Sciences and the Arts* 2, no. 1 (Spring 1971), pp. 7-21.

Althusser, Louis. *For Marx.* Middlesex: Penguin Book, 1969.

Althusser, Louis, and Etienne Balibar. *Reading Capital.* London: New Left Books, 1970.

Alvarez, Rodolfo. "The Psycho-Historical and Socioeconomic Development of the Chicano Community in the United States." In Rodolfo O. De La Garza, Frank D. Bean, Charles M. Bonjean,

Ricardo Romo, and Rodolfo Alvarez (eds.), *The Mexican American Experience: An Interdisciplinary Anthology*, pp. 33-56. Austin, TX: University of Texas Press, 1986.

"Asian Americans: A Model Minority." *Newsweek* (December 6, 1982), pp. 39-51.

Auletta, Ken. *The Underclass*. New York: Random House, 1983.

Avineri, Shlomo (ed.). *Varieties of Marxism*. The Hague: Martinus Nijhoff, 1977.

Bailey, Thomas A., and David M. Kennedy. *The American Pageant*, vol. 11, 7th ed. Lexington, MA: D. C. Heath, 1983.

Baldwin, John, and Janice I. *Beyond Sociobiology*. New York: Elsevier, 1981.

Balibar, Etienne. "Paradoxes of Universality." In David Goldberg (ed.), *Anatomy of Racism*, pp. 283-294. Minneapolis, MN: University of Minnesota Press, 1990.

Banfield, Edward. *The Unheavenly City: The Nature and Future of our Urban Crisis*. Boston: Little, Brown, 1970.

Banton, Michael. "Epistemological Assumptions in the Study of Racial Differentiation." In John Rex and David Mason (eds.), *Theories of Race and Ethnic Relations*, pp. 42-63. London: Cambridge University Press, 1986.

——. *The Idea of Race*. Boulder, CO: Westview Press, 1977.

——. *Race Relations*. London: Tavistock, 1967.

——. *Racial and Ethnic Competition*. Cambridge: Cambridge University Press, 1983.

——. *Racial Minorities*. London: Fontana, 1972.

——. *Racial Theories*. Cambridge: Cambridge University Press, 1987.

Banton, Michael. "1960: A Turning Point in the Study of Race Relations." *Daedalus* 103, no. 2 (Spring 1974), pp. 31-44.

Banton, Michael, and Jonathan Harwood, *The Race Concept*. New York: Praeger Pub., 1975.

Barker, Martin. "Biology and the New Racism." In David Goldberg (ed.), *Anatomy of Racism*, pp. 18-37. Minneapolis, MN: University of Minnesota Press, 1990.

Barrera, Mario. *Race and Class in the Southwest: A Theory of Racial Inequality.* South Bend, IN: University of Notre Dame Press, 1979.

Barth, Frederik. "Introduction." In Frederik Barth (ed.), *Ethnic Groups and Boundaries: The Social Organization of Culture Differences*, pp. 9-38. Boston: Little, Brown, 1969.

Barzun, Jacques. *Race: A Study in Modern Superstition.* New York: Harcourt, Brace and Co., 1937.

Bazant, J. *A Concise History of Mexico: From Hidalgo to Cardenas, 1805-1940.* New York: Cambridge University Press, 1977.

Becker, Gary. *The Economics of Discrimination.* Chicago: University of Chicago Press, 1957.

——. *Human Capital: A Theoretical and Empirical Analysis with Special Reference to Education.* Chicago: University of Chicago Press, 1981.

Bendix, Reihnard S., and Seymour Lipset (eds.). *Class, Status and Power: Social Stratification in Comparative Perspective.* New York: Free Press, 1966.

Bennett, Lerone, Jr. *Before the Mayflower: A History of Black America.* Chicago: Johnson Pub. Co., 1982.

van den Berghe, Pierre L. *Man in Society.* New York: Elsevier, 1975.

——. *Race and Ethnicity.* New York: Basic Books, 1970.

——. "Race and Ethnicity: A Sociobiological Perspective." In Norman Yetman (ed.), *Majority and Minority: The Dynamics of Race and Ethnicity in American Life*, 4th ed, pp. 54-61. London: Allyn and Bacon, 1985.

——. *Race and Racism: A Comparative Perspective.* New York: John Wiley, 1967.

Bernardi, Bernado (ed.). *The Concept and Dynamics of Culture.* The Hague: Mouton Pub., 1977.

Berreman, Gerald D. "Race, Caste, and Other Invidious Distinctions." In Norman Yetman (ed.), *Majority and Minority: The Dynamics of Race and Ethnicity in American Life*, 4th ed., pp. 21-39. London: Allyn and Bacon, 1985.

Berry, Brewton. *Almost White.* London: Collier-Macmillan, 1963.

——. *Race and Ethnic Relations*. Boston: Houghton Mifflin, 1958.

Berry, Mary Frances. *Black Resistance/White Law: A History of Constitutional Racism in America*. New York: Appleton-Century-Crofts, 1971.

Berry, Mary Frances, and John W. Blassingame. *Long Memory:The Black Experience in America*. New York: Oxford University Press, 1982.

"The Black Conservatives." *Newsweek* (March 9, 1981), pp. 29-33.

Blalock, Hubert M., Jr. *Toward a Theory of Minority-Group Relations*. New York: Wiley, 1967.

Blauner, Robert. *Racial Oppression in America*. New York: Harper and Row, 1972.

Block, Alan R., and Frank R. Scarpitti. *Poisoning for Profit: The Mafia and Toxic Waste in America*. New York: William Morrow, 1985.

Bloom, Allan. *The Closing of the American Mind*. New York: Simon and Schuster, 1986.

Blum, Alan, and P. Mc Hugh. "The Social Ascription of Motives." *American Sociological Review* 36, no. 1 (February 1971), pp. 98-109.

Boas, Franz. *The Mind of Primitive Man*. New York: Macmillan, 1938.

——. *Race, Language and Culture*. New York: Macmillan, 1948.

Boggs, Carl. *Gramsci's Marxism*. London: Pluto Press, 1976.

Boggs, James. *Racism and the Class Struggle*. New York: Monthly Review Press, 1970.

Bonacich, Edna. "Class Approaches to Ethnicity and Race." In Norman Yetman (ed.), *Majority and Minority: The Dynamics of Race and Ethnicity in American Life*, 4th ed., pp. 62-78. London: Allyn and Bacon, 1985.

——. "The Past, Present and Future of Split Labor Market Theory." In C. B. Marrett and Cheryl Leggon (eds.), *Research in Race and Ethnic Relations*, vol. 1, pp. 17-64. Greenwich, CT: Jai Press, 1979.

Bose, Arun. *Marxian and Post-Marxian Political Economy*. Middlesex: Penguin, 1975.

Boston, Thomas D. *Race, Class and Conservatism*. Winchester, MA: Unwin Hyman, 1988.

Boswell, Thomas D, and James R. Curtis. *The Cuban American Experience: Cultures, Images, and Perspectives*. Totowa, NJ: Rowman and Allanheld, 1984.

Boxill, Bernard. *Blacks and Social Justice*. Totowa, NJ: Rowman and Allanheld, 1984.

Briggs, Vernon M., Jr. *Immigration Policy and the American Labor Force*. Baltimore: John Hopkins University Press, 1984.

——.*Walter Fogel, and Fred H. Schmidt. The Chicano Worker*. Austin, TX: University of Texas Press, 1986.

Brody, William, and Sophie. *The Indian: America's Unfinished Business*. Norman, OK: University of Oklahoma Press, 1966.

Bush, Rod (ed.). *The New Black Vote*. San Francisco, CA: Synthesis Publications, 1984.

Butler, J. S. "Institutional Racism: Viable Perspective or Intellectual Bogey." *The Black Sociologist* 7, no. 3/4 (1978), pp. 5-25.

Callinicos, Alex. *Althusser's Marxism*. London: Pluto Press, 1976.

Carmichael, Stokely, and Charles V. Hamilton. *Black Power: The Politics of Liberation in America*. New York: Jonathan Cape, 1968.

Castles, Stephen, and Godula Kosack. *Immigrants and the Class Structure in Western Europe*. London: Oxford Unversity Press, 1973.

Cheng, Lucie, and Edna Bonacich (eds.). *Asian Workers in the United States: Labor and Immigration under Capitalism*. Los Angeles, CA: University of California Press, 1984.

Churchill, Ward (ed.). *Marxism and Native Americans*. Boston: South End Press, 1983.

Cicourel, A. V. *Cognitive Sociology*. Glencoe, IL: Free Press, 1974.

Cohen, G. A. *Marx's Theory of History*. Oxford: Clarendon Press, 1978.

Cohen, Jean L. *Class and Civil Society: The Limits of Marxian Critical Theory*. Amherst, MA: University of Massachusetts Press, 1982.

Cohen, Percy. "Need There be a Sociology of Race Relations?" *Sociology* 6, no. 1 (1972), pp. 100-108.

Coleman, James S., Ernest Q. Campbell, Carol J. Hobson, James McPartland, Frederic D. Weinfeld, and Robert L. York. *Equality of Educational Opportunity*. Washington, DC: U.S. Department of Health, Education, and Welfare, 1966.

Collins, Janet, and Martha Giminez (eds.). *Work Without Wages: Domestic Labor and Self-Employment Within Capitalism*. New York: State University of New York Press, 1990.

Commoner, Barry. *The Politics of Energy: The Poverty of Power*. New York: Knopf, 1979.

Conrad, Earl. *The Invention of the Negro*. New York: Paul Eriksson, Inc., 1966.

Cornelius, Wayne A. *Mexican Migration to the United States: Causes, Consequences and U.S. Responses*. Cambridge, MA: Center for International Studies, 1978.

Corwin, Arthur F. "Mexican Policy and Ambivalence Toward Labor Emigration to the United States." In Arthur F. Corwin (ed.), *Immigrants — and Immigrants: Perspectives on Mexican Labor Migration to the United States*, pp. 25-37. Westport, CT: Greenwood Press, 1978.

Cottrell, Allin. *Social Classes in Marxist Theory*. New York: Henley and Melbourne, 1984.

Cox, O. C. *Caste, Class and Race: A Study in Social Dynamics*. New York: Monthly Review Press, 1959.

———. *Race Relations: Elements and Social Dynamics*. Detroit, MI: Wayne State University Press, 1976.

Cross, Barry (ed.). *Reverse Discrimination*. New York: Prometheus, 1977.

Cross, Theodore. *The Black Power Imperative*. New York: Faulkner, 1984.

Crouch, Stanley. *Notes of a Hanging Judge: Essays and Reviews, 1979-1989*. Oxford: Oxford University Press, 1990.

Cruse, Harold. *The Crisis of the Negro Intellectual*. New York: William Morrow, 1967.

Curtin, P. D. *The Atlantic Slave Trade: A Census*. London: University of Wisconsin Press, 1969.

——. *The Image of Africa: British Ideas and Action, 1789-1850*, vol. 2. Madison, WI: University of Wisconsin Press, 1964.

Cutler, Anthony, Barry Hindess, Paul Q. Hirst, and Athar Hussain. *Marx's Capital and Capitalism Today*, vol. 1. London: Routledge and Kegan Paul, 1977.

Davis, Cary, Carl Haub, and JoAnne Willette. "U.S. Hispanics: Changing the Face of America." In Norman Yetman (ed.), *Majority and Minority: The Dynamics of Race and Ethnicity in American Life*, 4th ed., pp. 464-489. London: Allyn and Bacon, 1985.

Davis, D. Brion. *The Problem of Slavery in Western Culture*. New York: Cornell University Press, 1966.

Degler, Carl. *Neither Black Nor White*. New York: Macmillan, 1971.

Desan, Wilfrid. *The Marxism of Jean Paul Sartre*. New York: Doubleday, 1965.

Devereux, George. "Ethnic Identity: Its Logical Foundations and Its Dysfunctions." In George de Vos and Lola Romanucci-Ross (eds.), *Ethnic Identity: Cultural Continuities and Change*, pp. 42-70. Palo Alto, CA: Mayfield, 1975.

Dewart, Janet (ed.). *The State of Black America 1990*. New York: National Urban League, 1991.

Dewey, John. *Logic: The Theory of Inquiry*. New York: Henry Holt, 1926.

Dollard, John. *Caste and Class in a Southern Town*. New York: Doubleday, 1937.

Dinnerstein, Leonard, and David M. Reimers. *Ethnic Americans: A History of Immigration and Assimilation*. New York: Dodd and Mead, 1975.

Diop, Cheikh Anta. "Africa: Cradle of Humanity." In Ivan van Sertima (ed.), *Nile Valley Civilizations*, pp. 23-28. Atlanta, GA: Morehouse College, 1984.

——. *The African Origin of Civilization*. New York: Lawrence Hill and Co., 1974.

——. *The Cultural Unity of Black Africa*. Chicago: Third World Press, 1978.

——. "Speech by Cheikh Anta Diop." In Ivan van Sertima (ed.), *Great African Thinkers: Vol. I. Cheik Anta Diop*, pp. 320-321. New Brunswick, NJ: Transaction Press, 1987.

D'Souza, Dinesh. *Illiberal Education: The Politics of Race and Sex on Campus*. New York, Free Press, 1991.

Du Bois, W.E.B. *The Conservation of Races*. Washington, DC: American Negro Academy, 1897.

——. *The Souls of Black Folk*. Chicago: McClurg, 1904.

——. *The World and Africa: An Inquiry into the Part Which Africa Has Played in World History*. New York: International Pub., 1980.

Edsall, Thomas B, and Mary D. *Chain Reaction: The Impact of Race, Rights and Taxes on American Politics*. New York: W. W. Norton, 1991.

Ehrlich, Paul R., Loy Bilderback, and Anne H. Ehrlich. *The Golden Door: International Migration and the United States*. New York: Wideview Books, 1981.

Eitzen, D. Stanley, and Maxine Baca Zinn. *In Conflict and Order: Understanding Society*. Boston: Allyn and Bacon, 1991.

Elkins, Stanley. *Slavery: A Problem in American Institutional and Cultural Life*. Chicago: University of Chicago Press, 1964.

Engel, S. Morris. *With Good Reason: An Introduction to Informal Fallacies*. New York: St. Martin's Press, 1986.

Enloe, Cynthia. *Ethnic Conflict and Political Development*. Boston: Little, Brown, 1973.

——. "The Growth of The State and Ethnic Mobilization: The American Experience." In Norman Yetman (ed.), *Majority and Minority: The Dynamics of Race and Ethnicity in American Life*, 4th ed., pp. 79-88. London: Allyn and Bacon, 1985.

Fairchild, Halford. "Chicano, Hispanic, or Mexican American: What's in a Name?" *Hispanic Journal of Behavioral Sciences* 3, no. 2 (1981), pp. 191-198.

Faris, Robert. *Chicago Sociology 1920-1932*. Chicago: University of Chicago Press, 1970.

Farmer, James. *Lay Bare The Heart.* New York: Arbor House, 1985.

Farrakhan, Louis. *Back Where We Belong: Selected Speeches by Minister Louis Farrakhan,* edited by Joseph D. Eure and Richard M. Jerome. Philadelphia: PC International Press, 1989.

Feagin, Joe R. *Racial and Ethnic Relations.* Englewood Cliffs, NJ: Prentice-Hall, 1986.

———. *Social Problems,* 2nd ed. Englewood Cliffs, NJ: Prentice-Hall, 1986.

Fenton, C. Stephen. "Race, Class and Politics in the Work of Emile Durkheim." In UNESCO, *Sociological Theories: Race and Colonialism,* pp. 143-181. Paris: UNESCO, 1980.

Flynn, J. R. *Race, IQ, and Jensen.* London: Routledge and Kegan Paul, 1980.

Foner, Laura, and Eugene Genovese (eds.). *Slavery in the New World.* Englewood Cliffs, NJ: Prentice-Hall, 1969.

Forsythe, Dennis. "Marxism, Blacks and Radicalism in Sociology: The Necessary Reconciliation." *The Black Sociologist* 7, no. 1 (1977), pp. 14-22.

Franklin, Raymond S., and Solomon Resnik. *The Political Economy of Racism.* New York: Holt, Rinehart and Winston, 1973.

Franklin, Raymond S. and William K. Taab. "The Challenge of Radical Political Economics." *Journal of Economic Issues* 8, no. 1 (March 1974), pp. 127-150.

Frazier, E. Franklin. *Black Bourgeoisie: The Rise of a New Black Middle Class in the United States.* New York: Free Press, 1962.

———. "The Impact of Urban Civilization Upon Negro Family Life." In Paul K. Host and Albert J. Reiss, Jr. (eds.), *Cities and Society,* pp. 490-499. New York: Free Press, 1951.

Fredrickson, George M. "Toward a Social Interpretation of the Development of American Racism." In Nathan Huggins, Martin Kilson, and Daniel Fox (eds.), *Key Issues in the Afro-American Experience: Vol. I to 1877,* pp. 240-257. New York: Harcourt Brace Jovanovich, 1971.

Freeman, Richard. *The Black Elite: The New Market for Highly Qualified Blacks.* New York: McGraw-Hill, 1977.

Friedman, Murray. "Is White Racism the Problem?" In Peter

Rose (ed.), *Nation of Nations: The Ethnic Experience and the Racial Crisis*, pp. 279-293. New York: Random House, 1972.

Fussell, Paul. *BAD: Or the Dumbing of America*. New York: Summit Books, 1991.

Gabriel, John, and G. Ben-Tovim. "Marxism and the Concept of Racism." *Economy and Society* 7, no. 2 (1978), pp. 118-154.

Garfinkel, Harold. *Studies in Ethnomethodology*. Englewood Cliffs, NJ: Prentice-Hall, 1967.

de la Garza, Rodolfo O., Frank D. Bean, Charles M. Bonjean, Ricardo Romo, and Rodolfo Alvarez (eds.). *The Mexican American Experience: An Interdisciplinary Anthology*. Austin, TX: University of Texas Press, 1986.

Gatewood, William B. *Aristocracies of Color*. Bloomington, IN: Indiana University Press, 1990.

Gates, Henry L. "Critical Remarks." In David Goldberg (ed.), *Anatomy of Racism*, pp. 319-329. Minneapolis, MN: University of Minnesota Press, 1990.

Geertz, Clifford. *The Interpretation of Cultures*. New York: Basic Books, 1973.

Genovese, Eugene. *Roll Jordan Roll: The World the Slaves Made*. New York: Pantheon, 1974.

——. *The World the Slaveholders Made: Two Essays in Interpretation*. London: Penguin Press, 1969.

Gerth, Hans, and C. Wright Mills (eds.). *From Max Weber: Essays in Sociology*. London: Oxford University Press, 1953.

Geschwender, James A. *Racial Stratification in America*. Dubuque, IA: William C. Brown, 1980.

Giddens, Anthony. *Capitalism and Modern Social Theory: An Analysis of the Writings of Marx, Durkheim and Max Weber*. Cambridge: Cambridge University Press, 1971.

——. *New Rules of Sociological Method: A Positive Critique of Interpretative Sociology*. New York: Basic Books, 1976.

Gilbert, Dennis, and Joseph A. Kahl. *The American Class Structure: A New Synthesis*. Homewood, IN: Dorsey Press, 1982.

Gilroy, Paul. "One Nation Under a Groove, The Cultural Politics of 'Race' and Racism in Britain." In David Goldberg (ed.), *Anat-*

omy of Racism, pp. 263-282. Minneapolis, MN: University of Minnesota Press, 1990.

Glasgow, Donald. *The Black Underclass*. San Francisco, CA: Jossey-Bass, 1980.

Glazer, Nathan. *Affirmative Discrimination: Ethnic Inequality and Public Policy*. New York: Basic Books, 1975.

——. "Blacks and Ethnic Groups: The Difference, and the Political Difference It Makes." In Nathan Huggins, Martin Kilson, and Daniel Fox (eds.), *Key Issues in the Afro-American Experience*, vol. 2, pp. 193-211. New York: Harcourt Brace Jovanovich, 1971.

de Gobineau, Arthur J. *The Inequality of Human Races*, trans. Adrian Collins. New York: Fertig, 1977.

Goldberg, David. "The Social Formation of Racist Discourse." In David Goldberg (ed.), *Anatomy of Racism*, pp. 295-318. Minneapolis, MN: University of Minnesota Press, 1990.

Goldman, A. H. "Limits to the Justification of Reverse Discrimination." *Social Theory and Practice* 3, no. 3 (Spring 1975), pp. 289-306.

Gomberg, Paul. "IQ and Race: A Discussion of Some Confusions." *Ethics* 85, no. 3 (1974-75), pp. 258-266.

Gossett, Thomas. *Race: The History of an Idea in America*. New York: Schocken Books, 1965.

Gough, Ian. "Marx's Theory of Productive and Unproductive Labor." *New Left Review*, no. 16 (November-December 1972), pp. 47-72.

Gouldner, Alvin. *The Two Marxisms*. New York: Seabury Press, 1980.

Greeley, Andrew M. "The Ethnic Miracle." In Norman Yetman (ed.), *Majority and Minority: The Dynamics of Race and Ethnicity in American Life*, 4th ed., pp. 268-277. London: Allyn and Bacon, 1985.

——. *Ethnicity in the United States: A Preliminary Reconnaisance*. New York: John Wiley, 1974.

——. *Why Can't They Be Like Us? America's White Ethnic Groups*. New York: E. P. Dutton, 1971.

Green, Robert L. *The Urban Challenge: Poverty and Race.* Chicago: Follett Pub., 1977.

Greene, John C. "The American Debate on the Negro's Place in Nature, 1780-1815." *Journal of the History of Ideas* 15 (June 1954), pp. 384-396.

Grenier, Gilles. "Shifts to English as Usual Language by Americans of Spanish Mother Tongue." In Rodolfo de la Garza, Frank D. Bean, Charles M. Bonjean, Ricardo Romo, and Rodolfo Alvarez (eds.), *The Mexican American Experience: An Interdisciplinary Anthology*, pp. 346-358. Austin, TX: University of Texas Press, 1985.

Guillaumin, Colette. "The Idea of Race and Its Elevation to Autonomous Scientific and Legal Status." In UNESCO, *Sociological Theories: Race and Colonialism*, pp. 37-67. Paris: UNESCO, 1980.

Hall, Gus. *Fighting Racism.* New York: International Pub., 1985.

Hall, Raymond L. *Black Separatism in the United States.* Hanover, NH: University Press of New England, 1978.

Hall, Stuart. "Gramsci's Relevance for the Study of Race and Ethnicity." *Communication Inquiry* 10, no. 2 (Summer 1986), pp. 26-27.

——. "Race, Articulation and Societies Structured in Dominance." In UNESCO, *Sociological Theories: Race and Colonialism*, pp. 305-345. Paris: UNESCO, 1980.

Hansen, Niles. *The Border Economy.* Austin, TX: University of Texas Press, 1986.

Hanushek, Eric. "Ethnic Income Variations: Magnitudes and Explanations." In Thomas Sowell (ed.), *Essays and Data on American Ethnic Groups*, pp. 139-166. Washington DC: Urban Institute, 1978.

Hare, Nathan. *The Black Anglo-Saxons.* London: Collier-Macmillan, 1970.

Harmon, Alexandra. "When Is an Indian Not an Indian? The Friends of the Indian and the Problems of Indian Identity." *Journal of Ethnic Studies* 18, no. 2 (1990), pp. 95-123.

Harris, Donald J. "Capitalist Exploitation and Black Labor: Some Conceptual Issues." *Review of Black Political Economy* 8, no. 2 (Winter 1978), pp. 133-151.

Hernandez, J. A. *Mutual Aid for Survival: The Case of the Mexican American.* Marabar, FL: Robert E. Krieger, 1983.

Hindess, Barry. *Philosophy and Methodology in the Social Sciences.* Atlantic Highlands, NJ: Humanities Press, 1977.

Hindess, Barry, and Paul Q. Hirst. *Pre-Capitalist Modes of Production.* London: Routledge and Kegan Paul, 1974.

Hirsch, S. Carl. *The Riddle of Racism.* New York: Viking Press, 1972.

Hoare, Quintin, and Geoffrey N. Smith (eds.). *Antonio Gramsci, Selections from Prison Notebooks.* New York: International Pub., 1971.

Hobbes, Thomas. *Leviathan.* New York: E. P. Dutton, 1950.

Hodge, John L. "Equality: Beyond Dualism and Oppression." In David Goldberg (ed.), *Anatomy of Racism*, pp. 89-107. Minneapolis, MN: University of Minnesota Press, 1990.

Hohl, Donald. "The Indochinese Refugees: The Evolution of United States Policy." *International Migration Review* 12, no. 1 (Spring 1978), pp. 128-132.

Horsman, Reginald. *Race and Manifest Destiny: The Origins of American Racial Anglo-Saxonism.* Cambridge, MA: Harvard University Press, 1981.

Ignacio, Lemuel F. *Asian Americans and Pacific Islanders: Is There Such an Ethnic Group?* San Jose, CA: Philippino Development Associates, 1976.

Isaacs, H. "Basic Group Identity: The Idols of the Tribe." In Nathan Glazer and D. P. Moynihan (eds.), *Ethnicity: Theory and Experience*, pp. 29-52. Cambridge, MA: Harvard University Press, 1975.

Jackman, Mary R., and Mary S. Senter. "Images of Social Groups: Categorical or Qualified." *Public Opinion Quarterly* 44, no. 3 (Fall 1980), pp. 341-361.

Jacobs, Paul, and Saul Landau (eds.). *To Serve the Devil: Natives and Slaves, A Documentary Analysis of America's Racial His-*

tory and Why It Has Been Kept Hidden, vols. 1 and 2, p. 390.
New York: Random House, 1971.

Jacques-Garvey, Amy (ed.). *Philosophy and Opinions of Marcus Garvey*. New York: Atheneum, 1970.

Jaffe, A. J., Ruth M. Cullen, and Thomas D. Boswell. *The Changing Demography of Spanish Americans*. New York: Academic Press, 1980.

James, George G. M. *Stolen Legacy*. San Francisco, CA: Julian Richardson Associates, 1976.

Jencks, Christopher, and Paul E. Peterson. *The Urban Underclass*. Washington, DC: Brookings Institution, 1991.

Jensen, Arthur. *Genetics and Education*. New York: Harper and Row, 1972.

———. *Straight Talk about Mental Tests*. New York: Free Press, 1981.

Jiobu, Robert M. "Earnings Differentials Between Whites and Ethnic Minorities: The Case of Asians, Blacks and Chicanos." *Sociology and Social Research* 61, no. 1 (October 1976), pp. 24-38.

Jones, James M. *Prejudice and Racism*. London: Addison-Wesley, 1972.

———. "Racism in Black and White: A Bicultural Model of Reaction and Evolution." In Phyllis Katz and Dalmas Taylor (eds.), *Eliminating Racism: Profiles in Controversy*, pp. 117-136. New York: Plenum Press, 1986.

Jordan, Winthrop D. *White over Black: American Attitudes Towards the Negro, 1550-1812*. Chapel Hill, NC: University of North Carolina Press, 1968.

Jordan, Zbigniew A. (ed.). *Karl Marx: Economy, Class and Social Revolution*. London: Nelson, 1971.

Jorgensen, Joseph. "Indians and the Metropolis." In Jack O.Waddell and O. Michael Watson (eds.), *The American Indian in Urban Society*, pp. 66-113. Boston: Little, Brown, 1971.

Karenga, Maulana. *Essays in Struggle*. San Diego, CA: Kawaida Publications, 1978.

———. *Introduction to Black Studies*. Inglewood, CA: Kawaida Publications, 1982.

Katznelson, Ira. *Black Men White Cities: Race, Politics and Migration in the United States, 1900-1930 and Britain, 1948-1968.* London: Oxford University Press, 1973.

——. "Power in the Reformulation of Race Research." In Peter Orleans and William Ellis, Jr. (eds.), *Race, Change and Urban Society*, vol. 5, pp. 51-82. New York: Sage Pub., 1971.

Kautsky, Karl. *The Class Struggle*, trans. William E. Bohm. New York: Norton, 1971.

Kerbo, Harold R. *Social Stratification and Inequality: Class Conflict in the United States.* New York: McGraw-Hill, 1983.

Kim, Kwang Ghing, and Won Moo Hurh. "Korean Americans and the Success Image: A Critique." *Amerasia* 10, no. 2 (1983), pp. 3-22.

Kinloch, Graham C. *The Dynamics of Race Relations: A Sociological Analysis.* New York: McGraw-Hill, 1974.

Kitano, Harry H. L. "Asian Americans: The Chinese, Japanese, Koreans, Philipinos, and Southeast Asians." In Milton Gordon (ed.), *America as a Multicultural Society*, pp. 125-138. Philadelphia: American Academy of Political and Social Sciences, 1981.

Kitano, Harry H. L., and Stanley Sue. "The Model Minorities." *Journal of Social Issues* 29, no. 2 (1973), pp. 1-9.

Klass, Morton, and Hal Hellman. *The Kinds of Mankind.* New York: J. B. Lippincott, 1971.

Knowles, Louis, and Kenneth Prewitt. "Introduction." In Louis Knowles and Kenneth Prewitt (eds.), *Institutional Racism in America.* Englewood Cliffs, NJ: Prentice-Hall, 1969.

Kolakowski, Leszek. *Main Currents of Marxism: Its Rise Growth and Dissolution.* London: Oxford University Press, 1978.

Kozol, Jonathan. *Illiterate America.* New York: Anchor, 1985.

——. *Savage Inequalities: Children in America's Schools.* New York: Crown Pub., 1991.

Kroeber, Alfred. *The Nature of Culture.* Chicago: University of Chicago Press, 1952.

Kroeber, Alfred and Clyde Kluckhohn. *Culture, A Critical Review of Concepts and Definitions.* Cambridge, MA: Harvard University

Peabody Museum of American Archeology and Ethnology Papers, 1952.

Kuhn, Thomas. *The Structure of Scientific Revolutions*. Chicago: University of Chicago Press, 1962.

Kuper, Leo. *Race, Class and Power: Ideology and Revolutionary Change in Plural Societies*. New York: Aldine, 1975.

Kushner, James A. *Apartheid in America*. Frederick, MD: Associated Faculty Press, 1980.

LaDuke, Winona, and Ward Churchill. "The Political Economy of Radioactive Colonialism." *Journal of Ethnic Studies* 13, no. 3 (Fall 1985), pp. 107-132.

Lal, Barbara B. "The Chicago School of American Sociology, Symbolic Interactionism, and Race Relations Theory." In John Rex and David Mason (eds.), *Theories of Race and Ethnic Relations*, pp. 280-298. London: Cambridge University Press, 1986.

Landry, Bart. *The New Black Middle Class*. Berkeley, CA, University of California Press, 1987.

Lang, Susan S. *Extremist Groups in America*. New York: Franklin Watts, 1990.

Lee, Thea. "Trapped on a Pedestal: Asian Americans Confront Model-Minority Stereotype." In John A. Kromowski (ed.), *Racial and Ethnic Relations 91/92*, pp. 95-98. Guildford, CT: Duskhin Pub. Group, 1991.

Leech, Kenneth. "Diverse Reports and the Meaning of Racism." *Race and Class* 28, no. 2 (Autumn 1988), pp. 82-87.

Lenin, V. I. *What Is to Be Done?* Moscow: Progress Pub., 1923.

Levine, Irvin. "Statement." In U.S. Commission on Civil Rights, *Civil Rights Issues of Euro-Ethnic Americans in the United States: Opportunities and Challenges*. Washington, DC: U.S. Government Printing Office, 1979.

Levy, Daniel, and Gabriel Szekely. *Mexico: Paradoxes of Stability and Change*. Boulder, CO: Westview Press, 1983.

Lichtheim, George. *The Concept of Ideology and Other Essays*. New York: Random House, 1967.

Lieberson, Stanley. *A Piece of the Pie: Blacks and White Immigrants Since 1880*. Berkeley, CA: University of California Press, 1980.

Loury, Glenn C. "Beyond Civil Rights." *The New Republic* 193, no. 15 (October 1985), pp. 22-25.

———. "Economics, Politics, and Blacks." *Review of Black Political Economy* 12, no. 3 (Spring 1983), pp. 43-54.

———. "Internally Directed Action For Black Community Development: The Next Frontier for The 'Movement'." *Review of Black Political Economy* 13, nos. 1-2 (Summer-Fall 1984), pp. 31-46.

Luhman, Reid, and Stuart Gilman. *Race and Ethnic Relations: The Social and Political Experience of Minority Groups*. Belmont, CA: Wadsworth Pub. Co., 1980.

Lukacs, George. *History and Class Consciousness: Studies in Marxist Dialectics*, trans. Rodney Livingston. Cambridge, MA: MIT Press, 1972.

Lukes, Steven. *Power: A Radical View*. London: Macmillan, 1974.

Lyman, Stanford. *Chinese Americans*. New York: Random House, 1974.

Madhubuti, Haki R. *Enemies: The Clash of Races*. Chicago: Third World Press, 1978.

Malcolm X. *Malcolm X on Afro-American History*. New York: Pathfinder Press, 1967.

———. *Malcolm X Speaks: Selected Speeches and Writings and Statements*. New York: Pathfinder Press, 1967.

Mann, Michael. *Consciousness and Action Among the Western Working Class*. London: Macmillan, 1973.

Mannheim, Karl. *Ideology and Utopia*. London: Routledge and Kegan Paul, 1972.

Manuel, H. *Spanish-Speaking Children of the Southwest*. Austin, TX: University of Texas Press, 1965.

Marable, Manning. "The Beast Is Back: An Analysis of Campus Racism." *The Black Collegian* 19, no. 1 (September/October 1988), pp. 52-54.

———. *How Capitalism Underdeveloped Black America*. Boston: South End Press, 1983.

Marcuse, Herbert. *Essays on Liberation*. Boston: Beacon Press, 1969.

——. *One-Dimensional Man*. Boston: Beacon Press, 1966.

Marger, Martin. *Race and Ethnic Relations*. San Francisco: Wadsworth, 1991.

Marwick, Arthur. *Class: Image and Reality in Britain, France and the U.S.A. Since 1930*. New York: Oxford University Press, 1980.

Marx, Karl. *Capital*, vol. 1. London: Lawrence and Wishart, 1972.

——. *Capital*, vol. 3. London: Lawrence and Wishart, 1974.

——. *A Contribution to the Critique of Political Economy*. New York: International Publishers, 1971.

——. *The Eighteenth Brumaire of Louis Bonaparte*. New York: International Pub., 1969.

——. *The Poverty of Philosophy*. Chicago: Charles Kerr, 1913.

Marx, Karl, and Frederick Engels. *The Communist Manifesto*. London: Lawrence and Wishart, 1970.

——. *The German Ideology*. London: Lawrence and Wishart, 1965.

——. *Selected Works*, vol. 1. Moscow: Progress Publishers, 1969.

——. *Selected Writings*, edited by David McClellan. Oxford: Oxford University Press, 1977.

Matthews, Fred. "Cultural Pluralism in Context: External History, Philosophic Premises and Theories of Ethnicity in Modern America." *Journal of Ethnic Studies* 12, no. 2 (Summer 1984), pp. 63-79.

McCarthy, Kevin F., and Robert Valdez. *Current and Future Effects of Mexican Immigration in California*. Santa Monica, CA: Rand, 1985.

McCuen Gary E. (ed.). *The Racist Reader: Analyzing Primary Source Readings by American Race Supremacists*. Anoka, MN: Greenhaven Press, 1974.

McKee, Jesse O. (ed.). *Ethnicity in Contemporary America: A Geographical Appraisal*. Dubuque, IA: Kendall/Hunt Publishing Corp., 1985.

Medawar, Peter. *Pluto's Republic*. New York: Oxford University Press, 1982.

Meister, Richard J. (ed.). *Race and Ethnicity in Modern America.* Lexington, MA: D. C. Heath, 1974.

Melendy, H. Brett. *Chinese and Japanese Americans.* New York: Hippocrene Books, 1984.

——. *The Oriental Americans.* New York: Twayne Pub., 1972.

Merton, Robert. "Discrimination and the American Creed." In Norman Yetman (ed.), *Majority and Minority: The Dynamics and Ethnicity in American Life*, 4th ed., pp. 40-53. London: Allyn and Bacon, 1985.

Miles, Robert. *Capitalism and Unfree Labour: Anomaly or Necessity?* London: Tavistock, 1987.

——. "Class, Race and Ethnicity: A Critique of Cox's Theory." *Ethnic and Racial Studies* 3, no. 2 (1980), pp. 169-187.

——. *Racism.* London: Routledge and Kegan Paul, 1989.

——. *Racism and Migrant Labour.* London: Routledge and Kegan Paul, 1982.

Mirandé, Alfredo. *The Chicano Experience: An Alternative Perspective.* Notre Dame, IN: University of Notre Dame Press, 1985.

Montagu, Ashley. *Man's Most Dangerous Myth: The Fallacy of Race.* New York: Columbia University Press, 1945.

——. *Race, Science and Humanity.* New York: D. Van Nostrand, 1963.

Montagu, Ashley (ed.). *The Concept of Race.* New York: Macmillan, 1964.

—— (ed.). *Statement on Race.* New York: Oxford University Press, 1972.

Montero, Daniel. *Vietnamese Americans: Patterns of Resettlement and Socioeconomic Adaptation in the United States.* Boulder, CO: Westview Press, 1979.

Moore, Carlos. "Were Marx and Engels White Racists? The Prolet-Aryan Outlook of Marxism." *Berkeley Journal of Sociology* 19 (1974), pp. 125-155.

Moore, Joan W. "Colonialism: The Case of the Mexican Americans." *Social Problems* 17, no. 4 (Spring 1970), pp. 463-473.

——. "Minorities in the American Class System." In Norman Yetman (ed.), *Majority and Minority: The Dynamics and Ethnicity in American Life*, 4th ed., pp. 502-522. London: Allyn and Bacon, 1985.

Moore, Joan W., and Harry Pachon, *Hispanics in the United States*. Englewood Cliffs, NJ: Prentice-Hall, 1975.

Moynihan, Daniel P. "The Negro Family: The Case for National Action." In Lee Rainwater and William Yancey (eds.), *The Moynihan Report and the Politics of Controversy*, pp. 39-124. Cambridge, MA: MIT Press, 1967.

Murguia, Edward. *Assimilation, Colonialism, and the Mexican American People*. New York: University Press of America, 1989.

Murray, Albert. *The Omni Americans: New Perspectives on Black Experiences and American Culture*. New York: Outerbridge and Dienstfrey, 1970.

Murray, Charles. *Losing Ground: American Social Policy 1950-1980*. New York: Basic Books, 1984.

Myrdal, Gunnar. *An American Dilemma: The Negro Problem in Modern Democracy, Vol. I*. New York: Harper and Row, 1944.

Nader, Ralph, Richard Brownstein, and John Richard. *Who's Poisoning America: Corporate Pollution and Their Victims in the Chemical Age*. San Francisco, CA: Sierra Club Books, 1981.

Nagel, Gordon. *The Structure of Experience: Kant's System of Proof*. Chicago: University of Chicago Press, 1983.

Nakanishi, Don S. "Seeking Convergence in Race Relations Research: Japanese-Americans and the Resurrection of the Internment." In Phyllis Katz and Dalmas A. Taylor, *Eliminating Racism: Profiles in Controversy*, pp. 159-180. New York: Plenum Press, 1988.

National Hispanic Center for Advanced Studies and Policy Analysis. *The State of Hispanic America*, vol. 1. Oakland, CA: Babel, Inc., 1981.

National Urban League. "The State of Black America 1977." *Black Scholar* 9, no. 1 (September 1977), pp. 2-8.

Newman, Donald G. *Promises to Keep: African-Americans and the Constitutional Order, 1776 to the Present*. New York: Oxford University Press, 1991.

North, David S., and Marion F. Houston. *The Characteristics and Role of Illegal Immigration on the U.S. Labor Market: An Exploratory Study.* Washington, DC: U.S. Department of Labor, 1976.

Norton, Eleanor Holmes. "Foreword." In Gail E. Thomas (ed.), *U.S. Race Relations in the 1980's and 1990's: Challenges and Alternatives*, pp. xvii-xviii. New York: Hemisphere Pub., 1990.

Novak, Michael. *The Rise of the Unmeltable Ethnics: Politics and Culture in the Seventies.* New York: Macmillan, 1975.

Oakes, James. *The Ruling Race: A History of American Slaveholders.* New York: Knopf, 1982.

Ogbu, J. V. *Minority Education and Caste: The American System in Cross-Cultural Perspectives.* New York: Academic Press, 1978.

O'Hare, William P. and Judy C. Felt, "Asian Americans: America's Fastest Growing Minority," *Population Trends and Policy,* no. 19 (February 1991), pp. 2-16.

O'Hare, William, Taynia Mann, Katryn Porter, and Robert Greenstein. *Real Life Poverty in America: Where the American Public Would Set the Poverty Line.* Washington, DC: Center on Budget and Policy Priorities, 1990.

Oliver, Melvin. "The Enduring Significance of Race." *Journal of Ethnic Studies* 4 (1980), pp. 79-91.

Omi, Michael, and Howard Winant, *Racial Formation in the United States.* New York: Routledge and Kegan Paul, 1986.

Orozco, Edward. *Republican Protestantism in Aztlan.* New York: Petereins Press, 1980.

Ossofsky, Gilbert. *The Burden of Race.* New York: Harper Torchbooks, 1967.

Ossowski, Stanislaw. *Class Structure in the Social Consciousness*, trans. Sheila Patterson. London: Routledge and Kegan Paul, 1979.

Outlaw, Lucius. "Toward a Critical Theory of 'Race'." In David Goldberg (ed.), *Anatomy of Racism*, pp. 58-82. Minneapolis, MN: University of Minnesota Press, 1990.

Padilla, Felix M. "On the Nature of Latino Ethnicity." In Rodolfo de la Garza, Frank D. Bean, Charles M. Bonjean, Ricardo Romo, and Rodolfo Alvarez (eds.), *The Mexican American Experience: An Interdisciplinary Anthology*, pp. 332-345. Austin, TX: University of Texas Press, 1985.

——. "Latino Ethnicity in the City of Chicago." In Susan Olzak and Joane Nagel (eds.), *Competitive Ethnic Relations*, pp. 153-171. New York: Academic Press, 1986.

Park, Robert. *Race and Culture*. New York: Free Press, 1950.

Parker, J. A. "Black America Under the Reagan Administration." *Policy Review*, no. 34 (Fall 1985), pp. 27-41.

Parkin, Frank. *Marxism and Class Theory: A Bourgeois Critique*. London: Tavistock, 1979.

——. *Max Weber*. London: Tavistock, 1982.

——. "Social Stratification." In Tom Bottomore and Robert Nisbet (eds.), *A History of Sociological Analysis*, pp. 599-632. London: Heinemann, 1979.

Patel, Dinker I. "Asian Americans: A Growing Force." In John A. Kromowski (ed.), *Racial and Ethnic Relations 91/92*, pp. 86-91. Guildford, CT: Duskhin Pub. Group, 1991.

Patterson, Orlando. *Ethnic Chauvinism: The Reactionary Impulse*. New York: Stein and Day, 1977.

——. *Slavery and Social Death: A Comparative Study*. Cambridge, MA: Harvard University Press, 1982.

Paul, Richard. *Critical Thinking: What Every Person Needs to Survive in a Rapidly Changing World*. Rohnert Park, CA: Center for Critical Thinking and Moral Critique, 1990.

Pawalko, Ronald M. "Racism and the New Immigtration: A Reinterpretation of the Assimilation of White Ethnics in American Society." *Sociology and Social Research* 65, no. 1 (October 1980), pp. 56-77.

Perlo, Victor. *The Economics of Racism U.S.A.* New York: International Pub., 1975.

Petersen, William. "Success Story, Japanese-American Style." *New York Times Magazine*, January 9, 1966, pp. 20-21.

Phizacklea, Annie, and Robert Miles. *Labour and Racism*. London: Routledge and Kegan Paul, 1980.

Pine, Gerald, and Asa Hilliard III. "Rx for Racism: Imperative for America's Schools." *Phi Delta Kappan* (April 1990), pp. 595-598.

Pinkney, Alphonso. *The Myth of Black Progress.* Cambridge: Cambridge University Press, 1986.

Plamenatz, John P. *Ideology.* New York: Praeger, 1970.

Pohlmann, Marcus. *Black Politics in Conservative America.* New York: Longman, 1990.

Pois, Robert (ed.). *Race and Race History and Other Essays by Alfred Rosenberg.* New York: Harper Torchbooks, 1974.

Popper, Karl. *Objective Knowledge: An Evolutionary Approach.* Oxford: Clarendon Press, 1972.

Portes, Alejandro, and Robert L. Bach. *Latin Journey: Cuban and Mexican Immigrants in the United States.* Berkeley, CA: University of California Press, 1985.

Poulantzas, Nicos. *Classes in Contemporary Capitalism.* London: New Left Books, 1975.

Przeworski, A. "Proletariat into Class: The Process of Class Formation from Karl Kautsky's *The Class Struggle* to Recent Controversies." *Politics and Society* 7, no. 4 (1977), pp. 343-401.

Quarles, Benjamin. *Black Abolitionists.* New York: Oxford University Press, 1969.

Quinney, Richard. *Class, Status and Crime.* New York: Longman, 1980.

Radin, Paul. *The Story of the American Indian.* New York: Liverwright, 1944.

Ransford, Edward H. *Race and Class in American Society: Black, Chicano and Anglo.* New York: Schenkman, 1983.

Reich, Michael. *Racial Inequality: A Political Economic Analysis.* Princeton, NJ: Princeton University Press, 1981.

Reminick, Ronald. *Theory of Ethnicity: An Anthropologist's Perspective.* Lanham, MD: University Press of America, 1983.

Rex, John. *Race and Ethnicity.* Milton Keynes: Open University Press, 1986.

——. *Race, Colonialism and the City.* London: Routledge and Kegan Paul, 1973.

————. *Race Relations in Sociological Theory.* 2nd ed. London: Weidenfield and Nicholson, 1983.

————. "The Role of Class Analysis in the Study of Race Relations — A Weberian Perspective." In John Rex and David Mason (eds.), *Theories of Race and Ethnic Relations,* pp. 64-83. London: Cambridge University Press, 1986.

————. "The Theory of Race Relations — A Weberian Approach." In UNESCO, *Sociological Theories: Race and Colonialism,* pp. 117-142. Paris: UNESCO, 1980.

Rex, John, and Sally Tomlinson. *Colonial Immigrants in a British City: A Class Analysis.* London: Routledge and Kegan Paul, 1971.

Reynolds, Vernon. "Biology and Race Relations." *Ethnic and Racial Studies* 9, no. 3 (July 1986), pp. 373-381.

Ricoeur, Paul. *Lectures on Ideology and Utopia.* New York: Columbia University Press, 1986.

Robertson, Ian. *Sociology,* 3rd ed. New York: Worth Pub., 1987.

Rodriguez, Clara E. "Prisms of Race and Class." *Journal of Ethnic Studies* 12, no. 2 (Summer 1984), pp. 99-120.

Romo, Richard. *East Los Angeles: History of a Barrio.* Austin, TX: University of Texas, 1986.

Russett, Cynthia E. *Darwin in America: The Intellectual Response 1865-1912.* San Francisco, CA: W. H. Freeman, 1976.

Sabel, Charles F. "Ambiguities of Class and the Possibility of Politics." In Andre Liebich (ed.), *The Future of Socialism?* pp. 257-279. Montreal: Interuniversity Center for European Studies, 1979.

Salmon, Jaslin U. *Black Executives in White Businesses.* Washington DC: University Press of America, 1979.

Sartre, Jean-Paul. *Critique of Dialectical Reasoning: Theory of Practical Ensembles,* trans. Alan Sheridan-Smith. London: New Left Books, 1976.

Schermerhorn, Richard A. *Comparative Ethnic Relations: A Framework For Theory and Research.* New York: Random House, 1970.

Schlesinger, Arthur, Jr. *The Disuniting of America: Reflections on a Multicultural Society.* Knoxsville, TN: Whittle, 1991.

Schuman, Howard. "Sociological Racism." *Trans-Action* 7, no. 2 (December 1969), pp. 44-48.

Seecombe, Wally. "Housework Under Capitalism." *New Left Review,* no. 83 (January/February 1974), pp. 3-24.

Seliger, Martin. *The Marxist Conception of Ideology.* London: Cambridge University Press, 1977.

Seligmann, Herbert J. *Race Against Man.* New York: G. P. Putnam's Sons, 1939.

van Sertima, Ivan (ed.). *African Presence in Early America.* New Brunswick, NJ: Transaction Books, 1987.

———. *Great African Thinkers: Cheikh Anta Diop.* New Brunswick, NJ: Transaction Books, 1987.

Skinner, Kenneth A. "Vietnamese in America: Diversity in Adaptation." *California Sociologist* 3, no. 2 (Summer 1980), pp. 103-124.

Smith, Adam. *The Wealth of Nations.* New York: The Modern Library, 1937.

Sowell, Thomas. *Black Education: Myths and Tragedies.* New York: David McKay, 1972.

———. *Civil Rights: Rhetoric or Reality?* New York: William Morrow and Co., 1984.

———. "Culture — Not Discrimination — Decides Who Gets Ahead." *U.S. News and World Report* 91, no. 15 (October 12, 1981), pp. 74-75.

———. *The Economics and Politics of Race: An International Perspective.* New York: William Morrow, 1983.

———. *Ethnic America: A History.* New York: Basic Books, 1981.

———. *Markets and Minorities.* New York: Basic Books, 1981.

———. *Race and Economics.* New York: David McKay, 1975.

———. "Three Black Histories." In Thomas Sowell (ed.), *Essays and Data on American Ethnic Groups*, pp. 7-64. Washington DC: Urban Institute, 1978.

———. "The Use of the Government for Racial Equality." *National Review* 33, no. 17 (September 4, 1981), pp. 1000-1016.

—— (ed.). *Essays and Data on American Ethnic Groups*. Washington DC: Urban Institute, 1978.

Staples, Robert (ed.). *The Black Family: Essays and Studies*, 3rd ed. Belmont, CA: Wadsworth, 1986.

Steele, Shelby. *The Content of Our Character: A New Vision of Race in America*. New York: St. Martin's Press, 1990.

Steinberg, Stephen. *The Ethnic Myth: Race, Ethnicity and Class in America*. New York: Atheneum, 1981.

Stocking, George W., Jr. (ed.). *Malinowski, Rivers, Benedict and Others: Essays on Culture and Personality*. Madison,WI: University of Wisconsin Press, 1986.

——. "Introduction: The Basic Assumptions of Boasian Anthropology." In George Stocking (ed.), *The Shaping of American Anthropology, 1833-1911: A Franz Boas Reader*, pp. 1-20. New York: Basic Books, 1974.

Stuckey, Sterling. *Slave Culture: Nationalist Foundations of Black America*. New York: Oxford University Press, 1987.

Sung, Betty Lee. *A Survey of Chinese American Manpower and Employment*. New York: Praeger, 1976.

Suzuki, Bob H. "Education and the Socialization of Asian Americans: A Revisionist Analysis of the Model Minority Thesis." *Amerasia Journal* 4, no. 2 (1977), pp. 23-51.

Takaki, Ronald. *Strangers From a Different Shore: A History of Asian Americans*. New York: Penguin, 1990.

Talbot, Steve. *Roots of Oppression: The American Indian Question*. New York: International Pub., 1985.

Thompson, E. P. *The Making of the English Working Class*. London: Penguin, 1968.

de Tocqueville, Alexis. *Democracy in America*. New York: Anchor Books, 1969.

Touraine, Alain. *The Self-Production of Society*, trans. Derek Coltman. Chicago: University of Chicago Press, 1977.

Trimble, Joseph E. "Stereotypical Images, American Indians, and Prejudice." In Phyllis Katz and Dalmas Taylor (eds.), *Eliminating Racism: Profiles in Controversy*, pp. 181-201. New York: Plenum Press, 1986.

U.S. Bureau of the Census. *Census of Population and Housing.* Washington, DC: U.S. Government Printing Office, 1970.
——. *Census of Population and Housing.* Washington, DC: U.S. Government Printing Office, 1980.
——. *Current Population Reports: The Hispanic Population of the United States Series P-20, No. 446.* Washington DC: U.S. Government Printing Office, 1990.
——. *Current Population Reports, Series P-25, No. 1053, Projection of the Population of States by Age, Sex, and Race 1989-2010.* Washington, DC: U.S. Government Printing Office, 1990.
——. *Nonwhite Population, 1960.* Washington, DC: U.S. Government Printing Office, 1963.
——. *Statistical Abstract of the United States*, 105th ed. Washington, DC: U.S. Government Printing Office, 1985.
——. *Statistical Abstract of the United States*, 108th ed. Washington, DC: U.S. Government Printing Office, 1988.
U.S. Commission on Civil Rights. *Civil Rights Issues of Asian Americans.* Washington, DC: U.S. Government Printing Office, 1980.
——. *Civil Rights Issues of Euro-Ethnic Americans in the United States: Opportunities and Challenges.* Washington, DC: U.S. Government Printing Office, 1979.
U.S. Congress. House Committee on Post Office and Civil Service. *Decennial Census Improvement Act of 1991.* Washington, DC: U.S. Government Printing Office, 1991.
——. *Review Progress of Coverage Evaluation and Adjustment Procedures of the 1990 Census.* Washington, DC: U.S. Government Printing Office, 1991.
U.S. Department of Commerce, Bureau of The Census. *America's Black Population.* Washington, DC: U.S. Government Printing Office, 1983.
U.S. National Commission on Excellence in Education. *A Nation at Risk: The Imperatives for Educational Reform.* Washington, DC: U.S. Government Printing Office, 1983.
United Way. *Executive Summary: Asian Pacific Needs Assessment.* California: United Way, Inc. of Los Angeles, 1988.

Valdivieso, Rafael and Cary Davis, "U.S. Hispanics: Challenging Issues for the 1990's," *Population Trends and Public Policy,* no. 17 (December 1988).

Vogel, Lise. *Marxism and the Oppression of Women: Toward a Unitary Theory.* New Brunswick, NJ: Rutgers University Press, 1983.

Wade, Richard. *Slavery in the Cities: The South 1820-1860.* London: Oxford University Press, 1946.

Wang, L. Ling-chi. "Statement." In U.S. Commission on Civil Rights, *Civil Rights Issues of Asian and Pacific Americans: Myths and Realities.* Washington, DC: U.S. Commission on Civil Rights, 1979.

Warner, W. Lloyd. "American Caste and Class." *American Journal of Sociology* 42, no. 2 (1936), pp. 234-237.

Wax, Murray. *Indian-Americans: Unity and Diversity.* Englewood Cliffs, NJ: Prentice-Hall, 1971.

Weber, David J. (ed.) *Foreigners in Their Native Land: Historical Roots of the Mexican Americans.* New Mexico: University of New Mexico Press, 1973.

Weber, Max. "Class, Status and Party." In Hans Gerth and C. Wright Mills (eds.), *From Max Weber: Essays in Sociology*, pp. 150-195. London: Routledge and Kegan Paul, 1961.

——. *Economy and Society*, vols. 1 and 2. Edited by Guenther Roth and Claus Wittich. London: University of California Press, 1978.

——. "Ethnic Groups." In Talcott Parsons, Edward Shils, Kaspar D. Naegele, and Jesse R. Pitts (eds.), *Theories of Society: Foundations of Modern Sociology*, vol. 1, pp. 305-309. New York: Free Press, 1961.

——. *General Economic History.* London: Collier Books, 1961.

——. *The Methodology of Social Sciences*, trans. Edward A. Shils and H. A. Finch. New York: Free Press, 1949.

——. *The Protestant Ethic and the Spirit of Capitalism.* London: Unwin University Books, 1971.

———. *The Theory of Social and Economic Organization*, trans. A. M. Henderson and Talcott Parsons. New York: Oxford University Press, 1947.

Wellman, David. *Portraits of White Racism*. London: Cambridge University Press, 1977.

Welsing, Frances Cress. "The Cress Theory of Color-Confrontation." *The Black Scholar* 5, no. 8 (May 1974), pp. 32-40.

Werhane, Patricia H. *Adam Smith and His Legacy for Modern Capitalism*. New York: Oxford University Press, 1991.

Wilbanks, William. *The Myth of a Racist Criminal Justice System*. Monterey, CA: Brooks/Cole, 1987.

Willhelm, Sidney. "Black/White Equality: The Socioeconomic Conditions of Blacks in America, Part II." *Journal of Black Sociology* 14, no. 2 (December 1983), pp. 157-184.

———. "Can Marxism Explain America's Racism?" *Social Problems* 28, no. 2 (1980), 98-112.

———. *Who Needs the Negro?* Cambridge, MA: Schenkman, 1970.

Williams, Chancellor. *The Destruction of Black Civilization: Great Issues of a Race from 4500 B.C. to 2000 A.D.* Chicago: Third World Press, 1976.

Williams, Walter E. *America: A Minority Viewpoint*. Stanford, CA: Hoover Institution Press, 1982.

———. *The State Against Blacks*. New York: McGraw Hill, 1982.

Willie, Charles V. *The Continuing Significance of Race: A New Look at Black Families*, 2nd ed. New York: General Hall, 1981.

———. "The Inclining Significance of Race." In C. V. Willie (ed.), *The Caste and Class Controversy*, pp. 145-158. Bayside, NY: General Hall, 1979.

———. *Race, Ethnicity, and Socioeconomic Status*. New York: General Hall, 1983.

Wilson, William J. "The Black Community in the 1980's: Questions of Race, Class, and Public Policy." In Norman R. Yetman (ed.), *Majority and Minority: The Dynamics of Race and Ethnicity in American Life*, 4th ed., London: Allyn and Bacon, 1985.

——. *The Declining Significance of Race: Blacks and Changing American Institutions.* Chicago: University of Chicago Press, 1978.

——. "Race-Oriented Programs and the Black Underclass." In Clement Cottingham (ed.), *Race, Poverty and the Urban Underclass*, pp. 113-132. Lexington, MA: D. C. Heath, 1982.

——. "Studying Inner-City Dislocations." *American Sociological Review* 56, no. 1 (February 1991), pp. 1-14.

——. *The Truly Disadvantaged: The Inner City, the Underclass and Public Policy.* Chicago: University of Chicago Press, 1986.

Winks, Robin (ed.). *Slavery: A Comparative Perspective.* New York: New York University Press, 1972.

Wolpe, Harold. "Class Concepts, Class Struggle and Racism." In John Rex and David Mason (eds.), *Theories of Race and Ethnic Relations*, pp. 110-130. London: Cambridge University Press, 1986.

——. *Race, Class and the Apartheid State.* Paris: UNESCO, 1988.

Wong, Eugene F. "Asian American Middleman Minority Theory: The Framework of an American Myth." *Journal of Ethnic Studies* 13, no. 1 (Spring 1985), pp. 51-88.

Wood, Forrest G. *The Arrogance of Faith: Christianity and Race in America from the Colonial Era to the Twentieth Century.* New York: Knopf, 1990.

Woodward, C. Van. *The Strange Career of Jim Crow.* London: Oxford University Press, 1974.

Wortham, Anne. *The Other Side of Racism: A Philosophical Study of Black Race Consciousness.* Columbus, OH: Ohio State University Press, 1977.

Wright, Erik O. "Class Boundaries in Advanced Capitalist Societies." *New Left Review* (July-August 1976), pp. 3-41.

——. *Class, Crisis and State.* London: New Left Books, 1978.

——. "Varieties of Marxist Conceptions of Class Structure." *Politics and Society* 9, no. 3 (1980), pp. 323-370.

Yancey, William L,. Eugene P. Ericksen, and Richard N. Juliani. "Emergent Ethnicity: A Review and Reformulation." In Norman Yetman (ed.), *Majority and Minority: The Dynamics of*

Race and Ethnicity in American Life, 4th ed., pp. 185-194. London: Allyn and Bacon, 1985.

Yetman, Norman. "Statistical Appendix." In Norman Yetman (ed.), *Majority and Minority: The Dynamics of Race and Ethnicity in American Life*, 4th ed., pp. 532-554. London: Allyn and Bacon, 1985.

Yu, Eui-Young. "Korean Communities in America: Past, Present and Future." *Amerasia* 10, no. 2 (1983), pp. 33-51.

AUTHOR INDEX

SUBJECT INDEX